NATURAL FOODS COOKBOOK

NATURAL FOODS COOKBOOK

Bev Shaffer
in cooperation with
Mustard Seed Health Food Market, Inc.

PELICAN PUBLISHING COMPANY
GRETNA 2007

*The word "Pelican" and the depiction of a pelican are trademarks
of Pelican Publishing Company, Inc., and are registered in the
U.S. Patent and Trademark Office.*

Library of Congress Cataloging-in-Publication Data

Shaffer, Bev, 1951-
  Mustard seed market & café natural foods cookbook / Bev Shaffer.
     p. cm.
  Includes bibliographical references and indexes.
  ISBN 978-1-58980-465-4 (hardcover : alk. paper) 1. Cookery, American. I.
Mustard Seed Health Food Market. II. Title.
  TX715.S5255 2007
  641.5973—dc22
                                            2007018336

Photographs by John R. Shaffer

Page 2: Nothing says "fresh" better than a bucket full of organic blueberries just
harvested from Silver Creek Farm.

Printed in China
Published by Pelican Publishing Company, Inc.
1000 Burmaster Street, Gretna, Louisiana 70053

To all our customers who have passed through and continue to pass through our doors and support us . . . Thank you!

Locally grown organic squash at Nature's Acres farm.

CONTENTS

Our food is fresh, our customers are spoiled!

Phillip's signature red tennis shoes.

This book is more than just another cookbook. It contains our favorite and most cherished recipes, developed since 1981. It is a reflection of our mission to change the way Americans eat, farm, and think about food.

The journey began when we invested $60 in a stainless-steel cooking pot and began a vegetarian catering business. That business soon grew into a small health food store and then evolved into two natural foods supermarkets with full-service restaurants featuring banquet and catering facilities, as well as cooking schools. For additional information, check out www.mustardseedmarket.com.

Over the years, we have been able to feed thousands of families foods that are free from additives, setting new standards and challenging the status quo in the food industry. All the foods we sell meet our minimum standard of "natural." In addition, much of the foods we sell are also certified organic and locally produced. We prefer to purchase from locally owned family farms and businesses, providing the freshest foods available while contributing to the social fabric and sustainability of our local economy in the process.

We believe in the sacred nature of food. That is to say that food should be honored and elevated in its importance in our lives. Whether growing, preparing, presenting, or serving, food should be regarded as sacred. Throughout history humans have celebrated and honored special events with food rituals and traditions. Most religions have unique customs that involve food. In our daily lives, mealtimes are the times we remember most about family life. It is a time when we have guaranteed access to one another. We can measure our lives in the rhythms of mealtimes, seasonal harvests, and holidays.

Our food styles also directly impact our health. America has not been well nurtured by our chemically dependent, increasingly industrialized system of big agriculture and food processing. This system is unreasonably dependent on fossil fuels, with about 60 calories of energy invested to grow, process, and distribute just one calorie of food. The average bite of food travels on average more than 1,500 miles and is often over-packaged to support brand development. If half of the predictions about global warming and peak oil are true, our entire food system will have to radically and quickly change.

So, here's the challenge. Eat real food, whole food, not heavily processed food. Eat organic food produced locally or regionally. Do business with people who care about what they do. Maintain control of your health through a proper diet and regular exercise. Ideally, we should all start growing food. Think about a new landscaping plan for your yard that, like the victory gardens from World War II, will sustain you.

And, finally, enjoy what you are doing. Life is too short to work a job you don't like in order to buy things you don't need to impress people you don't care for!

—Phillip and Margaret Nabors, founders
Mustard Seed Market & Café, Inc.

A pickup full of locally grown organic cherry tomatoes.

PREFACE

This book has become my love letter to natural and organic foods. When I joined Mustard Seed Market in 1997 as the cooking school director, one of my goals was to help bridge the gap between the gourmet and health food worlds.

Teaching (and learning from my culinary students) is very satisfying for me. I continually ask myself, "How much impact does my cooking/teaching have on the people who taste and cook my recipes?" All too often, food is viewed as an end product, independent of the land that produced it, the hands that grew it, and those who prepared it. My hope is that after I've taught a seasonal cooking class for a club, whipped up a recipe using local, heirloom tomatoes on television, or given a talk and tasting to a bus tour that knew nothing about our store's philosophy or the natural and organic food industry, I have nurtured the human spirit through educational outreach (and, of course, unexpectedly great flavors!).

Consumers today feel as if they are entitled to the best of all possible worlds: both taste and nutrition. Our customers really do want to eat healthfully—it's just that they also want every meal to taste good! When I create recipes, I think irresistible. I think flavor. Food needs to be fun, and yet it's food you can feel good about. Our food is a living, evolving, cultural, nutritional initiative.

Selecting the recipes for this cookbook was, without question, a challenge . . . but as you turn the pages, deciding which dish to try first, my hope is that we have seduced you with exciting and flavorful options. The recipes are not stuffy or pretentious. I wrote this book casually, with real-world tips and suggestions. *Your* biggest challenge will be deciding which recipe to try first.

I invite you to cultivate a passion for cooking and the simple pleasures associated with a made-from-scratch meal, mindful of life's hectic pace. Food prepared with care epitomizes the love and sensory fulfillment you bring to your family and friends. Enjoy every natural morsel as you remember this:

Food: buy it with thought . . . cook it with care . . . serve just enough . . . save what will keep . . . eat what would spoil . . . locally grown is best . . . *don't waste it!*

Squash harvesting at Nature's Acres farm.

ACKNOWLEDGMENTS

Among the many pleasures I enjoyed over the course of writing this book was the unconditional generosity of my eclectic mix of coworkers. A sloppy kiss goes to all of them. They keep me warm, fuzzy, crazy, and laughing on a daily basis! Their kindness and patience made the writing possible, and much of what I share in the pages that follow is distilled from their recipes, ideas, and creativity.

Special thanks to Bruce Grimm and our varied and diverse collection of farmers for constantly teaching me something about farming and produce. Thanks to the farms we visited, Silver Creek Farm, Keim Family Farm, and Nature's Acres, for their generosity, warmth, and assistance.

I am grateful to a large handful of my coworkers who, usually with scant notice, agreed to whip up a recipe, answer a nagging question, or research a conundrum I had become obsessed with. In no special order I list them here and I am grateful to all of them for their contributions to this book: Keith Keyser, John Hermann, Bridget Cutshaw, Keith Jones, Jack Hickson, Alice Bulin, Christine Spiroch, Lisa Maglionico, Gary Cole, Karen Gaeta, Nancy Bohon, Derek Beltz, Heather Moke, Kyle Begue, Ric Juhas, Julie Palaski, Tammy Brooks, Kortez Wilson, Erin Veverka, Kate Heffner, Kimchi Thi Le, Keith Ezzo, Laura Miller-Hannah, Mike Schubert, Dan Buckholz, Rick Gedeon, Lisa Miller-Smiley, Alex Miller, Vicki Smith, Vicki Shepler, and Nancy Sieker.

My cooking school assistants are an invaluable part of my day-to-day existence, and I would be remiss if I did not single them out for their patience with me through this book-writing process and for their invaluable help in tackling the toughest of recipes and helping me test and restructure their unwieldy formats along the way. A special toast to these talented people: Annette Felton, Kelly Geosits, Vickie Getz, and Matt Ballard. I must also thank Vickie Getz and my husband, John, for unflinchingly reading and proofing the manuscript throughout the entire process.

My husband, John, has kept me excited about this book—and all my other ventures—through all its stages. He functions, among other things, as my general counsel and partner. He was the one who made me breakfast, lunch, and dinner when all I had time to do was test, write, and type. (A bigger and not-so-sloppy kiss goes to him!) I quite literally could not have written this book or coordinated the photography without him. I know you'll enjoy his creative photographs as much as I do. John's food photography and artistic food styling make the recipes in this book explode with life!

Warm thanks to everyone at Pelican Publishing Company for embracing this book and then lavishing it with extraordinary attention. In particular, I am indebted to Milburn Calhoun, Nina Kooij, Amy Kirk, Joseph Billingsley, Kathleen Calhoun Nettleton, Lindsey Reynolds, and everyone else at this extraordinary publishing house.

Heartfelt thanks to Margaret and Phillip Nabors for believing in my ability to pull this project together, and to Barb Schenk and Diana Rhoads for taming my occasional anxiety with patience, laughter, and love.

For me, gathering, cooking, sharing, eating, and talking food is all about connecting with other people. I think of this book as an all-natural culinary snapshot and hope you will too!

NATURAL FOODS COOKBOOK

MUSTARD SEED MARKET 101: A HISTORY

Mustard Seed Market & Café is thriving.

It's about our relationship to foods and food products as well as our relationship with our family of employees, with our customers, and with our purveyors—local folks tapping trees for maple syrup, harvesting the juiciest, drip-down-your-chin ripe Ohio peaches, or picking locally grown strawberries bursting with the flavor of sunshine.

It's about our connection—from the hands of our growers to the hands of our chefs to the hands of our servers to your table—whether at our market, at the café or cooking school, or in your own home!

Our goal is inspiration. We want this book to convey our knowledge and varied experiences and to inspire you to cook and enjoy these recipes!

We want you to know that every grocery purchase, every sip of coffee, tea or wine, and every bite of food makes a statement at our market and café. You support a cornucopia of natural, organic, sustainable, and fair-trade products.

So many of our suppliers are small, local growers and purveyors . . . We have this connection (and ultimately you do too) and direct contact. We can talk produce with these artisan producers—we can talk weather and soil and food. It fosters a sense of community and we love it!

A Look Back

In 1978, wife-and-husband team Margaret and Phillip Nabors started a home-based vegetarian catering business with $60 and a cooking pot. The couple catered many weddings for friends who followed a vegetarian diet and often had difficulty finding healthy living options in the northeast Ohio area.

In April 1981, the couple opened a 2,000-square-foot health food store in Akron, Ohio's Merriman Valley and named it Mustard Seed Market, drawing from the biblical metaphor that states that faith is like the tiny mustard seed from which a great tree grows.

Committed to helping individuals enjoy healthier lives through healthier eating habits, they even offered cooking classes out of their home. Margaret added a small menu of vegetarian fare to the store and soon discovered she couldn't feed customers fast enough. They realized that their mix of healthy, high-quality products were attractive and had the potential to convert mainstream shoppers.

Interest in the store grew and in March 1989 they relocated the market to an area more easily accessible from the freeway, adding "& Café" to the name. The new location was larger (9,000 square feet) and able to provide a wider selection of natural foods (all void of artificial colors, flavors, harmful preservatives, and additives). Seafood, poultry, and meat that met their stringent standards were soon added to the market's product mix.

In September 1996, Mustard Seed Market & Café added on to its location to create a 31,500-square-foot healthy shopping and dining area. The expansion resulted in a 14,000-square-foot retail space, a

120-seat restaurant, a 20-seat bar, and a banquet facility that holds up to 100 people. Upholding its commitment to helping individuals live healthier lives, Mustard Seed Market & Café offered an extensive list of cooking classes, lectures, and food demonstrations—all designed to improve and promote healthier eating and living habits.

The success of this one-stop natural shopping concept led to another expansion. In October 1999, Mustard Seed Market & Café opened a second location in Solon, Ohio. The 56,000-square-foot store and restaurant boasts a 191-seat restaurant and café, a whole-grain bakery, a fresh juice and cappuccino bar, an extensive prepared foods section, a cooking school, and banquet facilities.

While the size of the offerings and retail space may have changed, Mustard Seed Market & Café's vision has not. Both locations continue to set new standards and share knowledge of good food, good health, and sustainable living. Mustard Seed Market & Café is a locally owned family business with standards that state:

- No artificial flavorings
- No harmful chemical preservatives
- No saccharin or aspartame
- No meat or poultry raised with growth hormones
- No irradiated foods
- No artificial coloring
- Cruelty-free cosmetics

Join us. Our food is fresh, our customers are spoiled!

Natural

"Natural" is not defined by government regulation and some marketers play fast and loose with the term. At Mustard Seed Market & Café, we define natural foods as those free from artificial colors, flavors, and sweeteners such as saccharin or aspartame or other food additives and that do not contain any harmful chemical preservatives. The meat we sell is raised without added growth hormones, antibiotics, or animal byproducts.

Organic

The USDA's implementation of national standards is helpful in learning to navigate this terrain:
• 100 percent organic: Only products produced using organic methods and containing only organic ingredients are allowed to carry this label.
• Organic: Products made with at least 95 percent of the ingredients being organically produced may display this label.
• Made with organic: Products with 70-95 percent organic ingredients may carry this label.
• Products with less than 70 percent organic ingredients can list the organic items only in the ingredient panel, with no mention of organic on the main label.

Thanks to the above standards, organic products are nationally certified to have been produced and processed *without*:
• persistent synthetic herbicides/pesticides

• sewage sludge, a source of heavy metals, herbicides/pesticides, industrial solvents, and pathogens
• genetically modified organisms
• growth hormones and antibiotics, whose use in animal products is linked to antibiotic-resistant bacteria
• irradiation, whose use remains controversial

Ohio's First Certified Organic Market & Café

In September 2003, Mustard Seed Market & Café became Ohio's first certified organic retailer. This prestigious recognition assures you that we fulfill strict handling standards so that the organic products you purchase from us maintain their organic integrity from the farm to your table. The OEFFA (a federally recognized, independent third-party organization) certification process confirms that Mustard Seed Market & Café examines the organic certification status of our products; maintains an extensive audit trail and record-keeping process (assuring organic quality); appropriately protects our organic products from commingling with conventional products and contamination with prohibited materials; trains all staff in the safe handling practices of organic products; opens our stores to on-site inspections of OEFFA officials.

Fair Trade

Fair trade ensures that small-scale family farmers

Above and opposite: Organic zucchini and a cherry
bomb pepper, local and vine ripe.

in the developing world receive a fair price for their top-quality crops (crops such as coffee, tea, sugar, chocolate, and bananas). When you purchase Fair Trade Certified™ products, you are directly supporting a better life for these family farmers by allowing them to market their own harvests through direct, long-term contracts with international buyers. This exchange allows millions of people around the world to stay on their land, put food on the table, and keep their children in school. Fair trade empowers farming families to take care of themselves.

Basic Techniques from the Cooking School

Preparation prior to actual cooking is one of any culinary instructor or chef's most important steps. All of us in the kitchens refer to this as *mise en place*, literally "all things put in place." What does this mean for you? With these simple chef's techniques for the preparation and assembly of ingredients, pans, and utensils needed for the particular dish you're about to cook, it means an easier (and ultimately more enjoyable) cooking plan. Make your cooking a pleasurable experience by using *mise en place* and the following timesaving tips for your basic cooking tasks.

Keep a running shopping list in your kitchen, jotting down items when you are low.

Keep it clean: To avoid cross-contamination and prevent foodborne illnesses, follow these easy steps:
• Wash hands well in hot, soapy water before and after handling foods.
• Keep raw meat and meat juices from coming into contact with other foods during preparation.
• Wash all utensils, cutting surfaces, and counters with hot, soapy water after contact with raw meat.
• Do not use a platter or plate that held raw meat for cooked foods unless it has been washed in hot, soapy water.

Help from your freezer: Freeze small amounts of broth or stock in nonstick muffin pans or ice-cube trays. Once frozen, pop out and place "cups" or "cubes" in a plastic bag.

Freeze a stick of butter and use a vegetable peeler to shave slices onto food or grate the butter for use in mashed potatoes.

Partially frozen meat or poultry is easier to cut for stir-fries and soups.

Open both ends of a tomato paste can, then atop a piece of plastic wrap, carefully push one end with the lid to remove the paste. Wrap and freeze, then slice off pieces of the frozen paste as needed. (This helps eliminate the "what do I do with the rest of the can?" question.)

Technique help: There are lots of how-tos with each recipe, but here are a few can't-miss ideas as well.

To seed a cucumber or zucchini, slice it in half lengthwise then slowly glide a small spoon or melon baller down the center to scoop out the seeds. An ice-cream scoop works well for winter squashes.

Spraying your knife or grater first with an aerosol-free, nonstick cooking spray helps keep cheese from sticking. To make cleanup easier as well, I rinse these items first with cold water, then wash with hot, soapy water. You can also use this technique for chopping dried fruits, but I use kitchen scissors dipped repeated in hot water for ease in snipping dried fruits.

Store fresh mushrooms in a paper bag in the refrigerator, allowing them to breathe (ah!), keeping them from getting slimy (yuk!), and extending their life.

To chop a bell pepper efficiently (this always impresses people!), quickly slice the top off first, then the bottom, then stand the pepper up, slicing along the inside edges. This process easily separates the core and seeds from the sides.

When should I salt and pepper? Salt and pepper should be added before cooking to bring out the inherent flavors in food: if these seasonings are added after the cooking is complete, they have a tendency to overpower the finished dish's flavor. Experimenting with different flavors of herbs and spices allows for creativity, but don't forget the basics—the salt and pepper.

Zest, that citrus zing! When you grate the outer rind of a citrus fruit (not the bitter white pith), it releases aromatic essential oils that add a citrus flavor and fragrance to foods. Use a zester, grater, vegetable peeler, or paring knife . . . and finely chop as needed.

One of the handiest tools? A bench scraper (a piece of metal with a handle or a plastic piece about 4" x 6") allows me to easily remove cut items from a cutting board.

If your recipe calls for herbs and spices that are to be removed before the finished dish is served, put them in a mesh tea ball. Close the ball and hang it by the chain over the pot's side into the cooked item.

Toasting spices for boldness: A chef's secret has long been to toast seeds or spices to intensify their flavor. To do this stovetop, spread the seeds or spices in a shallow layer in a preheated, dry skillet and toss or shake the pan until a rich aroma arises. Transfer immediately to a large plate (this prevents scorching) and allow to cool. Once cool, grind as needed for your recipe. Watch carefully!—this will go from toasted to scorched in no time.

Toasting nuts for enhanced flavor: I store nuts in the refrigerator or freezer. To freshen their flavor, I simply spread the recipe's amount in a shallow layer in a dry skillet and again toss or shake the pan until a rich, nutty aroma arises. Remove skillet immediately from heat and allow to cool completely before chopping or using.

An easy way to chop nuts? Sure you can pull out the processor, the small grinder, or the chef's knife and cutting board, but you can also use a zip-top plastic bag and place the nuts inside, seal tightly, then roll or pound the nuts with a rolling pin. Easy clean up, too.

Read, read, read. In hands-on classes, I ask my students, "How can you cook it if you haven't read the recipe?" (and I'm not just talkin' ingredients!). Read through the entire recipe first before beginning preparation and then assemble all ingredients needed.

Sage advice on herbs: Follow these tips for long-lasting, flavorful results. Wash fresh herbs before you use them; shake off excess water over the sink, then roll in paper or cloth towels to dry on the counter.

Store basil at 44° F to 50° F (anything colder turns basil black). Store other herbs in a resealable plastic bag in the vegetable compartment of the refrigerator.

You'll get more flavor out of fresh herbs if you coarsely chop, as opposed to finely chop them. And I'm always asked, "Can you freeze herbs?" Yes, but it's not recommended, as they lose flavor and texture. If you do choose to freeze them, make a pesto or blend them with olive oil until the mixture becomes a thick puree then freeze.

U.S. Standard Measurement Equivalents

1 tablespoon	=	3 teaspoons
2 tablespoons	=	1 fluid ounce
4 tablespoons	=	¼ cup
5⅓ tablespoons	=	⅓ cup
8 tablespoons	=	½ cup
16 tablespoons	=	1 cup
1 cup	=	8 ounces
2 cups	=	1 pint
1 quart	=	2 pints
1 gallon	=	4 quarts

Substitutions, Yields, and Equivalents for Some Common Foods

Herbs	1 tablespoon fresh	=	1 teaspoon dried
Butter	1 cup	=	16 tablespoons (½ pound)
Cheese	1 pound	=	4-5 cups grated
Lemon	1 large	=	3-4 tablespoons juice
Lemon	1 large	=	1 tablespoon zest
Lime	1 large	=	2-3 tablespoons juice
Orange	1 medium	=	6 tablespoons juice
Beans (dried)	1 pound raw	=	2⅓ cups raw
Beans (dried)	2⅓ cups raw	=	6 cups cooked

Taste and flavor—what's the difference? Most of

us use the terms taste and flavor interchangeably, but they're actually different. Taste refers to the five basic receptors: sweet, salty, sour, bitter, and umami (a meaty texture and mouth feel—the one we didn't learn about in school!). Flavor, however, is a combination of taste plus the other sensations that influence our perception of food, such as aroma, texture, juiciness, mouth feel, and color.

Food In = Energy Out. Balance, variety, and moderation are important recipe ingredients when you're choosing foods to fuel your body. Mix up your menu with nutrient-rich foods that help you get through the day. No single food provides every nutrient you need. Fiber up. Make today's lunch sandwich with whole wheat or seven-grain bread, or enjoy making one of our grain recipes. Add to your food's color palette by eating colorful fruits and vegetables (the deeper the colors, the more nutrients they contain). Think of fat as a balancing act. Enjoy all foods, just balance high-fat options and low-fat options over time.

Have fun—cook something!

Field of organic leeks, Keim Family Farm.

BRUNCH FOR ANYTIME

Our brunch buffet transforms an ordinary Sunday into a special Sunday, without sacrificing the nice, lazy, expansive quality of that day of the week.

Brunch can be intimate yet informal, cozy yet boisterous, simple yet celebratory. Less serious than dinner, brunch is lighthearted but not lightweight. Brunch is very American, like pie a la mode, but in addition to the expected there are always the surprises that keep our customers coming back for more!

Bored with scrambled eggs? How about Andouille Chicken Sausage and Potato Omelet. Pancakes a little ho-hum? How about Pumpkin Cinnamon Pancakes. Love French toast but want something a little extra special? Don't miss our Sunday Brunch Crème Brûlée French Toast. And the selection goes on and on.

Brunch is a great time to razzle-dazzle 'em . . . to focus on new flavors and experiment with new dishes. Isn't it Sunday yet?

Somehow, one piece just isn't enough when you're enjoying our Sunday Brunch Crème Brûlée French Toast.

Three-Grain-and-More-Good-Stuff Granola

This is a tasty granola loaded with good things.
Delicious served atop (or under!) yogurt.

2 cups rolled oats
1 cup hulled barley
1 cup flaked rye or rye berries
2 cups coarsely chopped walnuts
½ cup raw wheat germ
½ cup unsalted hulled sunflower seeds
½ cup dry milk powder
1 tbsp. ground cinnamon
⅔ cup honey
½ cup canola oil
1½ tsp. vanilla
1 cup chopped dried apples
½ cup seedless raisins

Heat oven to 300 degrees. In a 13x9" baking pan, combine the oats, barley, and rye.

Bake, stirring frequently, until toasted (about 15 minutes). Stir in the walnuts, wheat germ, and sunflower seeds. Bake for 10 minutes. Remove pan from the oven, let cool for 15 minutes, and then stir in the milk powder and cinnamon.

In a small saucepan, heat the honey, oil, and vanilla, stirring until blended. Add this mixture to the dry ingredients, stirring until well coated. Bake for an additional 10 minutes. Remove pan from the oven and stir in the dried apples and raisins. Let cool.

Store in a tightly sealed container at room temperature. Makes about 6 cups. Granola will keep at room temperature for 5 days.

Chef's Notes

About . . .
One of the world's oldest cereal crops, barley is most commonly available hulled or pearled. Hulled barley (also called whole grain) has had only the outer husk removed.

Also called old-fashioned oats, rolled oats are oat groats that have been steamed and flattened.

Similar in style to rolled oats, flaked rye is perfect for breakfast cereals.

The heart of the wheat berry, wheat germ becomes rancid quickly and is best stored refrigerated or frozen.

Coconut-Almond Granola

Tasty, sweet, and fresh . . . Make a batch for your brunch bunch today!

2 cups old-fashioned rolled oats
1 cup shredded coconut
1 cup sliced almonds
1 tsp. sea salt or kosher salt
¼ cup safflower oil, plus additional for greasing your pan
¾ cup pure maple syrup
¼ cup honey
½ cup seedless raisins, dried cranberries, or dried blueberries
½ cup dried apricots or dried mangoes, chopped

Chef's Notes

About . . .
Sea salt vs. kosher salt. It's all a matter of taste! Sea salt is the result of the evaporation of seawater, coming mechanically harvested or hand harvested with a coarse, flaked, or fine grind. Kosher salt is a coarse-grained salt prized by some for its texture and flavor.

Heat oven to 300 degrees. Spread the oats, coconut, and almonds on a large baking pan. Sprinkle with the salt and bake for 10 minutes, stirring often, until the ingredients are lightly toasted. Transfer ingredients to a large bowl.

Increase oven temperature to 350 degrees. Lightly grease the baking pan with oil. Combine the oil, maple syrup, and honey in a small bowl, whisking until well blended. Pour mixture atop the lightly toasted oat mixture, tossing to coat evenly. Spread the granola onto the baking pan and bake for 25 minutes or until the mixture is crispy and golden brown, stirring often while baking.

Let cool completely on a wire rack, breaking up any large pieces while mixture is still warm.

Once cooled completely, add the raisins and apricots (or other fruits) and toss to mix.

Store in a tightly sealed container at room temperature. Makes about 6 cups. Granola will keep at room temperature for 5 days.

Flax, Fruit, and Rolled Oats

Don't get caught passing on a taste of this . . . or everyone around you
will snatch it up and it will be gone. Delicious and healthful!

2 cups milk, 2 percent or skim
¾ cup old-fashioned rolled oats
⅓ cup seedless raisins, chopped pitted
dates, or dried cranberries
¼ cup flax seeds
⅓ cup low-fat vanilla yogurt
⅓ cup maple syrup

In a medium saucepan, stir together the milk, oats, and dried fruit. Bring to a simmer over medium heat, stirring constantly. Reduce heat to medium low and cook, stirring frequently, for 5 minutes or until creamy and thickened. Remove from heat, cover, and let stand for 2 minutes.

While oats are resting, coarsely grind flax seeds. Stir ground flax into hot oat mixture. Spoon into individual bowls, topping each with a spoonful of yogurt and just a drizzle of maple syrup. Dig in! Makes 3+ servings.

Chef's Notes

How to Do It . . .
You can either purchase ground flax or grind your own from flax seeds. Use a spice or coffee grinder dedicated solely for this purpose. Ground or seeds, store your flax well sealed and refrigerated to prevent rancidity.

Omelets, Your Way

3 large eggs
1 dash hot pepper sauce
½ tbsp. canola oil

Optional Fillings

Sliced mushrooms
Grated cheese
Coarsely chopped ham
Seeded and diced fresh tomato
Sliced pitted black olives
Coarsely chopped green bell pepper
Finely diced firm tofu

Place eggs in small bowl with the hot pepper sauce. Whisk until the egg whites and yolks are blended.

Place oil in an 8" nonstick skillet and warm over medium heat. Add eggs to skillet, using a heat-resistant spatula to lift the eggs along the edges until most of the egg is cooked. Flip eggs over to allow them to finish cooking for about 30 seconds.

Fill with desired filling, fold in half, and then, using spatula, slide onto a plate. Serves 1.

Chef's Notes

About . . .
An eggshell's color, brown vs. white, is simply determined by the breed of the hen that laid it.

How to Do It . . .
Always refrigerate your eggs, storing them in the carton in which they came to prevent exposure to odors and damage. The best flavor comes from eggs used within a week.

Veggie Frittata

This Italian-style omelet is a great introduction to eggs for the novice cook, as it utilizes an assortment of cooking techniques and delicious flavor profiles.

2 tbsp. extra-virgin olive oil
9 oz. small zucchini, cut into matchstick strips
¾ cup finely chopped yellow onion
2 cloves garlic, finely chopped
Sea salt and freshly ground black
pepper to taste
5 large eggs
5 tbsp. milk, whole or 2 percent
½ cup finely chopped fresh chives, divided

Chef's Notes

About . . .
Superior olive oils depend on the variety of olive, how and where it was cultivated, where the olives were picked, and most importantly, how it was processed. The first cold pressing of olives yields the best-tasting and most healthful oil. Only oil containing less than 1 percent acids can be labeled extra virgin.

In Season . . .
When fresh tomatoes are juicy, ripe, and dropping off the vine, serve this frittata with a spoonful of freshly made tomato sauce.

Heat oil in a 9-10" nonstick skillet over medium heat. Add the zucchini, onion, and garlic and sauté until the veggies are tender. Season to taste with salt and pepper.

In a small bowl, whisk the eggs with the milk. Add *half* of the chives to the egg-milk mixture and pour over the zucchini mixture.

Lift the pan, swirling so that the egg-milk mixture spreads evenly. Cook over low heat until the eggs are set. (High heat tends to toughen the eggs quickly.)

Invert the frittata onto a plate—or an upside down lid—and slide it back into the skillet to brown the other side, about 5 more minutes. (Too scary? You can omit this step!)

Cut frittata into wedges, top with remaining chives, and serve. Serves 4 as an appetizer or 2 as an entrée.

Chicken Andouille Sausage and Potato Omelet

For those who like their omelet with a little heat and a kick, this is the dish.

1 tbsp. extra-virgin olive oil
1 cup (½-inch cubes) peeled red skin or
Yukon gold potatoes
½ cup (⅛-inch cubes) chicken andouille sausage
¼ cup chopped red bell pepper
¼ cup chopped yellow onion
2 tbsp. minced scallions
¼ tsp. ground cumin
6 large eggs, lightly beaten
½ tsp. sea salt
¼ tsp. freshly ground black pepper
1 tbsp. butter

Heat oil in a 12" sauté pan over medium heat. Add potatoes and sauté until golden brown. Add sausage, bell pepper, and onion and sauté until veggies are soft, about 6 minutes. Stir in scallions and cumin. Remove from heat and keep warm.

Heat oven to 375 degrees. Whisk eggs, salt, and pepper in a large bowl until well blended. Melt butter in a 12" ovenproof skillet over medium heat. Pour in egg mixture and cook until eggs are almost set in the center, tilting pan and lifting edge of omelet with a heat resistant-spatula for 3 minutes. Sprinkle sausage mixture over top. Transfer skillet to the oven and bake until eggs are completely set, about 4 minutes.

Run spatula under outer edge of omelet to loosen and slide onto serving plate. Makes 2 servings.

Chef's Notes

About . . .
Andouille sausage is a spicy, heavily smoked sausage of French origin and a specialty of Cajun cooking. The version we sell is made with chicken instead of the traditional pork.

How to Do It . . .
Tilting the pan and lifting the edge of an omelet with a heat-resistant spatula does more than exercise your arms—it allows the uncooked portion of egg flowing underneath the cooked portion to, you guessed it, cook!

Soufflé Cornmeal Pancakes for a Crowd

These are light and airy with a little bit of a cornmeal crunch.

Pancake Base

1 1/4 qt. half-and-half or whole milk, divided
18 large egg yolks
6 oz. unsalted butter, melted
1/3 cup Grand Marnier
1 tbsp. granulated sugar
1 tbsp. ground cinnamon
1 tsp. sea salt
2 cups unbleached, all-purpose flour
1 1/2 cups finely ground yellow cornmeal

To Cook for a Crowd

1 1/2 qt. egg whites (about 44 large eggs)
1/2 cup granulated sugar
3/4 cup clarified butter
Assorted fresh seasonal fruit, cleaned and cut as desired
Sifted confectioners' sugar, as needed

For the Pancake Base: Using a whisk attachment and an electric mixer, mix *2 cups* of half-and-half, yolks, butter, Grand Marnier, sugar, cinnamon, and salt until blended. Gradually add flour and cornmeal, mixing just until combined (leaving batter lumpy). Stir in remaining half-and-half. Cover and refrigerate until ready to use. Yields about 9 cups.

For each Soufflé Pancake: Heat oven to 400 degrees. Using a whisk attachment and an electric mixer, beat *3/4 cup* of the egg whites with *1 tsp.* of the sugar to soft peaks; set aside. In another bowl, place 1 cup of the Pancake Base and gently fold in beaten whites.

In a small (7-8") heatproof nonstick skillet, heat 1 tbsp. of the clarified butter over medium heat until hot. Add batter; cook about 4 minutes or until edges are set. Transfer skillet to oven; bake 10 to 12 minutes or until Soufflé Pancake is lightly browned and center is set. Serve garnished with assorted fresh seasonal fruit and a sprinkling of sifted confectioners' sugar. Full recipe for a crowd makes 24+ servings.

Chef's Notes

About . . .
(Very) simply put, maple syrup is sap from the maple tree that has been boiled until much of the water has evaporated and the sap becomes thick and syrupy. Buy locally for optimum flavor!

Egg whites are now available in cartons and can be kept frozen for several months or refrigerated for 5 days once opened.

Clarified butter. Why do I need it? Because the milk solids (which make butter burn when used in hot applications such as frying) have been removed, clarified butter has a higher smoke point than regular butter and may be used to cook at higher temperatures.

How to Do It . . .
Freezing the Pancake Base is easy. Simply place leftovers in a freezer-safe container; when ready to serve the crowd, thaw overnight in the refrigerator and then whisk mixture well before using.

To make clarified butter, melt unsalted butter slowly in a saucepan, which will evaporate most of the water and separate the milk solids (which sink to the bottom of the pan) from the liquid on the surface. After foam is skimmed off the top, the clear (clarified) butter is poured or skimmed off the milky residue on the bottom and used in cooking. Keeps well in the freezer in a well-sealed container for future use.

In Season . . .
Fresh blueberries, red raspberries, and sweet strawberries are delicious fruits to serve with this soufflé pancake when they're at their peak.

Worth gathering a crowd for, these Soufflé Cornmeal Pancakes are fun to make upon request.

Buttermilk Whole-Wheat Pancakes

Everyone loves pancakes, and this whole-wheat version
has a delightfully pleasant nutty flavor.

¾ cup whole-wheat flour
¾ cup unbleached, all-purpose flour
3 tbsp. granulated sugar
¼ tsp. sea salt
2½ tsp. baking powder
1 tsp. baking soda
1 tbsp. maple syrup, plus extra for serving
1 large egg
1 cup buttermilk
¾ cup milk, 2 percent or skim
2½ tbsp. canola oil, plus extra for cooking
1 cup fresh seasonal berries or other
chopped fruit

In a large bowl, combine the flours, sugar, salt, baking powder, and baking soda. In a medium bowl, combine maple syrup, egg, buttermilk, milk, and oil, whisking until well blended. Add wet ingredients to the dry ingredients, mixing until smooth.

Lightly coat a griddle or large skillet with a little canola oil. Heat on medium until hot. Pour 3 tbsp. of the batter onto skillet and sprinkle with 1 tbsp. of the fruit. Cover with 1 additional tbsp. of the batter and cook until bubbles form.

Carefully flip and cook until bottom side is golden brown. Serve immediately with maple syrup. Makes 4+ servings.

Chef's Notes

How to Do It . . .
The drier the fruit, the more success you'll have with this recipe. If using fresh berries wash them gently and dry them thoroughly with paper towels or a clean cloth before cooking.

Peanut Butter with Jelly Pancakes

Kids of all ages—including the kid in you—will love these peanutty pancakes.

1 ¼ cups unbleached, all-purpose flour
3 tsp. baking powder
1 tbsp. granulated sugar
½ tsp. sea salt
1 large egg, lightly beaten
1 cup milk, whole or 2 percent
2 tbsp. melted butter, cooled
½ cup peanut butter, smooth or chunky
Jelly for topping

In a medium bowl, sift together flour, baking powder, sugar, and salt. In a small bowl, combine egg, milk, and butter, whisking until combined. Add wet ingredients to dry ingredients, stirring just until moistened.

Heat large nonstick skillet until hot. Pour ¼ cup batter onto skillet, adding 1 tbsp. peanut butter to the center, flattening it out with a spoon. Flip pancake when top side is bubbly and peanut butter begins to melt. When bottom side is golden brown, serve and top with jelly. Makes 6+ pancakes.

Chef's Notes

About . . .
Grape or strawberry jelly seems to be the perfect flavors for these pancakes, but feel free to experiment.

Pumpkin Cinnamon Pancakes

As soon as the weather turns cool, requests from customers abound for pumpkin flavors. Close your eyes while enjoying these fall-flavored pancakes and picture those vibrantly colored leaves on Ohio's trees.

2 cups unbleached, all-purpose flour
½ cup granulated sugar
½ tsp. salt
2 tsp. baking powder
2 tsp. baking soda
½ tsp. cinnamon
½ tsp. vanilla
3 large eggs
1 cup plain, low-fat yogurt
¾ cup milk, whole or 2 percent
1 cup pumpkin puree

In a medium bowl, combine flour, sugar, salt, baking powder, baking soda, and cinnamon. In another bowl, combine vanilla, eggs, yogurt, milk, and pumpkin puree. Mix well. Pour the wet ingredients into the dry ingredients and stir just until blended.

Heat oiled griddle or large nonstick skillet until hot. Pour ¼ cup batter for each pancake onto skillet. Cook pancakes slowly over a low-medium heat, flipping when top side is bubbly and edges are lightly golden. Remove from skillet when bottom of pancake is golden. Makes about 12 pancakes.

Chef's Notes

In Season . . .
Pumpkin or squash? Feel free to use your favorite fall squash puree (butternut, acorn, or any of the heirloom varieties) as a substitute for the pumpkin in this recipe.

Banana-Cream Pancakes

*This light, fluffy version of everyone's favorite brunch "bread"
is a decadent treat served with the banana cream.*

Pancakes

3 cups buttermilk
2 large eggs, separated
2½ cups unbleached, all-purpose flour
2 tbsp. granulated sugar
1½ tsp. baking powder
1 tsp. baking soda
1 tsp. sea salt
6 tbsp. unsalted butter, divided
4 firm-ripe medium bananas, thinly sliced

Banana Cream

1 cup apple juice
4 ripe bananas, peeled and sliced
2 tbsp. lemon juice
1½ cups heavy (whipping) cream
⅔ cup confectioners' sugar, sifted

<table>
<tr><td>

Chef's Notes

</td></tr>
</table>

About . . .
Feel good about your food choices and use fair trade
bananas and organic heavy cream.

For the Pancakes: Whisk buttermilk and egg yolks in
a large bowl to blend. Whisk flour, sugar, baking
powder, baking soda, and salt in a medium bowl to
blend. Combine flour mixture and buttermilk mixture, whisking until blended.

Beat egg whites in a bowl with an electric mixer until
stiff but not dry. Gently fold whites into batter.

Heat oven to 250 degrees. Melt 2 tbsp. of the butter
in a large nonstick skillet over medium heat.
Working in batches, drop batter by ½ cupfuls onto
the skillet. Sprinkle 4 to 5 banana slices atop each
pancake. Cook until pancakes are lightly golden on
underside, about 3 minutes, then carefully flip and
continue cooking until pancake is golden and
cooked through, 3 to 4 additional minutes. Transfer
to a baking sheet and keep warm in the oven while
cooking remaining pancakes, adding more butter to
the skillet as needed, or serve as you make them. Top
served pancakes with dollops of Banana Cream.
Makes 4+ servings.

For the Banana Cream: In a small saucepan, cook
apple juice until reduced to ¼ cup to concentrate flavors. Set aside to cool completely.

Toss bananas in lemon juice; set aside.

Whip cream in a bowl with an electric mixer until
very soft peaks form. Continue whipping while slowly
adding the confectioners' sugar until stiff peaks form.

Toss the cooled apple juice with the bananas in a
medium bowl. Fold the whipped cream, one-third at
a time, into the banana mixture. Serve with the pancakes. Makes about 2 cups.

Sunday Brunch Crème Brûlée French Toast

I developed this recipe for an appearance on our local public television station. It was such a decadent success that our Sunday brunch patrons have been enjoying it ever since.

½ cup unsalted butter
1 cup packed light brown sugar
2 tbsp. brown rice syrup
9" round loaf of country-style bread
5 large eggs
1½ cups half-and-half
1 tsp. vanilla
1 tsp. Grand Marnier
¼ tsp. sea salt
Confectioners' sugar, sifted, for garnish

In a small saucepan, melt butter with brown sugar and syrup over medium heat, stirring until mixture is smooth. Pour into a 13x9x2" baking dish.

Cut six ¾"-thick slices from the center portion of the bread, reserving ends for immediate snacking or for another use. Arrange bread slices in one layer in baking dish, squeezing them to fit.

In a medium bowl, whisk together the eggs, half-and-half, vanilla, Grand Marnier, and salt until well combined; slowly pour mixture evenly over bread. Cover and chill overnight.

Bring bread mixture to room temperature for 30 minutes. Heat oven to 350 degrees. Bake uncovered in the middle of the oven until puffed and edges are golden, 35 to 40 minutes. Sprinkle with confectioners' sugar and serve immediately. Serves 4+.

Chef's Notes

About . . .
Brown rice syrup, a natural substitute for corn syrup, is my syrup of choice because it lacks that sickeningly sweet flavor of corn syrup. It's just sweet enough. Brown rice syrup is derived from rice and imparts a hearty, earthy sweet flavor.

How to Do It . . .
I love to use our Olde World French Bread for this, while our café often uses our Baguette. How to choose? You'll just have to try the recipe both ways.

French Toast Stuffed with Tofu

French toast with a tofu twist . . . and delicious flavor!

½ cup natural apple juice
¼ cup seedless raisins
¼ cup dried cranberries
¼ cup dried mangoes
1 lb. loaf day-old Italian bread,
cut into 1" slices
1 lb. refrigerated, firm tofu,
drained and crumbled
2 tsp. finely grated lemon zest
3 large eggs
1 cup vanilla soy milk
1 tsp. vanilla
Canola oil for cooking
Maple syrup or freshly sliced seasonal
fruit for serving

Chef's Notes

How to Do It . . .
Use the refrigerated, firm tofu for this recipe as it will hold its crumble; silken tofu will simply "disappear"!

Heat apple juice to a simmer in a medium saucepan; remove from heat. Soak the raisins, cranberries, and mangoes in the apple juice for 30 minutes.

Gently pull centers from each bread slice, leaving about ¾" bread around the crust. Crumble center of bread into pieces and place in a large bowl. Add tofu crumbles, lemon zest, and drained soaked fruit.

In a large bowl, beat eggs, soy milk, and vanilla until combined. Add ½ cup of this mixture to the bread mixture and toss.

Place remaining egg mixture in a shallow bowl. Dip each bread slice gently in egg mixture to coat. Set aside on a baking sheet.

Heat an oiled, large nonstick skillet over medium heat until hot. Arrange a few of the soaked bread slices on the skillet and fill the centers with some of the tofu mixture, pressing gently with a heat-resistant spatula to pack. Cook until golden brown on bottom, about 4 minutes. Gently turn and cook until golden brown. Serve at once with maple syrup, fruit, or (why not!) both. Makes 4+ servings.

Blueberry Blintzes

A popular Sunday brunch item, the hardest part of this
recipe is deciding how many to make.

Blintzes

1 cup unbleached, all-purpose flour
1 cup milk, whole or 2 percent
3 large eggs
2 tbsp. unsalted butter, melted,
plus additional for cooking
2 tsp. granulated sugar
Pinch of sea salt
1 tsp. canola oil for cooking
Sour cream for serving

Blueberry Filling

2 cups fresh or frozen blueberries, divided
2 tbsp. lemon juice
1 tsp. finely grated lemon zest
2 tbsp. granulated sugar
½ tsp. ground ginger
¼ tsp. ground cinnamon

Chef's Notes

About . . .
A blintz is a thin, tender pancake (similar to a crepe)
that's rolled to enclose its sweet or savory filling,
sautéed until golden, then traditionally served with
sour cream.

For the Blintzes: Combine the flour, milk, eggs, butter, sugar, and salt in a blender or food processor until smooth. Pour the batter into a pitcher or batter bowl with a pouring lip. Cover with plastic wrap and let stand at a cool room temperature for 30 minutes or refrigerate for up to 2 days.

Place a 7½" nonstick skillet over medium heat. Coat the pan with a little unsalted butter. Stir the batter and pour 3 tbsp. into the pan, lifting the pan off the heat and tilting and rotating it so that the batter forms an even layer.

Cook until the top is dry and set (but not completely cooked) and the underside is golden. Remove the blintz to a piece of waxed paper. Continue cooking the rest of the blintzes, buttering the pan and stirring the batter before each one. Stack the finished blintzes between sheets of waxed paper. Use as soon as they are cool enough to fill and roll, or let cool and wrap airtight, freezing for up to 1 month. Enough for 10 to 12 7½" blintzes.

For the Blueberry Filling: In a medium saucepan, bring *1 cup* of the berries, juice, zest, sugar, ginger, and cinnamon to a boil over medium heat, stirring constantly. Continue to boil until most of the berries have popped and the mixture is the consistency of jam. Stir in the remaining 1 cup of berries and cook for 1 minute. Transfer to a bowl and let cool to room temperature.

Spoon some of the filling in the center of the uncooked side of 6 or more of the blintzes. Fold the sides of each blintz around the filling to form a rectangular package. In a large nonstick skillet, heat over medium heat a little of the butter and 1 tsp. canola oil. When the butter has melted and the bubbles subside, add the blintzes, seam side down, and cook until golden brown on both sides. Transfer the blintzes to paper towels to drain for just a moment. Serve immediately with sour cream. Makes 6+ servings.

Mango-Pear Crisp

*This out-of-the-ordinary crisp is worth the
tango with a fresh mango in your kitchen.*

6 medium, firm ripe pears
2 ripe mangoes
¾ cup unbleached, all-purpose flour
½ cup granulated sugar
½ tsp. sea salt
8 tbsp. cold unsalted butter,
cut into small pieces
¼ cup diced crystallized ginger

Chef's Notes

About . . .
Crystallized ginger is fresh ginger that's been cooked
in sugar syrup and coated with coarse sugar.

How to Do It . . .
The mango tango—don't let this fruit intimidate
you. Repeat after me: "I am in charge in my kitchen."
Stand the mango upright on a cutting board and slice
through the flesh on one of the flatter sides, cutting
around the seed. Repeat on the other side to make
two cuts from the fruit plus a third center section
with the seed. You can use a sturdy kitchen spoon
and ease it between the ripe mango skin and the
fruit's flesh to separate, then place the fruit on the
cutting board, flat side down, to slice.

Heat oven to 375 degrees, positioning rack in the
lower third of the oven. Grease a 2-qt. baking dish
that's 2" deep.

Peel and core the pears. Slice them in half and then
cut each half into 4 wedges. Place in the baking dish.
Peel and cut mangoes into ½" slices. Toss with the
pears.

In a small bowl, stir together the flour, sugar, and salt.
Cut the butter into the flour mixture until it resembles coarse crumbs. Stir in the crystallized ginger.
Scatter the crumb topping evenly over the fruit. Tap
the dish gently on the counter once or twice to settle the crumbs.

Bake until the topping is golden brown, the fruit
juices are bubbling, and the fruit is tender when
pierced with a toothpick or skewer, about 45 minutes. Serve warm. Serves 4+.

Hashed Sweets

Delicate and crumbly, these lacy cakes have a sweet-salty
flavor that only sweet potatoes can provide.

1¼ lb. yellow or other starch sweet
potato (not orange)
½ tsp. sea salt
4 tbsp. unsalted butter

Chef's Notes

About . . .
The sweet potato vs. the yam. There are many varieties of sweet potato, but the two we're most familiar with are the pale sweet potato and the darker-skinned variety Americans erroneously refer to as a "yam." (True yams are not related to the sweet potato.)

Heat oven to 250 degrees.

Peel sweet potatoes then coarsely shred, tossing with salt in a large bowl.

Melt and heat 1 tbsp. of the butter in a small non-stick skillet over medium heat. When foam subsides, add ¾ cup of the potato mixture, spreading gently but evenly into a 6 or 7" round. Shaking skillet occasionally, cook potatoes until golden brown on the underside, about 4 minutes.

Flip potato cake over by covering skillet with flat side of a lid or plate at least 8" in diameter, then inverting the potato pancake onto the lid. Slide the pancake back into the skillet and cook until the second side is golden brown, 3 or 4 additional minutes. Keep warm on a baking sheet in the oven until all are cooked. Serves 3+.

Baked Breakfast Fruits

The aroma of this homespun fruit casserole will put a smile on anyone's face as they enter your home.

2 medium pears, cut into bite-size chunks
1 medium apple, cut into bite-size chunks
2 tbsp. snipped, pitted dates
2 tbsp. dried cranberries
1 tsp. ground cinnamon
¾ cup apple juice
2 tbsp. raspberry fruit spread
½ cup granola

Heat oven to 350 degrees.

In a 2-qt. casserole, combine the pears, apple, dates, and cranberries. Sprinkle with the cinnamon and then pour the apple juice over the mixture.

Bake, covered, for 20 to 25 minutes or until fruit is slightly tender.

While fruit is baking, heat fruit spread in a small saucepan until softened. Drizzle fruit spread over baked fruit and sprinkle with granola before serving. Serve warm. Makes 2 servings.

Chef's Notes

About . . .
Remember those great granola recipes at the beginning of this chapter? This is the perfect place to use one of them.

How to Do It . . .
A cup of hot water and some kitchen shears make easy work out of snipping pitted dates (snip, dip, then snip again!).

Pumpkin-Orange Spice Bread

The texture and flavor of pumpkin pairs well with orange for a bright, light, flavorful combination. You'll see this combo often in our recipes.

¾ cup granulated sugar
⅓ cup canola oil
2 large eggs
1 cup pumpkin puree
½ cup orange marmalade
1½ cups + 2 tbsp. unbleached, all-purpose flour
½ tsp. salt
½ tsp. baking soda
2 tsp. ground cinnamon
1 tsp. ground ginger
½ tsp. freshly grated nutmeg
¼ tsp. ground cloves
½ cup dried cranberries
¼ cup coarsely chopped toasted pecans

Heat oven to 350 degrees. Generously grease a 9x5" loaf pan.

With an electric mixer, beat the sugar with the oil in a large mixing bowl until well combined. Beat in the eggs. Add the pumpkin and marmalade, beating until smooth.

Combine the flour, salt, baking soda, cinnamon, ginger, nutmeg, and cloves in a medium bowl, whisking until mixture is evenly blended. Add the flour mixture to the egg mixture a little at a time, stirring until completely incorporated. Stir in cranberries and pecans.

Scrape the batter into the prepared loaf pan and bake for 1 hour or until a toothpick inserted in the center of the loaf comes out clean. Cool pan on a wire rack for 15 minutes. Invert the pan and gently shake to release the bread. Cool the bread completely on the wire rack. Makes 1 loaf.

Chef's Notes

How to Do It . . .
Cooled completely and wrapped in plastic wrap, this loaf keeps for up to 3 days at room temperature.

Apple Quick Bread with Praline Topping

This bread is more like a dessert—moist, sweet, with a crunch-and-crumble top. One slice is hardly enough.

Quick Bread

1 cup granulated sugar
8 oz. sour cream
2 large eggs
2 tsp. vanilla
2 cups unbleached, all-purpose flour
2 tsp. baking powder
½ tsp. baking soda
½ tsp. sea salt
1¼ cups chopped, peeled tart apples
1 cup chopped pecans, toasted, divided

Topping

¼ cup unsalted butter
¼ cup packed light brown sugar

Chef's Notes

About . . .
What exactly is quick bread? It's bread that is quick to make because it doesn't require rising time (from yeast) or kneading.

In Season . . .
Choose your favorite seasonal apple for this bread. Some of my preferences would include Gala, Granny Smith, or Fuji—but there's always a new, crisp variety available in our produce departments. I simply ask, "What's your best organic apple right now?"

Heat oven to 350 degrees. Lightly grease a 9x5x3" loaf pan.

For the Quick Bread: In a large mixing bowl, beat together the sugar, sour cream, eggs, and vanilla with an electric mixer on low speed until well combined, stopping to scrape bowl. Beat on medium speed for 2 minutes.

In a small bowl, stir together the flour, baking powder, baking soda, and salt; add to the sour-cream mixture, beating on low speed until combined. Stir in the apple and *½ cup* of the pecans.

Turn batter into prepared loaf pan. Sprinkle top with remaining pecans, pressing them lightly into batter.

Bake for 55-60 minutes or until a toothpick inserted in the center comes out clean. (If loaf looks like it's overbrowning, cover loosely with foil for the last 15 minutes to keep it from burning.) Remove pan from oven; cool bread in pan on a wire rack for 15 minutes.

For the Topping: Prepare topping while loaf is cooling. In a small saucepan, combine butter and brown sugar, cooking and stirring until mixture comes to a boil. Reduce heat and boil gently for 2 minutes.

Slide a piece of waxed paper under the wire rack. Carefully remove bread from pan and place bread on wire rack. Drizzle top with brown sugar mixture; cool. Makes 1 loaf (serves 8+).

Opposite: This moist quick bread would be a perfect gift from your kitchen when organic apples are at their peak.

Flavorful Fruit Muffins

These are moist and fruity and best enjoyed warm.
Perfect for a gluten-free or wheat-free friend.

⅔ cup brown rice flour
⅔ cup white rice flour
3 tbsp. tapioca flour
¼ cup potato starch
½ tsp. sea salt
2 tsp. (gluten-free) baking powder
½ tsp. ground cinnamon
⅔ cup (gluten-free) milk, cow or rice
⅓ cup unsweetened applesauce
3 tbsp. soft pitted prunes, finely chopped
⅔ cup (gluten-free) brown rice syrup
½ tsp. alcohol-free vanilla extract
½ cup ground flax seed
½ medium banana
1½ cups fresh blueberries

Heat oven to 375 degrees. Line 10 muffin tins with muffin paper.

In a large bowl, combine flours, potato starch, salt, baking powder, and cinnamon. Mix well. In a blender, combine the milk, applesauce, prunes, rice syrup, vanilla, ground flax, and banana and puree until well mixed, stopping to scrape sides of blender often. Pour into dry ingredients and gently but thoroughly mix. Fold in blueberries with a spatula.

Fill muffin cups two-thirds full and bake for 20 to 25 minutes or until golden brown. Makes 10 muffins.

Chef's Notes

How to Do It . . .
Specialty flours such as those used in this recipe are best kept well sealed in a plastic bag and refrigerated or frozen.

Sugar-Crusted Sweet-Potato Biscuits

Whole-wheat pastry flour adds some whole grain while
maintaining a lightness to these moist biscuits.

1 cup whole-wheat pastry flour
1 cup unbleached, all-purpose flour
3 tsp. baking powder
½ tsp. sea salt
4 tbsp. firmly packed light brown sugar, divided
3 tbsp. trans-fat-free shortening or
unsalted butter
⅔ cup milk, 2 percent or skim
½ cup mashed, cooked (orange-fleshed)
sweet potato
⅓ cup sour cream, regular or low fat

Chef's Notes

How to Do It . . .
Tender biscuits result from a soft touch. Mix gently
and quickly and just until dry ingredients are moistened.

Heat oven to 375 degrees. Line a cookie sheet with
parchment paper or use a nonstick cookie sheet.

In a medium bowl, combine flours, baking powder,
salt, and *2 tbsp.* of the brown sugar; mix well. Using
a pastry blender or fork, cut in shortening/butter
until mixture is crumbly.

In a small bowl, combine the milk, sweet potato, and
sour cream; blend well. Add to flour mixture all at
once, stirring just until moistened. (If dough is too
dry, add milk 1 tsp. at a time until all dry ingredients
are moistened.)

To form each biscuit, drop ¼ cup of the dough onto
cookie sheet. Sprinkle with remaining 2 tbsp. of the
brown sugar.

Bake for 15 to 20 minutes or until peaks and bottom
of biscuits are golden brown. Serve warm. Makes 12
biscuits.

White-Chocolate and Dried-Cherry Scones

Although these are delicious any time of year, they're the perfect holiday scone dotted with colorful dried cherries and chunks of white chocolate.

Scones

1¾ cups unbleached, all-purpose flour
¼ cup granulated sugar
2 tsp. baking powder
¼ tsp. baking soda
¼ tsp. salt
¼ cup unsalted butter
½ cup dried cherries
½ cup coarsely chopped white chocolate
1 tsp. finely grated orange zest
½ cup low-fat vanilla yogurt
⅓ cup buttermilk

Topping

2 tbsp. buttermilk
1 tbsp. granulated sugar
½ teaspoon finely grated orange zest

Chef's Notes

About . . .
If you enjoy giving gifts from your kitchen, this is a perfect gift.

How to Do It . . .
If you're giving these scones as a gift, wrap completely after cooling and include a card with directions for reheating. (Wrap in foil and heat at 300 degrees for 10 to 12 minutes.)

Heat oven to 375 degrees. Line cookie sheet with parchment paper or use a nonstick cookie sheet.

For the Scones: In a large bowl combine the flour, sugar, baking powder, baking soda, and salt. Using a pastry blender or fork, cut in the butter until mixture resembles coarse crumbs. Stir in cherries, white chocolate, and orange zest.

In a small bowl, mix together the yogurt and buttermilk until blended. Stir into the dry ingredients just until moistened.

Shape dough into a ball and place on cookie sheet. Roll or pat dough into an 8" circle. Cut into 6 or 8 wedges; do not separate.

For the Topping: Brush dough with the buttermilk. In a small bowl, combine the sugar and orange zest. Sprinkle over dough.

Bake for 18 to 25 minutes or until edges begin to turn golden brown. Cool 5 minutes. Cut into wedges; serve warm. Makes 6 to 8 scones.

Pumpkin Scones

Once again, whole-wheat pastry flour adds whole-grain goodness while maintaining that light texture. These moist scones brighten up any brunch menu.

1 cup whole-wheat pastry flour
1 cup unbleached, all-purpose flour
1 tbsp. baking powder
½ tsp. salt
½ tsp. ground ginger
½ tsp. ground cinnamon
¼ tsp. freshly grated nutmeg
3 tbsp. + 1 tsp. granulated sugar, divided
4 tbsp. unsalted butter, cut into pieces
½ cup milk, whole or 2 percent
½ cup pumpkin puree
¾ cup fresh or dried cranberries,
tossed with 1 tbsp. flour

Chef's Notes

In Season . . .
When fresh cranberries are in season, buy an extra bag or two to stick in your freezer. They're perfect for this recipe, and they can be measured and used frozen.

Heat oven to 400 degrees.

In a mixing bowl, combine flours, baking powder, salt, ginger, cinnamon, nutmeg, and 3 *tbsp.* of the sugar; stir to blend. Using a pastry blender or fork, cut the butter into the dry ingredients until mixture resembles coarse crumbs.

In a small bowl, combine the milk with the pumpkin puree, blending well. Stir the milk mixture and cranberry mixture into the dry ingredients just until dough begins to come together. Turn the dough out onto a lightly floured surface, gather it together, and knead lightly just to blend. Do not overwork the dough or the scones will become tough.

Flatten the dough into a round about 1" thick and place on a cookie sheet. Cut into 8 to 10 wedges; do not separate. Lightly sprinkle them with the remaining tsp. of sugar.

Bake until golden on top, 15 to 18 minutes. Cool on a wire rack for a few minutes, then serve warm. Makes 8 to 10 scones.

Breakfast Tortilla Wrap

The perfect "eat on the run" morning wake up!

1 strip bacon, turkey bacon or
veggie bacon, chopped
2 tbsp. chopped green bell pepper
⅛ tsp. sea salt
⅛ tsp. ground cumin
⅛ tsp. crushed red pepper flakes
1 large egg and 1 large egg white,
lightly beaten
2 tbsp. chopped tomato
Few dashes of hot pepper sauce
1 warmed 8" flour tortilla

In a 10" nonstick skillet, cook bacon until crisp. Add green bell pepper, salt, cumin, and crushed red pepper flakes. Cook for 4 additional minutes.

Add eggs and cook for 2 minutes or until almost cooked through. Stir in tomato and hot pepper sauce. Spoon onto tortilla and roll up. Makes 1 serving.

Chef's Notes

About . . .
Cumin is used to make curries and chili powders, but I love it in many dishes. It has an aromatic, complex, nutty, peppery flavor and aroma. For optimum flavor, toast cumin seeds (see "Basic Techniques from the Cooking School") and grind after cooling.

Turkey Waldorf Salad

Try this salad on a bed of assorted greens or (the way we like it)
as the topping for an open-faced sandwich on toasted seven-grain
bread with freshly made cranberry sauce.

Dressing

2 cups canola mayonnaise
3 tbsp. white wine vinegar
½ cup peeled and chopped tart apple
½ cup crumbled, mild chèvre
2 tbsp. chopped fresh chives or parsley
Sea salt and freshly ground black pepper to taste

Salad

3 lb. roasted boneless turkey breast
½ cup chopped dried apricots
¼ cup dried tart cherries
2 celery ribs, coarsely chopped
1 tart apple, cored and thinly sliced
½ cup coarsely chopped pecans, toasted
2 cups Dressing
¼ cup chopped fresh Italian (flat-leaf) parsley
¼ cup chopped fresh chives
Sea salt and freshly ground black pepper to taste

For the Dressing: Place the mayonnaise and vinegar in a food processor fitted with a metal blade, pulsing to combine. Add the apple, chèvre, and chives or parsley, pulsing again just until blended. Season with salt and pepper.

Cube the turkey breast into large pieces and place in a serving bowl. Add the apricots, cherries, celery, apple, pecans, and Dressing and mix gently until combined. Add the parsley and chives and toss, mixing with salt and pepper to taste.

Serve immediately or refrigerate in a covered container until ready to serve. May be prepared 1 day in advance. Serves 6+.

Chef's Notes

About . . .
French for "goat," chèvre is a white goat cheese with a tart, tangy flavor. I love to buy it from our local purveyors just when it arrives . . . the creamy flavor is divine.

In Season . . .
You might try smoked turkey or chicken in place of the roasted turkey. Or, if you're feeling adventuresome, try currants or dried cranberries or grapes, halved, for the dried apricots. Not in the mood for apples? Firm, sweet tart pears are a tasty substitute.

Spinach Cheese Strata

Think of it as lasagna without the pasta. This layered dish of spinach, cheese, and eggs is the perfect do-ahead for your next gathering.

10 oz. package frozen spinach, thawed
1½ cups finely chopped yellow onion
3 tbsp. unsalted butter
1 tsp. sea salt, divided
½ tsp. freshly ground black pepper, divided
¼ tsp. freshly grated nutmeg
8 cups cubed (1" size) Italian bread
2 cups coarsely grated Gruyere
1 cup finely grated Parmigiano-
Reggiano cheese
2¾ cups milk, whole or 2 percent
9 large eggs
2 tbsp. Dijon mustard

Chef's Notes

About . . .
Swiss Gruyere is a cow's milk cheese with a rich, sweet, nutty flavor.

Parmigiano-Reggiano, with the name stenciled on the rind, hails from Italy and is aged much longer (usually about 2 years) than the Parmesan cheese we're accustomed to. It has a rich, sharp flavor and granular texture that melts in your mouth!

How to Do It . . .
Nothing compares to nutmeg that's been freshly grated. The small, hard, egg-shaped nutmeg seed (available in jars or in our bulk food sections) is easy to grate with a fine rasp (such as a nutmeg grater) or a specifically designed nutmeg grinder. Once you try the freshly grated flavor and smell the delicately warm, spicy, and sweet aroma, you'll never turn back!

Squeeze handfuls of the spinach to remove as much liquid as possible. Finely chop.

In a 12" skillet, cook onion in butter over medium heat, stirring until soft. Add *½ tsp.* of the salt, *¼ tsp.* of the pepper, and the nutmeg and cook, stirring for 1 minute. Stir in chopped spinach and remove skillet from heat.

Spread one-third of the bread cubes in a greased 3-qt. gratin dish or other shallow baking dish and top evenly with one-third of the spinach mixture. Sprinkle with one-third of each cheese. Repeat layering twice, ending with cheeses.

Whisk together the milk, eggs, mustard, and remaining salt and pepper in a large bowl; pour evenly over the layers in baking dish. Cover and chill at least 8 hours to allow bread to absorb custard.

Heat oven to 350 degrees. Let strata stand at room temperature for 30 minutes, then bake uncovered in the middle of the oven until puffed, golden brown, and cooked through, 45 to 55 minutes. Let stand 5 minutes before serving. Makes 6 to 8 servings.

Ratatouille

*Surely there should be a children's song by this name,
it's so musical . . . ra-tuh-TOO-ee!*

1 cup extra-virgin olive oil, plus more
as needed for cooking
1 large eggplant, unpeeled and cut
crosswise into 1" slices
1 large yellow onion, diced
2 medium-size zucchini, diced
5 large garlic cloves, peeled and minced
2 cups firmly packed fresh basil leaves,
measured then chopped
½ cup fresh lemon juice
2½ tsp. finely grated lemon zest
¼ tsp. sea salt
¼ tsp. freshly ground black pepper
¼ cup chopped Italian (flat-leaf) parsley

Heat ¾ *cup* of the oil in a large skillet over medium-high heat. Add several eggplant slices and sauté, turning occasionally, just until golden. Remove from the skillet and set aside. After all eggplant has finished cooking, cut slices into 1" cubes. Place cubes in a deep, 3-qt. casserole.

Heat oven to 350 degrees. Quickly sauté the onion and zucchini in the remaining ¼ cup of the oil in the same skillet just until lightly golden. Remove to the casserole.

Add the garlic, basil, lemon juice, lemon zest, salt, and pepper to the veggies, stirring gently to mix. Bake covered for 1 hour. Taste and adjust seasonings, then stir in the parsley. Serves 3+.

Chef's Notes

In Season . . .
Although the vegetables can vary with the cook, fresh eggplant is the star in this French-inspired dish.

Crab Salad to Top Your Waffle

What? Crab salad with my waffle? Just once, skip the maple syrup and top your waffle with this edible luxury. (Great, huh?!)

1 lb. lump crabmeat, cartilage removed, then flaked
6 scallions, white part only, trimmed and thinly sliced
2 tbsp. snipped fresh chives
1½ tbsp. lemon juice, plus more to taste
⅔ cup mayonnaise
2 tbsp. ketchup
Sea salt and freshly ground black pepper to taste
Hot pepper sauce to taste

Put the crabmeat in a medium bowl and, using a fork, toss it with the scallions, chives, lemon juice, mayonnaise, and ketchup until evenly blended. Season with salt, pepper, and hot pepper sauce. If desired, additional lemon juice may be added to brighten and lighten the flavor. Cover with plastic wrap and refrigerate while making waffles. Serve one waffle to a plate with a scoop of Crab Salad in the center. Serves 6+.

Chef's Notes

In Season . . .
Scallions vs. green onions. It's all in the name, but they're both the same. Choose scallions with crisp, bright green tops and a firm, white base.

SATISFYING SOUPS

Soups and stews warm, sustain, and soothe us. They whet our appetites, stick to our ribs, and make us feel better when we're under the weather. They can be simple or elegant, hearty or light, hot or cold. Soups are one-pot meals that need only the accompaniment of one of our artisan breads fresh from the oven and a crisp, green organic salad to be complete.

In this savory and sweet selection of recipes, there are satisfying soups that reflect their ethnic origins, those that mirror a regional heritage, and those that are contemporary and inviting. The best thing about these soups is not the convenience of making them but how good they taste.

Soups make a warm, healthy, satisfying lunch to take to work or to heat up when you don't have the time to cook. A soup can also be a light, comforting late-night supper. Hearty soups, like the Curried Vegetable Soup in this collection, are the perfect choice for a crowd, not just because they are easy to prepare but because you can make them a day in advance—and they taste even better the next day!

How to Do It . . . a Little Chef's Magic for Your Kitchen

Like some things in life, making soup is not an exact science. Experiment with these recipes depending on the season and what you have on hand; soup is almost impossible to mess up! Here are some tips from the cooking school to help you along.

Soup recipes are easily doubled: Freeze some for later or bring some to a friend. Make chili and bean soups when you have some extra time . . . you'll be happy to have them in the refrigerator or freezer for a quick, healthy meal.

Select recipes by the season: Especially with pureed soups, which are all about the concentration of flavors, the natural flavors of the fresh ingredients you start with will make all the difference.

Garnish or accent: provide contrasting flavors and textures. Make the "same ol' soup" more interesting and elegant (even if it's just for you). Some inspiration:
- a spoonful of orange relish on top (especially anything with black beans)
- a swirl of extra-virgin olive oil
- diced pieces of avocado
- toasted pumpkin seeds
- of course, a dollop of the usual sour cream (or low-fat yogurt) with some chopped chives

Vegetable trimmings from your soup makings? These "scraps" are perfect for making a quick broth. Place the trimmings in a saucepan while you prep the vegetables for the soup. Add just enough cold water to cover the trimmings, salt and pepper, and two bay leaves and simmer for 30 minutes. Strain and you will have a delicious broth for this soup or the next.

Don't forget that a vegetable pureed soup also makes a delicious sauce for grilled fish, chicken, or tofu.

Is It a . . . ? Terms for Soups and Beyond

Bisque: A rich cream or pureed soup, often made with shellfish or poultry.

Broth: The liquid obtained by simmering meat or poultry, bones, and/or vegetables in hot water. Broth is usually seasoned, strained, and degreased for use as the base for soups, stews, and sauces. The terms broth and stock are used interchangeably.

Chili (con carne): A highly seasoned Mexican American dish of beef, tomatoes, and oftentimes beans. There are many variations, and the name is ordinarily shortened to chili.

Chowder: A milk-based thick soup made from fish, shellfish, or vegetables. Diced potatoes are usually included.

Minestrone: A rich, thick vegetable soup usually containing dried beans and pasta.

Stew: A combination of meat or fish, vegetables, and a small amount of liquid that is simmered or slowly boiled in a covered container. It is characterized by tender meat and well-mingled flavors.

Stock: See Broth.

There's a variety of flavor profiles in this Asian Mushroom and Leek Soup, but they all add up to one thing—delicious!

Wild Rice and Chicken Chowder

Hearty flavors combine to make this one-pot meal perfect for
weeknights and special enough for entertaining.

2 baking potatoes (about 4 oz. each), peeled
and coarsely chopped
1 large yellow onion, chopped
2 large garlic cloves, pressed or finely minced
2 small jalapeños, cored, seeded, and chopped
4 cups chicken broth
3 tbsp. extra-virgin olive oil
½ cup diced celery
½ cup diced red bell pepper, plus
more for garnish
¾ cup diced sweet potato
¾ cup corn kernels (frozen if not in season)
Sea salt and freshly ground black pepper to taste
½ cup milk, whole or 2 percent
1½ cups cooked wild rice, plus more for garnish
2 cups diced, cooked chicken
¼ tsp. Worcestershire sauce

Chef's Notes

About . . .
Technically not a rice at all but a long-grain marsh
grass native to the northern Great Lakes area, wild
rice is known for its luxuriously nutty flavor.

Sea Salt gives food an earthy, substantial quality; it
tends to enhance a dish rather than overpower it.
Sea salt is produced from tidal pools of concentrated
saline and is often hand harvested.

How to Do It . . .
Use gloves when cutting up hot chilies like jalapeños
so capsaicin won't burn your skin.

In a large saucepan, stir together the potato, onion,
garlic, jalapeños, and broth. Bring to a boil. Reduce
heat to a simmer and cook until the veggies are
extremely soft, about 45 minutes. Cool slightly, then
puree until smooth, straining if desired for a
smoother texture. Rinse out the saucepan.

While the soup base is cooking, heat the oil in a 12"
skillet until hot. Add the celery, bell peppers, sweet
potato, and corn and sauté over medium-high heat
until soft and slightly browned, 10 to 15 minutes.
Season with salt and pepper to taste.

Return the pureed soup base to the saucepan. Add
the milk and bring the mixture to a simmer. Add the
cooked wild rice, chicken, and sautéed veggies.
Season with a little more salt as needed and add the
Worcestershire sauce. Simmer (do not boil) for 15
minutes, giving the flavors a chance to blend.

Serve hot, garnished with some wild rice and diced
peppers. Makes 6 to 8 cups.

Chipotle Chicken Stew

Spicy, warm, and stick-to-your-ribs goodness . . . This full-bodied stew is perfect with a square of cornbread from our bakery.

1 medium yellow onion, diced
3 celery ribs, diced
½ cup canola oil
¼ cup unbleached, all-purpose flour
4 qt. chicken broth
2½ lb. cooked chicken pieces, cubed
4 cups seeded, diced tomato
4 large Idaho potatoes, cooked, cooled, and diced
2 tbsp. chipotle powder
2 oz. hot pepper sauce
Sea salt and freshly ground black pepper to taste

In a large stockpot, sweat onion and celery in canola oil until soft and lightly golden in color. Add flour, stirring to toast. Add broth, stirring to thicken. Combine chicken, tomatoes, and potatoes in broth. Stir in chipotle powder, hot sauce, and salt and pepper. Simmer for 25 minutes to allow flavors to blend, then serve. Serves 10+.

Chef's Notes

About . . .
Hot sauce, a common brand of which is Tabasco, is a fiery-hot commercial sauce made of red chili peppers, vinegar, and salt. The sauce is aged (oftentimes in oak barrels) before being bottled.

Chipotle powder is made from smoked jalapeño peppers, brownish-red chili peppers with wrinkled skin, and ground into a powder.

How to Do It . . .
To sweat the onion and celery is a technique by which ingredients, particularly vegetables, are cooked in a small amount of fat over low heat. The ingredients are covered directly with a piece of foil, parchment, or waxed paper, then the pot is tightly covered. This method allows the ingredients to both soften without browning and cook in their own juices.

In Season . . .
Can I still buy an Idaho potato if I don't live in Idaho? Sure, we'll just call it a russet potato.

Split-Pea Soup with Spiced Yogurt

When I was a kid, I always thought it would be fun to have a job splitting peas! This is a hearty, flavorful soup perfect for a cold winter day.

Soup

1 cup dry split peas
4 cups vegetable broth
¼ tsp. dried rosemary, crushed
1 bay leaf
½ cup coarsely chopped yellow onion
1 cup sliced celery
1 cup chopped carrots
2 garlic cloves, pressed or finely minced
2 tbsp. dry sherry

Spiced Yogurt

½ cup plain, low-fat yogurt
¼ tsp. ground turmeric
¼ tsp. sweet paprika
¼ tsp. ground cumin
⅛ tsp. cayenne pepper

For the Soup: Pick through peas to check for small stones; rinse peas and drain. In a large saucepan, combine the split peas, vegetable broth, rosemary, and bay leaf. Bring to a boil. Reduce heat, cover, and simmer for 1 hour, stirring occasionally.

Stir in the onion, celery, carrots, and garlic. Return to a boil then reduce heat. Cover and simmer 20 minutes more or until the veggies are crisp-tender. Discard bay leaf. Stir in sherry.

For the Spiced Yogurt: In a small bowl, stir together the yogurt, turmeric, paprika, cumin, and cayenne. Serve each cup or bowl of soup with a dollop of the Spiced Yogurt. Makes 4+ servings.

Chef's Notes

About . . .
Split peas are a variety of yellow or green peas grown specifically for drying. When dried and split along the natural seam, they are called (you guessed it) split peas. Whole they are referred to as field peas.

Chickpea and Escarole Soup with Garlic-Toasted Bread

A hearty, good-for-you soup with a European flair.

Soup

3 tbsp. extra-virgin olive oil
1 cup finely diced yellow onion
1 garlic clove, peeled and finely chopped
3 tbsp. chopped fresh Italian (flat-leaf) parsley
2 tsp. chopped fresh marjoram, divided
½ lb. plum tomatoes, peeled, seeded, and coarsely chopped
2 cups cooked chickpeas with their liquid
4 cups vegetable broth or chicken broth
Sea salt and freshly ground black pepper to taste
½ of a small head of escarole, tough outer leaves removed, leaves julienned

Bread

4 slices artisan bread, such as our bakery's Pain au Levain or Olde World French
Extra-virgin olive oil
2 garlic cloves, peeled and halved
Freshly grated Parmigiano-Reggiano cheese, plus additional for soup garnish

Chef's Notes

About . . .
Chickpeas—not just for chicks! These are also known as garbanzo, ceci (Italy), and chana dal (India).

In Season . . .
Escarole, the sturdy, broad-leafed variety of endive, has a strong, slightly bitter flavor that's less pronounced in the creamy white center leaves. Kale is also a delicious substitute for escarole in this recipe.

For the Soup: Heat the oil in a large saucepan over medium heat. Add the onion and cook over low heat until the onion softens. Add the garlic, parsley, and *1 tsp.* of the marjoram. Cook for 3 minutes, stirring occasionally. Add the tomatoes and cook an additional 5 minutes.

With the vegetables, combine the chickpeas, their liquid, and the broth; bring to a boil. Simmer for 30 minutes, seasoning with salt and freshly ground pepper as needed. Add the escarole and cook just until the escarole is tender.

For the Bread: While soup is cooking, prepare the bread. Brush the slices with some olive oil, then rub each slice with a garlic half. Discard garlic or finely chop it and sprinkle atop the garlic-rubbed bread slices. Sprinkle with cheese. Toast in a 350-degree oven for 15 minutes or until bread is crisp. Cool.

To serve: Arrange a slice of the toasted bread in the bottom of each of four shallow soup bowls. Ladle soup over the bread. Sprinkle with remaining marjoram and additional cheese. Serve immediately. Serves 4.

Soba Noodles in Vegetable Broth

Japanese buckwheat or soba noodles offer an interesting
whole-grain flavor to this veggie-packed broth.

5 oz. soba noodles
6 cups vegetable broth
1 tbsp. peanut oil
½ cup sliced fresh mushrooms such as cremini
or white button
10 to 12 dried shiitake mushrooms, reconstituted
1 small carrot, julienned
1 small zucchini, julienned
2 cups shredded napa cabbage
7 oz. firm, refrigerated tofu, drained then cut
into ½" cubes
6 to 8 snow peas, strings removed, julienned
1½ tsp. soy sauce
6 to 8 fresh spinach leaves, stems removed,
then torn into bite-size pieces
1 tbsp. toasted sesame oil
Freshly ground white pepper

Chef's Notes

About . . .
Tofu, or bean (soy) curd, is soft and cheeselike with a
bland taste. It is available in soft, firm, and silken forms.

How to Do It . . .
To reconstitute dried shiitakes, soak (or reconstitute)
in hot water until soft, about 30 minutes. Strain to
remove grit (reserving soaking liquid for another use,
perhaps a mushroom broth for another soup), then
cut to desired size.

In Season . . .
Napa cabbage has pale green, oblong leaves and a
zesty, moist crispness.

Snow peas are one of the two types of edible pea
pods. These peas contain tiny peas inside flat, tender
3"- to 4"-long pods.

Cook the noodles according to package directions.
In a colander, drain and rinse the noodles with cold
water to stop the cooking process. Place the noodles
in a pan with ½ *cup* of the vegetable broth and hold
over low heat until needed.

Heat a wok or large skillet over high heat. Add oil
and stir-fry mushrooms, carrot, and zucchini for 2
minutes. Add cabbage, tofu, and snow peas and stir-
fry over high heat for another 2 minutes. Add
remaining vegetable broth and soy sauce. Just before
serving, stir in spinach, sesame oil, and pepper to
taste.

Place noodles in individual bowls. Top with stir-fried
veggies and broth. Makes 3+ servings.

Miso Soup

Miso (bean paste) is a Japanese culinary mainstay used in soups, sauces, marinades, as a table condiment, and more. It's easily digested and extremely nutritious. You'll find a miso soup selection on our café menus on a daily basis.

6 cups water
1 strip kombu
1 small yellow onion, halved then thinly sliced
1 medium carrot, cut into thin matchsticks
1 tbsp. instant wakame flakes
3 stalks of bok choy, green tops only, cut into large chunks
3 tbsp. barley miso
4 oz. refrigerated, firm tofu, cut into small cubes
3 scallions, finely chopped

In a medium saucepan, bring the water and kombu to a boil. Remove from heat and let steep for 10 minutes. Strain broth, discarding kombu.

Return strained broth to saucepan and add onion and carrots. Simmer for 8 minutes. Add flakes and bok choy, simmering for 3 minutes. Remove from heat.

Dilute miso in $\frac{1}{2}$ cup of the soup broth; add to the saucepan with the tofu. (Do not boil soup after miso has been added.) Garnish with scallions and serve. Serves 4+.

Chef's Notes

About . . .
Kombu is a long, dark-brown to grayish-black seaweed, which, after harvesting, is sun-dried and folded into sheets. Kombu is also referred to as kelp.

Wakame, a deep-green seaweed, is often used as a vegetable in soups and simmered dishes.

Bok choy, a mild vegetable that resembles a bunch of wide-stalked celery with long, full leaves, has crunchy white stalks and tender, dark-green leaves.

Asian Mushroom and Leek Soup

★

The intense flavors of dried shiitake or porcini mushrooms combine with sweet
leeks, coconut milk, and lemongrass to give this soup an Asian flair.

½ oz. dried shiitake or porcini mushrooms
3 tbsp. peanut oil, divided
2 medium shallots, minced
1 large leek, white and tender green, cleaned,
halved lengthwise, thinly sliced crosswise
4 oz. white button mushrooms, stems
discarded, caps thinly sliced
1 tbsp. minced fresh ginger
½ tsp. curry powder
6 cups vegetable broth
½ cup coconut milk
1 tsp. arrowroot
1 tbsp. water
Coarse sea salt to taste
Freshly ground black pepper to taste
½ lb. assorted wild mushrooms, thinly sliced
1 tbsp. minced fresh lemongrass, tender
white bulb only
1 tbsp. lemon juice
1 tbsp. coarsely chopped fresh chives

Chef's Notes

About . . .
Shiitake vs. Porcini Mushrooms. Shiitakes have a
meaty flavor; stems are not edible but can be used to
make broth. Porcini mushrooms are also referred to
as cepes. These earthy treasures have a smooth,
meaty texture and a pungent, woodsy flavor.

How to Do It . . .
When choosing leeks, select those with clean, white
bottoms and crisp, fresh-looking green tops. To
clean, cut off and discard root ends. Trim tops, leaving about 3" of green leaves. Beginning at the green
end, cut leeks in half lengthwise. Hold under cold
running water, separating leaves carefully to rinse out
any dirt. Pat dry with paper towels before using.

In a small bowl, cover the dried mushrooms with hot
water and let soak until softened, about 30 minutes.
Drain and rinse off any grit. Discard the stems and
thinly slice the mushrooms as needed.

Heat 1 *tbsp.* of the oil in a large saucepan. Add the
shallots and cook over high heat, stirring until gold-
en brown. Add the leek, white and dried mushrooms,
ginger, and curry powder and, stirring, cook over
medium heat for 4 minutes. Slowly pour in the vegetable broth and coconut milk and bring to a boil.

In a small bowl, whisk the arrowroot with the water
until smooth. Stir the paste into the soup and bring
to a boil over medium-high heat. Reduce the heat to
low, simmering the soup for 30 minutes. Season with
salt and pepper.

Heat the remaining oil in a skillet. Add the wild
mushrooms and sauté over high heat until softened.

To serve: Divide the sautéed mushrooms among soup
bowls. Stir the lemongrass and lemon juice into the
soup. Ladle the soup into individual bowls and garnish with chopped chives. Makes 4+ servings.

In Season . . .
Chives are hearty, perennial herbs prized for their
mild onion flavor. Their purple blossoms are also edible and make a colorful garnish for soups or salads.

Hot-Buttered Cauliflower Soup

Even non-cauliflower lovers enjoy this flavorful, creamy soup.

8 cups chicken broth
1 medium-size (about 1 ½ lb.) cauliflower,
cleaned and thinly sliced
2 medium leeks, green leaves trimmed, split
lengthwise, washed well, and thinly sliced
1 cup heavy (whipping) cream
½ tsp. freshly grated nutmeg, plus
more for garnish
Sea salt to taste
Freshly ground white pepper to taste
3 tbsp. unsalted butter, if desired

Chef's Notes

Do Ahead Tip:
Once you have added the cream, nutmeg, salt, and pepper to the puree, you can cover and chill the mixture for up to 3 days.

How to Do It . . .
To ready cauliflower for slicing, remove and discard outer leaves and carefully cut out core; rinse well. Break the cauliflower head into flowerets using your (clean) hands.

In a 5-qt. saucepan, combine broth, cauliflower, and leeks. Bring to a boil, then cover and simmer until cauliflower is very tender and will mash easily, about 30 minutes.

In a blender or with an immersion blender, puree mixture until smooth. If using a blender, return smooth mixture to saucepan. Add cream, nutmeg, and salt and pepper to taste. Heat to simmering.

Ladle into bowls and, if desired, add to each a small piece of butter to smooth the mixture and add a richer flavor. Sprinkle with freshly grated nutmeg for garnish. Serves 6+.

Curried Vegetable Soup

The flavors of this soup jump right off your spoon . . .

1½ tsp. extra-virgin olive oil
1 tbsp. curry powder
1 large leek, cleaned and chopped
4 cups chicken or vegetable broth
½ cup red lentils
1 medium red skin or Yukon Gold potato, peeled and diced
1 medium sweet potato, peeled and diced
1 medium turnip, diced
1 medium parsnip, sliced on the diagonal
1 carrot, sliced on the diagonal
¼ cup coconut milk
2 tbsp. chopped fresh cilantro
Sea salt to taste
⅛ tsp. to ¼ tsp. cayenne pepper

Heat the oil in a medium saucepan. Add the curry powder and leek and, stirring frequently, cook over low heat for 2 minutes. Add the broth and the lentils. Bring to a boil; reduce to a simmer and cook covered over medium heat until the lentils are soft, about 10 minutes. Add the potato, sweet potato, turnip, parsnip, and carrot. Simmer covered until the veggies are soft but not mushy, about 20 minutes.

Remove from heat, then stir in the coconut milk and cilantro. Season with salt and cayenne and serve. Makes 4+ servings.

Chef's Notes

About . . .
Coconut milk is made by combining equal parts water with shredded fresh coconut meat, simmered then strained. Available canned in regular and light versions.

In Season . . .
Yukon Gold potatoes are a yellow-fleshed, moist potato.

Turnips may be eaten from top to bottom, with the globe-shaped roots having a reddish-purple skin, crisp white flesh, and a sweet/hot flavor. Choose firm, smooth, small- to medium-size (2" to 3" diameter) turnips that feel heavy for their size. If the tops are still attached, the leaves should be bright green and tender.

Parsnips are a fair-skinned cousin of carrots with a delicately sweet, nutty taste. Choose small- to medium-size parsnips that are smooth, firm, and well shaped. Avoid large roots.

Cheesy Country Vegetable Chowder

This corn, veggie, and cheese chowder is full flavored and perfect with a side salad and a plate of fresh, seasonal organic fruits.

½ cup yellow onion, finely chopped
1 large garlic clove, finely minced
1 cup sliced carrots
1 cup sliced celery
3½ cups chicken broth or vegetable broth
1 cup diced potatoes
2 cups corn kernels, fresh in season or frozen
2 cups half-and-half
¼ cup unsalted butter
¼ cup unbleached, all-purpose flour
1 tbsp. Dijon mustard
¼ tsp. freshly ground black pepper
¼ tsp. sweet paprika
8 oz. cheddar cheese, shredded

In a large saucepan, combine the onion, garlic, carrots, celery, broth, and potatoes. Bring to a boil. Reduce heat to a simmer, cover, and cook for 20 minutes or until the potatoes are tender. Stir in corn and remove from heat.

In a small saucepan, warm half-and-half to a simmer (do not boil); set aside.

In a medium saucepan, melt butter over low heat. Add flour, stirring until smooth. Cook butter/flour mixture over low heat for 3 minutes, stirring constantly until thick and bubbly. Add the mustard, pepper, paprika, warm half-and-half, and cheese, stirring constantly until cheese melts.

Gradually add the cheese sauce to the vegetable soup. Stir until thoroughly combined and heated through. Makes 4+ servings.

Chef's Notes

In Season . . .
One Potato, Two Potato . . . I like to use Yukon Gold potatoes for this recipe. These boiling potatoes with a buttery yellow/golden flesh have a moist texture.

Tomato-Orange Soup

*This combo always draws attention with its name—then draws "wows"
when tasted!*

35-oz. can whole plum tomatoes or 2¼ lb. ripe
plum tomatoes in season, quartered
½ cup firmly packed fresh basil leaves
1 or several long strips of orange peel
2 tbsp. sliced scallions, white part only
1 cup orange juice
1 tbsp. cornstarch or arrowroot
2 tbsp. chopped fresh Italian (flat-leaf) parsley
¼ tsp. sea salt
⅛ tsp. freshly ground black pepper
Sour cream or plain, low-fat yogurt for garnish,
optional

Chef's Notes

About . . .
Arrowroot, a white powder from the root of a tropical
plant of the same name, is used as a flour or thickener.
It remains clear in cooking, is easily digested, and
doesn't break down when reheated.

In Season . . .
Substitute ripe, fresh tomatoes for canned when in
season. Store fresh tomatoes at room temperature to
maintain that sweet, fresh tomato flavor.

Combine the tomatoes, basil, orange peel, and scallions in a 5-qt. saucepan. Cover and bring to a boil. Lower the heat and simmer covered for 15 minutes.

Remove the peel then force the mixture through a food mill into a bowl, or whirl mixture in a blender or food processor then strain through a fine sieve. Discard the solids. Return liquid to saucepan.

Combine the orange juice and cornstarch/arrowroot in a small bowl, mixing until smooth. Add to the tomato mixture. Cook over medium heat, stirring constantly until mixture thickens slightly and comes to a boil. Cook 1 minute longer.

Season with parsley, sea salt, and pepper. Garnish each serving with sour cream/yogurt, if desired. Makes 4+ servings.

Fresh Tomato Soup with Red Wine

This couldn't be easier to make. Serve this simple, cold zesty soup as a first course on a warm summer night. Slices of a crusty, scratch-made baguette and a glass of red wine complete the course.

3 cups tomato juice, chilled
2 cups peeled, seeded, coarsely chopped
fresh tomatoes
1 cup coarsely chopped zucchini
¼ cup finely chopped green bell pepper or
red bell pepper
¼ cup finely chopped yellow onion
¼ cup dry red wine
1 tbsp. coarsely chopped fresh basil leaves
1 garlic clove, pressed
¼ tsp. sea salt
2 tsp. extra-virgin olive oil

In a large serving bowl, combine the juice, tomatoes, zucchini, bell pepper, onion, red wine, basil, garlic, and salt. Mix well. Just before serving, gently stir in the olive oil. Makes 3+ servings.

Chef's Notes

In Season . . .
Based on the ingredients—tomatoes, zucchini, bell peppers, basil—this is definitely a summertime soup with maximum flavor.

A gazpacho-type soup taken to the next tasty level!

Cream of Roasted Fennel Soup

Always a hit in our soups and stews cooking classes, this
flavor-packed soup is sure to warm you up.

1 large fennel bulb (1½ to 2 lb.),
trimmed and sliced
1 cup coarsely chopped white onion
2 tsp. extra-virgin olive oil
½ tsp. coarse sea salt or kosher salt
1 large russet potato, peeled and cut into ½" cubes
4 cups chicken broth
1 cup half-and-half
¾ tsp. ground cumin
2 tbsp. grapefruit juice
Freshly ground white pepper to taste
1 tbsp. fennel seeds
Edible flowers, optional

Chef's Notes

About . . .
Not all flowers are edible, and those that have been
sprayed with pesticides (such as those found at
florists) should never be eaten! Some of the more
popular edible flowers include: nasturtiums, chive
blossoms, pansies, violas, roses, marigolds, and violets.
Unlike black peppercorns, white peppercorns are
picked when ripe and the skin is removed. White
pepper is traditionally less aromatic than black.

How to Do It . . .
To cut the fennel, trim away tough stalks and bottom
stem from fennel bulb; reserve leafy tops for garnish,
if desired. Cut the bulb and tender stalks into ½"-
thick slices.

In Season . . .
Fennel has been a Mediterranean favorite since the
time of the Romans. The raw bulb of fennel is
crunchy and celery-like in texture. Both the bulb
and the leaves have a slightly sweet, licorice taste.

Heat oven to 375 degrees. Arrange fennel and onion
in a 13x9" baking pan. Drizzle with olive oil and
sprinkle with salt. Roast for 25 minutes or until veggies are just tender, but not brown.

Transfer roasted fennel and onion to a large
saucepan. Add potato and broth; bring to a boil.
Reduce heat and simmer, covered, for 10 minutes or
until potatoes are tender. Cool.

In a blender or with an immersion blender, puree
mixture until smooth. If using a blender, return all
mixture to saucepan. Stir in half-and-half, cumin,
and grapefruit juice. Heat through. Season to taste
with white pepper.

While soup is heating, toast fennel seeds in a small
skillet over medium-high heat until lightly browned
and fragrant, stirring frequently and watching carefully so seeds do not burn. Remove from heat.

To serve, ladle soup into individual bowls. Top each
serving with a sprinkle of toasted fennel seeds. Garnish
with edible flowers if desired. Makes 8 servings.

Roasted-Garlic Potato Soup

An old cook's trick rediscovered, this soup is thickened by mashed potatoes
and gets its hearty, smoky flavor from the addition of bacon and garlic.

5 whole garlic heads
Drizzle of extra-virgin olive oil, if desired
2 bacon slices, diced
1 cup diced yellow onion
1 cup diced carrot
2 garlic cloves, minced (in case there isn't
enough already!)
6 cups diced baking potato
4 cups chicken broth
½ tsp. sea salt
¼ tsp. freshly ground black pepper
1 bay leaf
1 cup milk, 2 percent or whole
¼ cup chopped fresh Italian (flat-leaf) parsley

Chef's Notes

About . . .
Roasting garlic produces a sweet, mellow, irresistible
garlic flavor.

Heat oven to 350 degrees.

Remove white, papery skin from each garlic head (do
not peel or separate cloves). Drizzle olive oil over
garlic if desired. Wrap each head separately in foil
and bake for 1 hour; let cool for 15 minutes. Separate
cloves and squeeze to extract the garlic pulp (this
should yield about ¼ cup). Discard the garlic skins.

Cook the bacon in a large saucepan over medium-
high heat until crisp. Add the onion, carrot, and
minced garlic and sauté 10 minutes. Add the potato,
broth, salt, pepper, and bay leaf; bring to a boil.
Cover and simmer for 25 minutes or until potato is
tender; remove bay leaf.

Combine garlic pulp and 2 cups of the potato mixture in a blender and puree until smooth. Return
puree to pan with remainder of potato mixture. Stir
in milk and cook over low heat until heated through.
Remove from heat and stir in chopped parsley.
Makes 4 servings.

Cold Sweet-Potato Soup

*Layers of flavors combine to make this soup perfect
as a starter course for any holiday meal.*

1½ cups vegetable or chicken broth
1 medium yellow or white onion, minced
1 tbsp. freshly grated ginger
1 leek, white part only, cleaned and
coarsely chopped
1 whole clove
¼ tsp. ground cinnamon
⅛ tsp. freshly grated nutmeg
1 large, orange-fleshed sweet potato, peeled
and finely diced
2 tsp. maple syrup
2 cups half-and-half
1 tbsp. arrowroot or cornstarch
1 tbsp. orange juice

Chef's Notes

How to Do It . . .
For fresh grated ginger, remove the skin of the ginger
by scraping with a spoon or peeling, then grate with
a sharp grater.

In Season . . .
Maple syrup is made from the sap of sugar maples and
other maple trees. These trees are tapped with a spig-
ot set into the tree trunk, and the sap begins to "run"
in late winter and is then boiled down into sweet
syrup.

Pour *¼ cup* of the broth into a large saucepan and
bring to a simmer over medium-high heat. Reduce
the heat to medium low and add the onion, ginger,
leek, clove, cinnamon, and nutmeg. Cook, stirring
often, until the veggies become very soft and the liquid is almost evaporated. Add the sweet potato and
the remaining broth. Cover and simmer until the
sweet potato is soft enough to puree, about 10 minutes.

Transfer the mixture to a blender or use an immersion blender to puree. If using a blender, return mixture to the saucepan. Stir in the maple syrup.

In a medium mixing bowl, whisk together the half-
and-half and arrowroot/cornstarch until well blended.
Stir this mixture into the puree and set saucepan
over medium heat, stirring often, until thickened.

Remove from heat and pour into a bowl. Fill another
larger bowl with ice and place the bowl with the soup
gently inside the ice bowl. Cover with foil and refrigerate until thoroughly cool.

Just before serving, stir in the orange juice. Serves 4+.

Carrot Soup with Caraway Breadcrumb Topping

Buttered breadcrumbs sautéed with caraway seeds provide a crisp,
flavorful topping for this soup's smooth, slightly sweet carrot puree.

Carrot Puree

¼ cup extra-virgin olive oil
2 medium yellow onions, thinly sliced
2 lb. carrots, thinly sliced (avoid large,
woody carrots)
1 tsp. dried tarragon, crumbled
4 cups chicken broth
⅓ cup orange juice
2 tbsp. lemon juice
Sea salt to taste
Freshly ground white pepper to taste

Topping

3 tbsp. extra-virgin olive oil
1 tbsp. butter
2 tsp. caraway seeds
⅔ cup finely ground, fresh white breadcrumbs
2 tbsp. finely chopped fresh Italian
(flat-leaf) parsley

Chef's Notes

How to Do It . . .
Fresh breadcrumbs are moist and flavorful. A simple process, tear several slices of bread and place in a food processor, pulsing until pieces turn into crumbs. Leftovers must be refrigerated or frozen to prevent mold.

For the Carrot Puree: Heat oil in a large saucepan over medium heat. Add the onions and sauté until translucent. Add the carrots and tarragon, reduce the heat to low, and simmer covered, stirring occasionally, about 15 minutes. Stir in the broth, orange, and lemon juices. Bring to a boil, then reduce heat to low, cover, and simmer until the carrots are very tender, about 10 additional minutes.

In a blender or with an immersion blender, puree the soup. If using a blender, return puree to the saucepan, season to taste with salt and pepper, and keep warm on low heat.

For the Topping: Heat the oil and butter over medium heat in a small skillet until butter is melted and mixture is blended. Add the caraway seeds and sauté for 2 minutes, then add the crumbs. Raise the heat to medium high and, stirring, sauté until golden brown.

Ladle the soup into individual bowls and scatter the Topping generously on top. Garnish with a sprinkling of parsley. Serves 6+.

Serve this with a decorative flair, in small hollowed-out
pumpkins or squash as your serving bowls.

Ginger-Pumpkin Bisque

With the aroma and flavors of autumn, this bisque is like eating warm
pumpkin pie with a spoon. (Whipped cream optional!)

¾ cup chopped shallots
½ cup coarsely chopped yellow onion
2 tsp. freshly grated ginger
2 tbsp. walnut oil
¼ cup unbleached, all-purpose flour
4 cups chicken broth
½ cup apple cider or natural apple juice
16 oz. pumpkin puree
⅓ cup maple syrup
2 bay leaves
¼ tsp. ground cinnamon, plus more for garnish
¼ tsp. dried thyme, crushed
¼ tsp. freshly ground black pepper
⅛ tsp. ground cloves
1 cup milk, 2 percent or whole
½ tsp. vanilla

In a large saucepan, cook shallots, onion, and ginger in hot oil over medium heat until tender but not brown. Stir in flour. Add broth and cider/juice, cooking and stirring over medium heat until slightly thickened and bubbly. Stir in pumpkin, maple syrup, bay leaves, cinnamon, thyme, pepper, and cloves. Return to a boil, then reduce heat, cover, and simmer for 20 minutes.

Remove from heat. Discard bay leaves. Cool slightly, and then using a blender or immersion blender, blend mixture until smooth. (If using a blender, blend in batches.) Return mixture to saucepan and then stir in milk and vanilla. Simmer (do not boil) until heated through.

Garnish each bowl or cup with a sprinkling of additional cinnamon. Serves 6+.

Chef's Notes

Do Ahead Tip:
You can cook and blend the pumpkin mixture up to 24 hours in advance. Chill. To serve, return the soup to the saucepan. Stir in the milk and vanilla, and heat through but do not boil.

About . . .
Dairy free? For a dairy-free version, feel free to replace the milk with soy milk in this recipe.

Walnut oil has a distinctively nutty flavor and fragrance and is an ideal way to enhance the overall bisque flavor. Keep refrigerated when not in use.

How to Do It . . .
If you had a choice between using the same saucepan and getting another container dirty, what would you choose? Introducing the immersion blender—plug it in, stick it in the bottom of the saucepan, press "on," and swirl gently . . . *Voila!* a smooth mixture without too much extra fuss.

In season . . .
Shallots, part of the onion family, are prized for their mild onion flavor.

Barley Minestrone

This rendition of the classic Italian vegetable and
bean soup uses barley instead of pasta.

2 tbsp. extra-virgin olive oil
¼ cup coarsely chopped nitrate-free bacon
2 cups diced large Savoy cabbage
1 cup medium-diced yellow onion
1 cup sliced carrot, ¼" thick
¼ cup medium-diced celery
2 large garlic cloves, minced
2 qt. chicken broth
14½-oz. can diced tomatoes with their juices
½ cup pearl barley, rinsed
2 large sprigs fresh rosemary
2"-square piece of Parmigiano-
Reggiano rind, optional
½ tsp. kosher salt
1 cup water
1 cup rinsed and drained canned kidney beans
Salt and freshly ground black pepper to taste
Freshly grated Parmigiano-Reggiano for serving

Heat oil in a 6-qt. stockpot over medium heat. Add the bacon and cook, stirring frequently until it becomes golden. Mix in the cabbage, onion, carrot, celery, and garlic. Stirring frequently, cook until the veggies begin to soften, about 8 minutes.

Add the broth, tomatoes with their juices, barley, rosemary, rind (if using), salt, and water. Bring to a boil over high heat, then reduce the heat to a simmer and cook until barley and veggies are tender, about 20 minutes.

Discard the rosemary sprigs and rind. Stir in the beans and season to taste with salt and pepper. Serve sprinkled with freshly grated cheese. Serves 6+.

Chef's Notes

About . . .
Simmering a piece of the rind from Parmigiano-Reggiano in the soup is a traditional way of adding flavor. When you finish off a wedge of Parmigiano, just stash the rind in a bag in the freezer so you always have it on hand when you need it.

How to Do It . . .
Barley has a mild flavor that's not as nutty as many other grains, but it has an unusually chewy texture. It can be used in just about every way that rice is used—in pilafs, soups, and even risottos. Whole hulled barley takes about an hour to cook; pearl barley and rolled barley need about 20 minutes to get tender; quick-cooking barley is usually done in 12 minutes.

In Season . . .
Savoy cabbage has crinkly, flexible green leaves. More tender than traditional green cabbage and milder in flavor, it's eaten both cooked and raw.

Red Bean Stew with Veggies and Chili Salsa

Don't let the steps in this recipe fool you. This stew is not difficult to prepare and the flavor profiles are incredible. It's worth every minute of your time.

Stew

2 medium dried chilies, wiped clean, reconstituted
⅓ cup extra-virgin olive oil
2 cups finely chopped white onions
2 tsp. coarse sea salt, divided
½ tsp. freshly ground black pepper
4 garlic cloves, pressed
2 cups dried small red beans, picked over to remove any stones and debris, rinsed, soaked overnight in water to cover, then cooked
2 medium parsnips, peeled and cut into ½" cubes
2 medium carrots, peeled and cut into ½" cubes
2 celery ribs, peeled and cut into ½" cubes
1 medium zucchini, cut into ½" cubes
1 medium yellow squash, cut into ½" cubes

Chili Salsa

4 medium dried chilies, wiped clean, stemmed, and seeded
1 jalapeño pepper, stemmed and seeded, diced
½ cup orange juice
1 tbsp. grapefruit juice
1 tbsp. lime juice
2 tsp. sea salt
½ tsp. freshly ground black pepper

Chef's Notes

Do Ahead Tip:
Salsa may be made 3 days ahead and chilled, covered. Bring salsa to room temperature before serving.

For the Stew: Drain the soaking chilies. Wearing rubber gloves, stem, seed, and tear them into bite-size pieces.

In a 5-qt. saucepan, heat oil over medium heat until hot. Stirring occasionally, cook onions with *half* of the salt and all of the pepper until golden. Add the garlic and cook until fragrant. Add beans with their cooking liquid, chilies, parsnips, and carrots and cook at a low boil for 10 minutes. Mix in celery, zucchini, yellow squash, and remaining salt and simmer until veggies are tender, about 15 minutes.

For the Chili Salsa: Using tongs, toast chilies in a nonstick skillet over medium heat, turning frequently until softened slightly and reddish brown, about 4 minutes. Wearing rubber gloves, cut chilies into 1" wide strips, then cut strips crosswise into very thin slivers.

In a bowl, stir together chilies, jalapeño, juices, salt, and pepper. Let stand at room temperature at least 30 minutes and as long as 2 hours. (Chilies will soften and expand, absorbing much of the liquid.) Makes about 1½ cups.

To serve, ladle stew in individual serving bowls and top each serving with a spoonful of the Chili Salsa. Serves 6+.

How to Do It . . .

To cook the beans, simmer beans in fresh water to cover in a 4-qt. saucepan for 45 minutes to 1 hour or until tender and creamy. Remove pan from heat and let beans stand for 10 minutes before using.

Reconstitute dried chilies, pour boiling water over dried chilies in a bowl and allow to steep for 30 minutes; strain to remove any grittiness.

In Season . . .

Parsnips, or I Wouldn't Know One if It Fell into My Cart in the Produce Department: parsnips look like a thick-topped, short white carrot (actually, they're cousins).

An assortment of fresh veggies combine with red beans, and a zesty chili salsa tops it all off.

Spicy Black-Bean Chili with Tortilla Chips

A deliciously spicy bean chili served with the smoothness of a dollop of sour cream and the crunch of salty tortilla chips. Bring on the flavor!

1 lb. dried black beans, picked over and rinsed
¼ cup canola or safflower oil
4 cups chopped yellow onion
8 large garlic cloves, chopped
2 jalapeño peppers, seeded and chopped
¼ cup chili powder (this packs a significant punch—you may use less to taste)
4 tsp. ground cumin
28-oz. can plum tomatoes with juices, chopped
2½ cups water
1 tbsp. granulated sugar
1 tsp. minced canned chipotle chili in adobo sauce
Sea salt to taste
Freshly ground black pepper to taste
Tortilla chips
Sour cream

Chef's Notes

About . . .
The hot chipotle chili is actually a dried, smoked jalapeño. It has a smoky, sweet, almost chocolaty flavor.

How to Do It . . .
Let's speed things up . . . using canned beans. It's okay, just choose your brand wisely, checking sodium content and rinsing and draining well before using.

Place beans in a large bowl, adding enough water to cover by 3". Let stand overnight; drain well before using.

After the beans have been soaked, place them in a large saucepan. Add enough fresh water to cover. Bring to a boil and cook until beans are almost tender, about 35 minutes. Drain.

Heat oil in a large stockpot over medium-high heat. Add onions, garlic, and jalapeños and sauté until tender. Mix in chili powder and cumin and stir until fragrant. Add beans, tomatoes with their juices, water, and sugar. Bring to a boil. Reduce heat to medium low and simmer for 20 minutes.

Add chipotle and, stirring frequently, simmer until chili is very thick, about 1 hour. Add more water by the ½ cupfuls if chili is dry. Season with salt and pepper.

Ladle chili into individual bowls; top with tortilla chips and a dollop of sour cream. Makes 6+ servings.

Mexican Meatball Soup

A spicier, south-of-the-border version of traditional Italian wedding soup.
Just a few of you? Recipe can easily be halved.

Meatballs

1 lb. lean ground turkey
¼ cup uncooked long-grain white rice
2 tsp. chili powder
½ tsp. sea salt
¼ tsp. dried oregano, crumbled
1 large garlic clove, pressed
1 large egg, lightly beaten

Soup

1 cup coarsely chopped yellow onion
½ cup sliced celery
2 large garlic cloves, pressed
2 tbsp. extra-virgin olive oil
8 cups beef broth
16 oz. tomato sauce
½ tsp. dried oregano, crumbled
1 cup chopped green or red bell pepper
1½ cups sliced zucchini
1½ cups corn kernels, fresh if in season or frozen
2 large or 3 medium tomatoes, peeled, seeded, and cut into ½" cubes
Shredded cheddar or Monterey Jack cheese

For the Meatballs: In a large bowl, combine meatball ingredients, mixing well. Shape into about 30 meatballs 1" in size. In a large nonstick skillet, thoroughly brown meatballs, shaking pan frequently to help maintain their round shape. Drain on a cooling rack placed atop a baking sheet.

For the Soup: In a 6-qt. stockpot, sauté onion, celery, and garlic in oil until tender. Stir in beef broth, tomato sauce, and oregano. Bring to a boil. Stir in meatballs and bell pepper. Reduce heat; cover and simmer 20 minutes.

Skim any fat from broth. Stir in zucchini, corn, and tomatoes. Simmer uncovered an additional 10 minutes or until zucchini is crisp-tender. Sprinkle a little cheese on top of each serving. Makes 6+ servings.

Chef's Notes

About . . .
Not all ground turkey is created equal, and some are fattier than others. Be sure to ask for 99 percent lean turkey ground from white meat without the skin.

How to Do It . . .
A scoop and a disher are handy tools for making uniform meatballs at a quick pace.

Chilled Fresh Blueberry Soup

A beautiful, refreshing soup—and a cooking school favorite—made at peak blueberry season during our Bluesberry Fest. Try this luscious fruit soup as a refreshing alternative to a rich dessert, served with your favorite crisp cookies.

4½ qt. fresh blueberries
1 cup apple juice
¾ cup honey, clover or orange blossom
½ cup lemon juice
1 tbsp. finely grated lemon zest
2 tsp. ground cinnamon
1 cup low-fat vanilla yogurt

Chef's Notes

How to Do It . . .
To zest a lemon, remove the fragrant outermost skin layer with the aid of a zester or grater, paring knife, or vegetable peeler. Only the colored portion of the skin (and not the white pith underneath) is used.

In Season . . .
We salute locally grown blueberries at the peak of their summer season (usually in July in Ohio) with a Bluesberry Fest, a one day celebration of all things blueberry-ish!

Chilled soups always surprise and delight first-time tasters, and the fresh, fruity flavors make this one irresistible.

In a blender or food processor, combine blueberries, apple juice, honey, lemon juice, lemon zest, and cinnamon. Puree or pulse until smooth then strain through a fine sieve over a large bowl. (Be patient—it takes time to extract all the juice and leave the seeds behind!) Chill mixture.

Serve soup in large chilled wine glasses or small bowls, with a swirl of yogurt. Makes 6+ servings.

Let the fireworks begin now that you have your serving
of this patriotic Red, White, & Blue Potato Salad!

SALADS OF THE SEASON: SIDES AND ENTRÉES

This chapter's recipes truly reflect the way we cook today. There is a definite layering and combining of flavors that make up these healthy, fresh-tasting dishes.

Salads can mean many things. In addition to the green salads that you'd most likely serve as a first course, a side salad like our Italian Rice Salad with Garlic Vinaigrette puts so many distinct flavors and textures on one plate that it's satisfying enough to the palate to be a light meal in itself. And the Caramelized Onions with Treasured Heirloom Tomatoes is an ode to the season's best. Although it has become a cliché to say you should cook with the seasons, it's true. Simply put, if the raw ingredients don't taste good, the finished dish won't taste good either.

Sensational Salads: Observations and Chef's Tips

Greens have reentered our culinary consciousness. This revival is a rediscovery of the joys of real, deep flavors found in fresh seasonal produce. Our new appreciation represents a victory over culinary closed-mindedness. The difference between a green and a weed is often in the eye of the beholder! To most Americans, many of the world's finest greens were little more than marginally edible weeds, mysterious ingredients best left that way. After all, dandelions to some are nothing but pests messing up neat lawns.

Whatever greens are used in a given recipe, you should always feel free to substitute and adapt to suit your own taste and what is available. One of the great things about salads is that they are easygoing and flexible.

Cleaning Greens: It's important to wash leafy greens well—there's nothing worse than biting down on some grit. If you're working with greens that come in a bunch, cut off all the stems in one chop while the greens are still gathered together. Fill a big bowl or the sink with cold water. Place the greens in the water and gently submerge them without stirring (yelling "dive, dive" as a warning to those around you—just kidding!). This process allows the grit to fall to the bottom. As they're soaking, go through and pinch off any remaining large stems. Let the greens soak for at least 10 minutes, giving the grit a chance to sink, then quickly lift the greens out of the water and into a colander. Rinse briefly one more time in the colander and let drain.

Drying and Storing Greens: Now we come to what may well be the most important thing about making a salad: drying the greens thoroughly after cleaning them. If you dry greens properly, they will keep in the refrigerator for 4 or 5 days. You'll have the greens cleaned and stored and ready to make excellent salads the rest of the week.

Why should the greens be well dried? Any water left on the greens will dilute your dressing, and water will prevent dressing from adhering to and coating the greens. As a result, you'll have a watery dressing that pools up separately from the greens. So—to dry your greens either roll them up in a cotton towel or whirl them in a salad spinner, fluff them up, and whirl them again.

Once they are washed and dried, store your greens in whole leaves; tear them only when you are about to make a salad. Greens should be kept in one of your refrigerator's vegetable storage bins in either a clean muslin bag, allowing air to circulate freely around the greens, or rolled loosely in paper towels after washing, then put into a plastic bag with a few holes poked into it.

Chicken Sesame Salad

This popular salad from our market's kitchen is
loaded with texture, crunch, and fresh flavors.

Salad

2 lb. boneless, skinless chicken breasts
¾ cup Korean sesame sauce
¾ lb. broccoli florets, coarsely chopped
⅓ lb. red bell pepper, cut into diamond-
shaped chunks
¼ cup sliced almonds, toasted
⅓ lb. sugar snap peas, strings removed
¼ cup thinly sliced red onion, halved
2 oz. package of tofu and miso ramen noodles,
lightly crushed by hand
1 tsp. sesame seeds
1 tsp. black sesame seeds

Dressing

Spice packet from 2-oz. package of tofu and
miso ramen
¼ cup toasted sesame oil
⅛ cup extra-virgin olive oil
⅛ cup canola oil
3 tbsp. rice vinegar

Heat oven to 375 degrees.

For the Salad: Toss chicken in sesame sauce in a large bowl. Place in a roasting pan, piled together to retain moisture, and roast just until cooked through and chicken is no longer pink, beginning to check after 25 minutes. Remove pan from oven and allow chicken to cool completely. Once cool, slice chicken into strips, cutting against the grain.

In a large serving bowl, toss together broccoli, red bell pepper, almonds, sugar snap peas, onion, ramen noodle packet, and sesame seeds. Add chicken.

For the Dressing: In a small bowl combine spice packet, oils, and rice vinegar, mixing to blend well. Top salad with dressing, tossing gently but well to coat ingredients. Serves 4.

Chef's Notes

How to Do It . . .
Some prefer this salad with a little less crunch but still full flavored. In that case, feel free to heat a teaspoonful of toasted sesame oil in a large skillet until hot, then quickly sauté over medium-high heat the sugar snap peas and red bell pepper, just long enough to take the raw crunch off them. Mix salad as above.

Pesto Chicken Salad

Not your ordinary chicken salad, this flavorful version gets some snap from a pesto vinaigrette. It's a wonderful summer meal (or great in the winter if you're longing for summer).

Pesto Vinaigrette

1 cup prepared pesto
3 tbsp. white wine vinegar
3 tbsp. fresh lemon juice
¼ cup extra-virgin olive oil
Sea salt to taste
Freshly ground black pepper to taste

Salad

7 cups cubed, cooked chicken
1 cup Pesto Vinaigrette
¼ cup pine nuts or walnut pieces, toasted
1 cup freshly grated Parmesan cheese
1 large bunch of fresh greens (my favorites are arugula or spinach), washed, stemmed, and torn into bite-size pieces
¼ cup thinly sliced fresh basil
Freshly ground black pepper to taste

For the Pesto Vinaigrette: In a medium bowl, whisk together the pesto, vinegar, and lemon juice. Add the oil, slowly whisking constantly until well blended. Season with salt and pepper to taste. Makes about 1½ cups, and any leftovers may be covered and refrigerated for 1 week.

For the Salad: In a large serving bowl, gently toss together the chicken, vinaigrette, nuts, and cheese.

Place greens on a serving platter. Top greens with chicken mixture and sprinkle sliced basil evenly atop chicken. Add a little freshly ground pepper and serve. Serves 6+.

Chef's Notes

How to Do It . . .
For moist, flavorful chicken I like to poach mine in a large sauté pan with just a little simmering water. Cover and cook the chicken just until the chicken is no longer pink when you cut into it and the juices run clear. Begin checking at 20 minutes and remove chicken from heat as soon as it's cooked in order to prevent it from overcooking and becoming tough.

In Season . . .
If your herb garden is overflowing with basil, by all means make your own pesto for this vinaigrette. Traditionally, pesto contains lots of fresh basil, garlic, pine nuts, Parmesan cheese, and olive oil.

Add this chicken-salad recipe to your cooking repertoire and begin to collect the compliments.

Warm Poached-Chicken Salad with Vinaigrette Choices

A simple salad made with your choice of deliciously easy vinaigrettes, perfectly prepared to suit the season and your taste buds. The Double Apple Vinaigrette is excellent in the fall and the Screamin' Strawberry is just the thing for a spring fling!

Salad

2 whole chicken breasts, poached in chicken broth just until cooked through
Assorted organic salad greens, cleaned and torn into bite-size pieces
2 tart, crisp apples, cut into 1" chunks
1 cup dried cranberries, dried apples, or dried strawberries

For the Salad: When chicken is cool enough to handle, skin, bone, and cut it into 1" chunks. Combine chicken, greens, apples, and dried fruits in a large bowl, tossing gently. Spoon onto a large serving platter and drizzle with some of one of the following vinaigrettes. Makes 4+ servings.

Chef's Notes

How to Do It . . .
When making the Screamin' Strawberry Vinaigrette: If the strawberries are not pureeing in the blender, add a tablespoon or two of the vinegar to coax it along.

Double-Apple Vinaigrette

¾ cup unsweetened applesauce
¼ cup apple cider vinegar
1 tbsp. Dijon mustard
2 large scallions, trimmed and sliced
¼ tsp. sea salt
⅓ cup extra-virgin olive oil

Process the applesauce, vinegar, mustard, scallions, and salt in a blender until smooth. With motor running, add oil in a thin, slow, steady stream until mixture is emulsified. Cover and refrigerate any leftovers. Makes 1½ cups.

Screamin' Strawberry Vinaigrette

1 lb. strawberries, stemmed and quartered
2½ tbsp. rice vinegar
2½ tbsp. fresh lemon juice
1 small garlic clove, minced
1½ tbsp. chopped fresh chives
1½ tbsp. chopped fresh basil
1½ tbsp. chopped fresh Italian (flat-leaf) parsley
1 tsp. sea salt
1 tsp. freshly ground black pepper

Puree strawberries in a blender or food processor. Add the vinegar, lemon juice, garlic, chives, basil, parsley, salt, and pepper; blend to combine. Cover and refrigerate any leftovers. Makes 2 cups.

Soy, Soy, and More Soy Salad

This soy-packed salad is perfect for lunch at work or a picnic side salad.

Salad

1 lb. extra-firm, refrigerated tofu, drained
2 cups peeled, seeded, and diced cucumber
1 cup diced red bell pepper
4 scallions, thinly sliced
Red leaf lettuce, cleaned and torn into
bite-size pieces
1 tsp. sesame seeds, toasted
1 tsp. black sesame seeds, toasted

Dressing

8½ oz. can black soybeans, drained
1 tbsp. vegetable broth
3 tbsp. tamari
2 tbsp. pickled ginger
1 tbsp. hot pepper sesame oil

Place tofu atop a plate lined with paper towel. Top tofu with another paper towel, then place a plate atop the covered tofu. Refrigerate for 30 minutes to 1 hour to remove some of the excess moisture from the tofu.

For the Dressing: Puree soybeans, broth, tamari, ginger, and oil in a blender until smooth.

For the Salad: Cut tofu into ½" dice. In a medium bowl combine tofu, cucumbers, red bell pepper, scallions, and dressing, tossing gently. Refrigerate for 30 minutes to allow flavors to blend.

When ready to serve, place red leaf lettuce on individual plates and top with tofu mixture. Sprinkle with sesame seeds and serve. Serves 4+

Chef's Notes

About . . .
Tamari, a sauce made from soybeans, is similar to but thicker than soy sauce. Some varieties are wheat free. If you've ever purchased sushi, chances are your serving came with pickled ginger. Simply put, pickled ginger is fresh ginger that has been preserved in sweet vinegar.

Black Bean, Corn, and Orzo Salad

The use of your favorite salsa helps dress this
pasta and bean salad in a hurry.

8 oz. orzo pasta
¼ tsp. salt
3 tbsp. + 1 tsp. extra-virgin olive oil
2 tbsp. freshly squeezed lime juice
¼ tsp. ground cumin
¼ tsp. freshly ground black pepper
1 cup cooked black beans
1 cup corn kernels, fresh if in season, frozen if not
1 small red bell pepper, halved, seeded, and cut into thin slivers
1 cup prepared salsa
2 scallions, coarsely chopped
3 tbsp. chopped fresh cilantro
2 tbsp. chopped fresh Italian (flat-leaf) parsley
⅓ cup toasted pecan halves or chopped pecan pieces

Bring a large pot of water to a boil. Add orzo and salt and stir, cooking for 8 to 10 minutes or until orzo is done but still firm to the bite. Drain; toss with 1 tsp. of the olive oil and set aside.

Whisk together the lime juice, remaining olive oil, cumin, and black pepper. Gently stir in orzo, black beans, corn, pepper strips, salsa, scallions, cilantro, and parsley.

Stir in toasted pecans and taste salad; adjust seasonings as desired. Serve at room temperature or chill 30 minutes prior to serving. Makes 4 servings.

Chef's Notes

About . . .
Orzo is a tiny, rice-shaped pasta that's great in soups and salads.

This flavorful bean, corn, and pasta salad is easy to put together . . . and even easier to enjoy.

Crunchy Tempeh Salad

★

A delightful vegetarian salad with a "meaty"
flavor and crunch and a spicy dressing.

Sesame Dressing

¼ cup brown rice vinegar
¼ cup sweet rice or rice miso
1 tbsp. honey
1 tbsp. toasted sesame oil
1 tsp. dried red pepper flakes
Apple juice to taste
Freshly ground white pepper to taste

Salad

1 tbsp. extra-virgin olive oil
1 package tempeh, cut into ¼" thick strips
10 shiitake mushrooms, stemmed
1 lb. Napa cabbage, shredded
3 medium carrots, shredded
1 medium red bell pepper, halved, seeded, and
cut into thin strips
1 cup peeled and shredded jicama
½ cup coarsely chopped fresh cilantro

For the Sesame Dressing: In a small bowl, whisk together the vinegar, miso, honey, sesame oil, and red pepper flakes, adding apple juice as needed and pepper to taste.

For the Salad: In a large nonstick skillet, heat the olive oil and sauté the tempeh and mushrooms until tempeh is lightly browned.

While tempeh and mushrooms are cooking, combine cabbage, carrots, bell pepper, jicama, and cilantro in a large bowl. Add enough dressing to lightly coat, tossing to blend well.

Arrange the tempeh and mushrooms on top of the salad mixture on individual plates. Serve at room temperature or chilled. Serves 6.

Chef's Notes

About . . .
Kome miso is made with soybeans and rice and is the sweetest of the misos. Shiro miso, sweet rice, is sometimes called "white miso" and has a light, sweet taste, suitable for use in a wide variety of dishes.

Tempeh is a fermented soybean cake with a nutlike texture and taste.

In season . . .
Jicama, a large, bulbous root vegetable often referred to as a Mexican potato, has a thin brown skin and white crunchy flesh.

Napa cabbage has crinkly, thickly veined leaves that are cream colored with brighter green tips. The flavor is crisp and delicately mild.

Herb-Marinated Mozzarella Salad

A sensational side or salad . . . easy to prepare and even easier to eat!
Always a hit when I show students this "what to do with your fresh mozzarella" recipe after a hands-on mozzarella-making cooking class.

Marinade

1 cup extra-virgin olive oil
¼ cup chopped fresh oregano leaves
1 tsp. crushed red pepper flakes
2 garlic cloves, pressed or finely minced
½ tsp. sea salt
½ tsp. freshly ground black pepper
10 oz. fresh mozzarella cheese, drained and sliced

For the Marinade: Mix together the oil, oregano, red pepper flakes, garlic, salt, and pepper in a small bowl. Arrange the cheese slices in a shallow pan just large enough to hold cheese in a single layer. Pour oil mixture over cheese, coating well. Cover and refrigerate overnight to allow flavors to develop.

To serve as a side:
2 very ripe, large tomatoes, cored and sliced
Golden balsamic or white wine vinegar to drizzle

On serving plates, alternate tomato slices and marinated mozzarella slices; drizzle with vinegar and serve. Serves 4+.

To serve as a salad:
Red wine vinegar or champagne vinegar to whisk
Assorted fresh salad greens
Cherry or grape tomatoes

Remove mozzarella slices from marinade with a slotted spoon. With a flexible rubber spatula, scrape remaining marinade into a small bowl. Whisk in just enough vinegar until mixture turns a mustard color.

In another bowl, drizzle vinaigrette mixture atop salad greens and tomatoes, tossing gently to coat. Plate greens and top with marinated mozzarella slices. Serves 4+.

Sizzling Goat Cheese Salad

This chef's technique of coating tender discs of goat cheese with a crumb mixture then cooking until crispy and warm makes this one sizzling recipe to try in your home kitchen. Perfect for entertaining!

Salad

4 cups cleaned and torn organic mixed greens
½ cup halved pitted ripe olives
12 whole sun-dried tomatoes in oil, drained and chopped
2 tsp. sliced scallions

Dressing

¼ cup + 1 tbsp. extra-virgin olive oil
¼ cup tarragon vinegar
2 tbsp. walnut oil
1 tbsp. Dijon mustard

Goat Cheese Sizzler

1 large egg
1 tbsp. water
4 tbsp. cornmeal
2 tbsp. fine dry breadcrumbs
1 tbsp. sesame seeds, toasted
2 tbsp. grated Parmesan cheese
10 oz. chèvre or a soft, mild goat cheese log of your choice
2 tbsp. unsalted butter

For the Salad: In a large serving bowl, toss together the greens, olives, tomatoes, and scallions. Cover and chill.

For the Dressing: In a small bowl whisk together the olive oil, vinegar, walnut oil, and mustard. Set aside.

For the Goat Cheese Sizzler: In a small bowl, whisk together the egg and water. In a shallow bowl, combine the cornmeal, breadcrumbs, sesame seeds, and Parmesan cheese. Divide the goat cheese log into 12 equal portions. Dip each "slice" into the egg mixture, then coat with the cornmeal mixture. Cover and chill at least 30 minutes.

When ready to serve, melt butter in a large skillet. Add cheese patties and cook over medium heat for 4 minutes or until golden, carefully turning once.

Arrange cheese atop greens mixture on individual serving plates. Whisk dressing and drizzle over greens and cheese. Serve immediately. Makes 4+ servings.

Chef's Notes

About . . .
Sun-dried tomatoes are also available packaged and in need of rehydrating. Place the quantity needed in a small bowl, pouring boiling water over shriveled tomatoes just to cover. Let steep for 30 minutes, then drain and continue with recipe.

Vegetable Salad with Roasted Lemon Vinaigrette

If the grill is hot, cook the veggies on the grill; if not,
roasting brings out their flavors as well.

Roasted Lemon Vinaigrette

2 large lemons
1 tsp. granulated sugar
1½ tsp. chopped fresh thyme
Sea salt to taste
Freshly ground white pepper to taste
⅔ cup grapeseed oil

Vegetable Salad

1 tsp. minced garlic
½ tsp. minced fresh oregano
½ tsp. minced fresh basil
2 tbsp. white vinegar
2 tbsp. extra-virgin olive oil
Sea salt
Freshly ground black pepper
1 large red bell pepper, seeded and sliced into 1½" strips
1 large yellow bell pepper, seeded and sliced into 1½" strips
1 zucchini, halved, then sliced lengthwise into ½" strips
1 yellow squash, halved, then sliced lengthwise into ½" strips
6 cups cleaned, assorted salad greens

For the Roasted Lemon Vinaigrette: Heat oven to 325 degrees. Wrap lemons tightly in foil and roast in the middle of the oven until soft, about 1 hour. (Place foil-wrapped lemons atop a baking sheet so you don't have to clean the oven after roasting!) Carefully open foil and cool the lemons just enough to handle. Halve lemons and juice them.

In a small bowl, whisk together the juice, sugar, thyme, and salt and pepper to taste. Add the oil in a slow stream, whisking until emulsified. Makes about 1 cup.

For the Vegetable Salad: In a small bowl combine the garlic, oregano, basil, and vinegar; whisk in the olive oil. Season with salt and pepper; set aside.

Combine the peppers, zucchini, and yellow squash in a shallow glass or ceramic bowl. Pour marinade over veggies, toss gently, and cover. Let marinate 1 to 2 hours.

Prepare a hot grill or heat oven to 400 degrees. Remove veggies from marinade and grill on a grid until crisp tender or bake on a parchment-lined baking pan for about 15 minutes or until crisp tender. Remove and slice veggies into 1" pieces.

To serve: Combine salad greens and veggies in a large serving bowl and toss gently with enough vinaigrette just to coat. Serve immediately. Serves 4+.

Chef's Notes

Do Ahead Tip.
Covered and refrigerated, this vinaigrette keeps 8 days.

About . . .
Roasting lemons intensifies the flavor. This will soon become your new, favorite, made-from-scratch vinaigrette!

Extracted from (you guessed it) grape seeds, grapeseed oil, mild in flavor, does not overpower the roasted lemons in this vinaigrette.

Caramelized Onions with Treasured Heirloom Tomatoes

This recipe is a party for your mouth, with an assortment of flavor profiles and textures. A few simple steps are all that are required to pull this together and enjoy.

Caramelized Onions

1 tbsp. extra-virgin olive oil
2 cups very thinly sliced sweet yellow onions
Sea salt and freshly ground black pepper to taste
1 tbsp. granulated sugar

Vinaigrette

½ tsp. Dijon mustard
Sea salt and freshly ground black pepper
to taste
2 tbsp. red or white wine vinegar
5 tbsp. extra-virgin olive oil
1 tbsp. minced fresh chives

Salad

1 cup packed mesclun greens or fresh baby
spinach, stemmed
2 medium, ripe heirloom tomatoes, each
cut into 8 wedges
1 cup golden pear tomatoes or yellow
cherry tomatoes, halved
1 cup red pear tomatoes or red cherry
tomatoes, halved
2 oz. soft goat cheese, crumbled

For the Caramelized Onions: Heat the oil in a large skillet over very low heat. Add the onions, salt, and pepper and stir well. Cover and cook for 15 minutes until a light golden brown, stirring occasionally. Remove the lid, sprinkle the sugar over the onions, and sauté uncovered for another 5 minutes, stirring frequently until the onions reach a rich, golden-brown color. Remove from heat and cool completely.

For the Vinaigrette: Mix the mustard, salt, and pepper in a small bowl. Add the vinegar, whisking in the oil until smooth. Mix in the chives and set aside.

For the Salad: Arrange the greens on a platter. Top with the tomatoes, alternating colors and shapes. Drizzle the vinaigrette atop the tomatoes and greens, then top with the onions and sprinkle with the goat cheese. Serves 4+.

Chef's Notes

Do Ahead Tip:
Onions can be made 24 hours ahead, then covered and refrigerated until ready to use.

About . . .
Chèvre is a pure-white goat's milk cheese that has a tart, fresh flavor. French for "goat," it can range in texture from moist and creamy to dry and semifirm. "Pur chèvre" on the label ensures that the cheese is made entirely from goat's milk.

Lettuce and Basil Salad with Sweet Carrot Dressing

*Carrot juice makes a refreshing, sweet salad
dressing that you'll soon find other uses for.*

Dressing
1 cup fresh carrot juice
2 tsp. minced garlic
½ cup extra-virgin olive oil
3 tbsp. rice vinegar
Sea salt and freshly ground black pepper
to taste

Salad
1½ heads Bibb lettuce, torn into bite-size
pieces (12 cups)
¾ cup shredded carrots
1 oz. whole fresh basil leaves, torn into
bite-size pieces (2 cups)
1 cup crumbled Maytag blue cheese, room
temperature

For the Dressing: Boil the carrot juice with minced garlic in a small saucepan until reduced by half. Cool.

In a medium bowl, whisk oil and rice vinegar until well blended. Whisk in carrot juice mixture. Season dressing to taste with salt and pepper.

For the Salad: Combine lettuce, carrots, and basil in a large serving bowl. Toss with enough dressing to coat. Divide equally among plates, sprinkle with crumbles of cheese, and serve. Makes 6 servings.

Chef's Notes

Do Ahead Tip:
Dressing can be prepared 1 day ahead, then covered and refrigerated. Bring to room temperature and whisk to combine before using.

About . . .
Maytag blue is a creamy, salty cheese from Iowa and makes converts out of "I don't like blue cheese" folks. Rice vinegars, made from fermented rice, are typically milder than most other vinegars.

Autumn Harvest Pumpkin Salad

A true seasonal treat from our café. Go for color when picking the organic produce to complement this made-from-scratch pumpkin dressing.

Creamy Pumpkin Dressing

¾ cup sour cream or plain, low-fat yogurt, drained
1½ cups pumpkin puree
2 tbsp. red wine vinegar
1 large garlic clove, pressed
1½ tbsp. honey, clover or orange blossom or a flavor profile you prefer
½ cup + 1 tbsp. mayonnaise
2 tbsp. Dijon mustard
2 tbsp. white wine
Sea salt and freshly ground white pepper to taste

Salad

4 cups mixed organic salad greens
2 firm ripe pears, halved, cored, then thinly sliced
1 yellow bell pepper, halved, seeded, then thinly sliced
1 cup thinly sliced red onion
1 cup yellow or red cherry tomatoes
1 white or striped beet, peeled then cut into matchstick pieces
1 cup roasted pumpkin seeds

For the Creamy Pumpkin Dressing: Whisk together the ingredients in a medium bowl, seasoning as necessary with salt and pepper.

For the Salad: Assemble the salad on serving plates and drizzle with the Creamy Pumpkin Dressing. Garnish each plate with the pumpkin seeds and serve immediately. Serves 2+.

Chef's Notes

How to Do It . . .
Leftover Dressing? Store, covered, in the refrigerator for up to 5 days.

In Season . . .
Don't miss the chance to use any winter squash puree in place of the pumpkin puree. And use a variety and assortment of firm ripe pears—Bosc, Crimson, d'Anjou, and more. Crisp!

Sweet-Potato Salad with Dried Fruits

These are festive flavors, and this salad is a natural for a Thanksgiving buffet. You can even make it a day ahead to allow the flavors to develop.

4 sweet potatoes (orange fleshed), peeled and cut into ½" dice
⅔ cup diced red onion
½ cup dried cranberries
⅓ cup dried currants or seedless raisins
⅔ cup coarsely chopped pecans, lightly toasted

Honey Mustard Dressing

1 tbsp. Dijon mustard
¼ cup cider vinegar
¼ cup honey
⅓ cup canola oil

In a vegetable steamer bring water to a boil. Put the sweet potatoes in the steamer basket, cover, and steam just until fork tender, about 25 minutes.

For the Honey Mustard Dressing: While potatoes are steaming, whisk together the mustard, vinegar, honey, and oil in a small bowl until smooth.

In a large bowl, combine the red onion, cranberries, and currants/raisins. Add the steamed sweet potatoes along with the honey mustard dressing, tossing to evenly coat the mixture. Chill for at least 1 hour. Just before serving, toss in the pecans and enjoy. Serves 6+.

Chef's Notes

About . . .
The currants I'm referring to in this recipe are the ones you'll find in our bulk department, a tiny, dark raisin—actually the seedless, dried Zante grape.

Sweet-Potato Salad with Crystallized Ginger

Orange juice and zest and pineapple chunks add sweet, light flavor to this creamy sweet-potato salad. It's perfect for a crowd!

6 lb. sweet potatoes (orange fleshed), peeled and cut into ½" dice
8 ribs of celery, sliced into ¼" pieces
2 cups walnut pieces, toasted
2 cups seedless raisins
2¼ lb. pineapple chunks (½" dice), fresh or canned
⅛ lb. crystallized ginger, finely diced

Dressing

2 oranges, zested and juiced
1⅓ cups mayonnaise
3 cups sour cream, light or regular
1½ tsp. sea salt

In a vegetable steamer bring water to a boil. Put the sweet potatoes in the steamer basket, cover, and steam just until fork tender, about 25 minutes.

In a large serving bowl, combine the celery, walnuts, raisins, pineapple, and sweet potatoes.

For the Dressing: Finely chop the orange zest. In a medium bowl, whisk together the mayonnaise, sour cream, salt, orange zest, and juice.

Gently stir the dressing into the potato mixture, tossing in the ginger at the final stir. Serves 8+.

Red, White, & Blue Potato Salad

Our market kitchen's patriotic salute to the holidays, and purple potatoes
are always a conversation starter at any picnic!

¾ lb. purple potatoes, cubed
¾ lb. red potatoes, cubed
½ lb. Yukon Gold potatoes, cubed
⅔ cup mayonnaise
3 tbsp. Dijon mustard
3 tbsp. cider vinegar
1 lb. tomatoes, seeded and diced
1 small red onion, diced
3 tbsp. sweet (pickle) relish
1½ tsp. sea salt, plus more to taste
1 tsp. freshly ground black pepper

Place cubed potatoes in a medium saucepan and cover with cold water. Bring to a boil, then lower heat and simmer potatoes about 14 minutes or just until tender. Drain and cool.

In a large serving bowl, whisk together mayonnaise, Dijon mustard, and cider vinegar until smooth. Add cooked potatoes, tomatoes, red onion, relish, salt, and pepper. Stir gently to blend. Makes 4+ servings.

Chef's Notes

In Season . . .
Purple potatoes are a perfect example of a reintroduced heirloom vegetable. These purples have a dense texture and are great for boiling. Yukon Gold potatoes have a moist texture. If you have a difficult time finding red-fleshed potatoes, substitute red skins instead.

Green Beans and Gold Potato Salad with Miso Dressing

*This is a beautiful salad . . . freshly steamed, in-season
green beans with wedges of Yukon Gold potatoes in a salty, flavorful
citrus miso dressing. Hurry, get out your shopping list!*

1½ lb. green beans, cut diagonally into
1½" pieces
1½ lb. Yukon Gold potatoes, cut into ¾" wedges
2 tbsp. white or yellow miso
2 tbsp. fresh lemon juice
2 tbsp. fresh orange juice
1 tbsp. canola oil or extra-virgin olive oil
1 tsp. umeboshi vinegar
½ cup chopped, fresh Italian (flat-leaf) parsley
Sea salt if desired

Chef's Notes

About . . .
Umeboshi vinegar is made from pickled Japanese plums picked prior to ripening and soaked in brine and red shiso leaves (which add flavor and a natural pink coloring).

Steam green beans in a steamer over boiling water just until tender, about 5 minutes. Transfer to a bowl and set aside.

On a large steamer rack over boiling water, steam potatoes, covered, just until tender, about 10 minutes. Transfer to a bowl and set aside.

In a large bowl, whisk together the miso, lemon juice, orange juice, oil, and vinegar. Add the steamed beans and potatoes. Toss in the parsley and gently mix all ingredients until well combined. Serves 4+.

Italian Rice Salad with Garlic Vinaigrette

This salad always stops them cold . . . and everyone, much to their surprise, always wants seconds and the recipe! It's my most requested recipe for special cooking classes and demonstrations.

Vinaigrette

1¼ cups canola or safflower oil
½ cup white wine vinegar
1¾ tsp. sea salt
1¾ tsp. freshly ground black pepper
1 to 2 tbsp. freshly minced garlic
1½ tsp. minced fresh basil or ½ tsp. dried basil, crumbled
1½ tsp. minced fresh oregano or ½ tsp. dried oregano, crumbled
¼ cup minced fresh Italian (flat-leaf) parsley

Rice Salad

6 cups cooked basmati rice, white or brown
2 cups finely chopped bell peppers (an assortment of yellow, orange, or red)
¾ cup finely chopped red onions
1 cup quartered, marinated artichoke hearts
¼ cup capers, drained
⅓ cup minced fresh Italian (flat-leaf) parsley
⅓ cup minced fresh dill
½ cup seedless raisins
Mixed organic greens

For the Vinaigrette: In a small bowl, whisk together the oil, vinegar, salt, pepper, garlic, basil, oregano, and parsley. Set aside.

For the Rice Salad: In a large serving bowl, combine the rice, peppers, onion, artichoke hearts, capers, parsley, dill, and raisins. Stir gently to blend.

Toss with the vinaigrette and let marinate for at least 1 hour, and up to 3 hours, covered and refrigerated. Serve on a bed of salad greens. Serves 6+.

Chef's Notes

About . . .
Capers, the flower bud of a bush native to parts of Asia and the Mediterranean, are picked, sun dried, and then usually pickled in a vinegar brine.

In Season . . .
Fresh herbs are so much more flavorful in this recipe, but if you must, use the dried herbs, being sure to crumble them between the palms of your hands to help release their essential oils. There is no suitable substitute for fresh parsley (even though dried parsley is available).

Quinoa Spinach Salad

When you're stuck in a pasta rut, think quinoa. This nutritious grain takes virtually no additional time to cook and has a delicate, nutty consistency that takes well to vinaigrettes. You'll enjoy the flavors and textures of this salad.

1½ cups quinoa
¼ cup extra-virgin olive oil
3 cups water
½ tsp. sea salt
3 tbsp. balsamic vinegar
1 small bunch fresh spinach, cleaned, stemmed, and torn into bite-size pieces
1 cup half-moon-size thin red onion slices
1 cup halved cherry tomatoes
Freshly ground black pepper to taste
⅓ cup crumbled feta cheese
Mixed organic salad greens

Chef's Notes

How to Do It . . .
Rinsing the quinoa . . . Don't skip this step! You are extracting the bitter saponins from this grain, a natural substance that coats quinoa. If you forget to do this . . . well, as I tell my cooking school students, you won't forget again!

Place the quinoa in a fine mesh sieve and rinse the grain thoroughly under cold water for several minutes. Let the quinoa drain well.

Heat *1 tbsp.* of the olive oil in a large skillet over medium-high heat. When hot, add the quinoa and toast the grain, stirring often for several minutes just until the quinoa smells toasted. Add the water and the salt. Bring the mixture to a boil, cover the pan, and reduce heat to low. Cook the quinoa for 15 minutes.

While the quinoa is cooking, combine the balsamic vinegar and remaining oil in a large serving bowl. Add the spinach, red onion, and tomatoes. Season the veggies with freshly ground black pepper.

When the quinoa is cooked, add it to the vegetables and vinaigrette in the bowl. Toss well, adding the feta. Serve warm on a bed of mixed organic greens. Serves 4.

The perfect way to introduce your family, friends, or even yourself to flavorful, nutritious quinoa.

Petite Pea Salad

There's lots of room for simple, tasty salads in our kitchens too. This quick and easy recipe is an adaptation of a favorite from our café's vegetarian buffet.

1¼ lb. frozen petite peas
1 lb. vegetarian bacon, cooked and crumbled
¼ cup finely chopped scallions
¼ cup finely chopped celery
1 tsp. freshly ground black pepper
¾ cup canola mayonnaise
7 oz. salted and roasted cashews, coarsely chopped

Combine peas, bacon, scallions, celery, black pepper, and mayonnaise in a large serving bowl, gently stirring to blend so as not to crush the peas. Cover and chill several hours until ready to serve. Toss in the cashews just before serving. Serves 6+.

Chef's Notes

How to Do It . . .
Cooking the peas is not a requirement for this recipe. The most labor-intensive pea production you'll have to do is snip the bag open and pour some peas into a bowl.

Tropical Salad with Kiwi-Honey Dressing

Combine the juiciest, ripest tropical fruits with this slightly sweet, tart
dressing for a taste of the tropics.

Salad

1 tbsp. fresh lemon juice
2 firm ripe bananas, peeled and sliced
10 asparagus stalks, cooked just until crisp,
then cut into 1" pieces
1 head Bibb or Boston lettuce, cleaned then
torn into bite-size pieces
1 cup large mango chunks
1 whole skinned and boned chicken breast,
poached then sliced or 10 sea scallops,
cooked, optional
1 large, firm ripe avocado, halved and sliced
3 kiwi fruit, peeled and sliced

Dressing

1 tbsp. corn or safflower oil
1 tbsp. fresh lemon juice
1 tsp. honey, orange blossom or clover
¼ tsp. sea salt
Freshly ground black pepper to taste
3 kiwi fruit, peeled and sliced

For the Salad: Gently toss the banana with the
lemon juice. Arrange the banana, asparagus, lettuce,
mango, chicken or scallops (if using), and avocado
atop individual serving plates.

For the Dressing: In a medium bowl whisk together
the oil with the lemon juice, honey, sea salt, and a
little pepper. Puree the kiwi fruit; whisk into the oil
until blended.

Drizzle dressing atop the salad, then top with slices of
kiwi fruit. Serves 4+.

Chef's Notes

In Season . . .
If fresh asparagus is not locally available, it may be
omitted from the salad. Add a tropical fruit in its
place, such as fresh pineapple cut into 1"-thick strips.

Honey Mustard Salmon Salad

This simply prepared, sit-down dinner salad is perfect when only the freshest seafood is what you're longing for!

Salad

4 pieces salmon fillet (1 lb. total)
1-2 tbsp. extra-virgin olive oil
¼ tsp. freshly ground black pepper
6-8 cups Boston or Bibb lettuce or red leaf lettuce, cleaned and torn into bite-size pieces
¼ cup pistachio pieces, toasted

Vinaigrette

½ cup white wine vinegar
2 tsp. Dijon mustard
¼ tsp. salt
2 tsp. honey, orange blossom or clover
1½ tbsp. extra-virgin olive oil
4 tbsp. dried cherries

Heat oven to 400 degrees. Line a baking sheet with parchment paper.

For the Salad: Brush salmon with olive oil, then sprinkle with pepper and roast in the oven for 5 to 10 minutes or just until cooked through.

For the Vinaigrette: In a small mixing bowl combine the vinegar, mustard, salt, and honey. Whisk in the oil until mixture is well blended; stir in the dried cherries. Set aside.

Divide lettuce among individual serving plates. Top with freshly roasted salmon fillets and drizzle with vinaigrette, being sure some cherries top each salad. Sprinkle pistachio pieces atop each serving. Makes 4 servings.

Chef's Notes

About . . .
Need a quick and easy version? Substitute smoked trout or smoked salmon for the roasted salmon fillets in this recipe.

How to Do It . . .
Ten minutes per inch is the general rule for cooking fish, but you want your fillet pieces to be moist, not dry and overcooked. Begin checking the fish after 5 or 6 minutes (depending on its thickness) and remove fish from oven just when it begins to lightly flake apart with a fork. Let fillet pieces sit a minute or two to allow them to finish cooking.

Planning a luncheon and need a simple, satisfying salad entrée? You've just discovered the perfect recipe.

Pasta, White Beans, and Tuna Salad

Reminiscent of a Tuscan lunch, this nutritious salad is perfect to throw
together with some of our very best ingredients off the grocery shelves.
Perfect with locally grown, organic asparagus in the spring.

Salad

3 cups sliced fresh asparagus
12 oz. canned tuna, drained and flaked
1½ cups cooked white beans
10 large pitted black olives, sliced
½ cup diced roasted red pepper
6 cups cooked corkscrew-shaped pasta

Dressing

⅓ cup balsamic vinegar
2 tbsp. extra-virgin olive oil
2 tsp. fresh lemon juice
1 tbsp. Dijon mustard
2 tbsp. minced red onion
Freshly ground black pepper to taste
Sea salt to taste

For the Salad: In a steamer basket set above boiling water, steam the asparagus just until tender but still firm. Immediately remove from heat and shock in ice water. Drain.

In a large bowl, combine the tuna and asparagus. Add the beans, olives, red pepper, and cooked pasta.

For the Dressing: In a small bowl whisk together the vinegar, oil, juice, mustard, and red onion. Season with pepper and salt to taste. Add the dressing to the salad, tossing gently. Refrigerate for 1 to 2 hours to allow flavors to blend. Makes 6 servings.

Chef's Notes

About . . .
Why bother? Can't I just cut up a red bell pepper? Sure, but if you want a sweet, distinct veggie flavor, roasted bell peppers are a must.

How to Do It . . .
To roast a bell pepper, seed and cut pepper in half and place on a broiler rack, cut side down. Broil, moving peppers around to distribute the heat evenly, until skin is charred black. Place blackened peppers in a plastic bag and seal. Allow to sit for 30 minutes and then peel as much of the blackened skin off as possible. Cut pepper as needed in recipe. This process can easily be done on a grill or directly over a gas flame. Short on time? Roasted red bell peppers are available in a jar on our grocery shelves.

VEGE-MAGIC: ENJOYING PRODUCE AT ITS PEAK

Few gustatory pleasures can match the treat of tiny peas in June, the tart sweetness of fresh blueberries in July, the luxury of ruby red, vine-ripened tomatoes, or the miracle of midsummer corn.

With our hectic schedules and the rush of day-to-day living, it's easy to forget that your favorite vegetable (asparagus, for example) or your guest's favorite fruit (raspberries, perhaps) is out of season. Of course, that doesn't necessarily mean it's unavailable. In this age of jet shipping in nitrogen, we can get almost whatever we want, whenever we want it. But, in addition to the outlandish prices, the inferior quality of out-of-season produce makes it a doubly poor choice. Your best bet is to plan a menu around the produce that is readily available at any given time of the year. Simply put, instead of serving your favorite dishes *every* season, try exploring favorite dishes *of the* season.

Our well-stocked produce departments yield a bounty of fresh-picked delights. Without question, frozen or canned vegetables will do in a pinch, but fresh produce should be on your table every day.

The most important word to think about (with respect to this chapter's recipes in particular) is "seasonal." Rely on simple cooking techniques designed to enhance the flavor of a seasonal vegetable—not mask it. Use the seasons as a guide for choosing a recipe. In the fall make Brown Rice Pilaf with Roasted Squash and Sautéed Shallots, while in the spring gravitate toward Asparagus Spears with Citrus Ginger Dip. Once you embrace this kind of thinking, it becomes second nature. Finding Sautéed Ramps on the menu shouts "Spring is here!"

Pesticides in Produce

When you're grocery shopping, it's easy to find labels that assist you in picking foods that help reduce cholesterol and saturated fats, avoid antibiotics, or keep clear of artificial colors and sweeteners. When it comes to pesticides, however, consumers have been left in the dark.

This guide to pesticides in produce (developed by analysts at the not-for-profit Environmental Working Group based on the results of more than 100,000 tests for pesticides on produce collected by the USDA and the U.S. Food and Drug Administration over a period of 9 years) lists the most popular fresh fruits and vegetables that are considered the most contaminated with pesticides as well as those fruits and vegetables that consistently have low levels of pesticides. If you are concerned about pesticides in your diet, this handy guide can help you choose produce that lowers exposure to pesticides for you and your family.

For the most contaminated items, we suggest substituting organically grown produce whenever possible. While washing and rinsing fresh produce may help reduce pesticide residues, it does not eliminate them. Peeling reduces exposure, but valuable nutrients often go in the compost with the peel. The best option is to eat a varied diet, wash all produce, and choose organic when possible to reduce exposure to potentially harmful chemicals.

Produce Highest in Pesticides
• apples, cantaloupe, bell peppers, celery, cherries,

grapes (imported), nectarines, cucumbers, apricots, green beans, peaches, pears, potatoes, red raspberries, spinach, and strawberries

Produce Lowest in Pesticides
• asparagus, avocados, bananas, broccoli, cauliflower, sweet corn, kiwi, mangoes, onions, papaya, pineapples, and sweet peas

Some Basics on Storing Your Produce

Properly storing produce can help it last longer while also preserving taste and nutrients. Here's a sampling of how to keep things fresh. Remember, the path to the compost pile is paved with good intentions!

Bananas: Keep them on a countertop, unbagged, to ripen at room temperature. Don't refrigerate an unripe banana—the cold causes the skin to turn brown (which is not a problem) and prevents the fruit from ripening properly (which is a problem).

Blueberries: Dry and unwashed, blueberries can be kept in their plastic container in the back of the refrigerator.

Carrots: Remove any greens and then place the carrots in a resealable plastic bag in your refrigerator's crisper.

Grapes: Store in a resealable plastic bag in the back of the refrigerator. Wash just before eating.

Lemons and other citrus fruits: Keep citrus unbagged in the refrigerator door, but let them sit at room temperature for a few hours before using.

Lettuce: Wrap lettuce, before or after washing, in damp paper towels and seal in a plastic bag. Put bagged lettuce in your refrigerator's crisper, which will keep it moist and cold.

Onions: Store in a cool, well-ventilated place out of direct sunlight. Storing in mesh bags is acceptable, but plastic bags do not allow air to circulate and will cause the onions to rot.

Pears: If unripe, store pears at room temperature in a paper bag for 2 to 5 days to ripen. If ripe, keep refrigerated and unbagged.

Scallions: Store in the refrigerator's crisper unwashed and in a plastic bag.

Strawberries: Store in the refrigerator, unwashed, atop paper towels on a platter or plate, covered with plastic wrap. Wash and remove the hulls when you're ready to enjoy them.

Tomatoes: Store at room temperature on a countertop, out of direct sunlight, stem side up. Refrigerating them will ruin their flavor and texture.

This is a small sampling of some of the more popular fruits and vegetables. Where appropriate, I've included more tips with the recipes.

Isn't it fun when you taste something so essentially simple—like these In-Season Tomatoes—that your mouth screams, "Wow! This is fresh."

Parsley Pecan Pesto Green Beans

This dish's success depends on having a pesto that really sings with flavor! Taste it once it's all put together . . . it may need a few more notes of lemon, salt, or oil.

¾ cup fresh Italian (flat-leaf) parsley
¾ cup fresh basil leaves
½ cup pecan halves
2 large garlic cloves, peeled and sliced
2 tbsp. fresh lemon juice
¾ cup extra-virgin olive oil
¼ tsp. sea salt
¼ tsp. freshly ground black pepper
2 lb. green beans, ends trimmed

Chef's Notes

How to Do It . . .
Some do and some don't, but we like to salt the green beans in the pot. Once the water is boiling, just add a little sea salt to taste before adding the green beans.

Combine the parsley, basil, pecans, garlic, and lemon juice in a food processor, pulsing to grind as finely as possible. With the motor running, pour the oil in a slow, steady stream through the feed tube. Add the salt and pepper and continue processing until blended, stopping to scrape down the sides of the work bowl. Pesto, made ahead, may be covered and refrigerated for a day or two. Makes 1 cup.

Bring a large pot of water to a boil. Add the beans and cook over high heat until barely tender but still firm, about 3 to 5 minutes. Drain the beans in a colander, then rinse under cool water. Set aside in the colander or transfer to a kitchen towel and gently pat dry to remove excess water.

Place the beans in a large serving bowl, toss with the pesto, and serve. Serves 6+.

Maple-Mustard Green Beans

The sweet flavor of maple syrup combines well with the
assertive flavors of balsamic vinegar and mustard.

2 lb. green beans, ends trimmed
2 tbsp. coarse-grained Dijon mustard
3 tbsp. balsamic vinegar
1½ tbsp. maple syrup
2 tsp. extra-virgin olive oil
2 tbsp. chopped scallions
Sea salt and freshly ground black pepper to
taste

In a saucepan, bring 2 qt. of water to a boil over high heat. Add beans and cook uncovered until crisp-tender (begin checking at 5 minutes). Drain and place beans in a serving bowl.

While beans are cooking, in a small bowl whisk together the mustard, vinegar, maple syrup, and oil. Pour over hot beans and mix to coat well, then sprinkle with scallions. Season to taste with salt and pepper. Makes 6+ servings.

Chef's Notes

In Season . . .
Choose slender, crisp green beans that are bright and blemish free. Avoid mature beans with large seeds and swollen pods.

Hot Pepper-Filled Peppers

What a delicious change of pace from rice- and beef-stuffed peppers.

4 large red bell peppers, halved, seeded, roasted, and peeled
4 large yellow bell peppers, halved, seeded, roasted, and peeled
1 small eggplant, roasted and peeled
2 cups ricotta cheese
⅔ cup freshly grated Parmesan cheese
3 tbsp. minced fresh basil
1 tsp. finely minced garlic
⅓ cup diced chili peppers

Heat oven to 425 degrees.

Place half of a red and half of a yellow pepper in the work bowl of a food processor along with the roasted eggplant, ricotta cheese, Parmesan, basil, and garlic. Process just until smooth. Mix in diced chili peppers.

Fill the remaining pepper halves with the cheese mixture and place, cut half up, in a shallow baking dish. Bake until light golden brown, about 25 minutes. Makes 4 servings.

Chef's Notes

How to Do It . . .
To roast peppers, place in a shallow pan under the broiler so that peppers are about 1" from heat source. Broil, turning frequently with tongs, until peppers are well blistered and charred on all sides. Place in a plastic bag, close tightly, and let the peppers sweat (this allows skin to loosen) for 20 minutes or until cool enough to handle. Peel and discard skins. These peppers may be kept refrigerated and tightly wrapped for up to 4 days. Bring to room temperature before baking.

In Season . . .
Chili peppers differ in flavor and hotness depending on the type. Among the most commonly available of those not for the timid are the short, tapering Fresno; thick-fleshed, cylindrical jalapeño; and the short, slim Serrano.

Holiday Peppers

Festive red and green bell peppers add a perfect
touch alongside your holiday meats.

1 tbsp. extra-virgin olive oil
3 red bell peppers, cut into 1½" squares
2 green bell peppers, cut into 1½" squares
3 large garlic cloves, minced or pressed
½ tsp. finely grated orange zest
⅓ cup fresh orange juice
1 tbsp. tomato paste
½ tsp. sea salt
½ tsp. dried oregano, crushed
½ tsp. freshly ground black pepper

In a large nonstick skillet, heat the oil over medium heat until hot but not smoking. Add the bell peppers and cook, stirring gently but frequently, until the peppers are almost tender, about 5 minutes. Stir in the garlic and cook about 1 minute or until the garlic is fragrant. Add the orange zest, orange juice, tomato paste, salt, oregano, and black pepper and cook, stirring gently but frequently, until the peppers are tender and glossy, about 3 minutes longer.

Spoon the peppers into a medium bowl and serve. Serves 4+.

Chef's Notes

About . . .
Did you know? Red bell peppers are simply green bells that have been allowed to fully ripen.

Zucchini Parmesan

A deliciously simple dish and an easy alternative to the
traditional breading and frying of other Parmesan recipes.

2 tbsp. extra-virgin olive oil
4 small zucchini (about 5" or 6" long), sliced
into thin medallions
1 cup halved, peeled, and thinly sliced
yellow onion
12 white mushrooms, cleaned and sliced
1 large garlic clove, finely minced
½ tsp. sea salt
½ tsp. freshly ground black pepper
½ cup freshly grated Parmesan cheese, divided
8 oz. tomato sauce
½ tsp. granulated sugar

Heat oven to 350 degrees.

Heat the olive oil in a large skillet over medium heat.
Sauté the zucchini, onion, and mushrooms for 5 minutes. Add the garlic and cook for an additional
minute. Add the salt and pepper and *half* of the
cheese, mixing well. Stir in the tomato sauce and
sugar.

Pour the entire mixture into a 3-qt. casserole dish.
Sprinkle with the remaining cheese and bake for 25
minutes or until cheese is golden. Serves 4.

Chef's Notes

About . . .
The sugar in this recipe helps remove any acidity
from the tomato sauce.

In Season . . .
The peak season for summer squash is July through
September in Ohio. When buying, select small- to
medium-size firm squash with smooth, glossy, tender
skin. Squash should feel heavy for their size.

Rice Pilaf with Roasted Squash and Sautéed Shallots

Butternut and acorn squash, whichever you prefer, lend a rich, creamy
flavor to this hearty grain dish.

1 lb. butternut or acorn squash,
peeled and seeded
2 tbsp. extra-virgin olive oil, divided
2 tsp. sea salt, plus more to taste
½ tsp. freshly ground black pepper, plus more
to taste
1 tbsp. unsalted butter
1¼ cups thinly sliced shallots
1 cup brown rice
3 cups chicken broth or vegetable broth

Chef's Notes

In Season . . .
Choose hard, thick-shelled squash that feel heavy for
their size. Store whole squash, unwrapped, in a cool
(50 degrees) dry, dark place with good ventilation for
up to two months.

Heat oven to 400 degrees.

Cut the squash into ½" cubes and place in a baking
pan. Drizzle with 1 tbsp. of the olive oil, sprinkle
with extra salt and pepper, and toss to coat. Stirring
occasionally, roast the squash for 40 minutes, until
tender and golden brown. Allow to cool slightly.

Melt the butter in the remaining olive oil in a medium saucepan over medium heat. Add the shallots
and cook to soften, about 5 minutes. Add the rice
and stir, cooking 2 additional minutes. Stir in the
broth, the 2 tsp. salt, and the ½ tsp. pepper. Bring to
a boil over medium-high heat. Reduce to low, cover,
and simmer for 35 to 40 minutes or until all the liquid is absorbed and the rice is fluffy.

Remove saucepan from the heat. Serve warm. Serves
4+.

Praline-Topped Orange Yams

This fluffy, creamy yam dish with a sweet, crunchy topping is destined to become a regular family tradition at your home.

Yams

8 lb. cooked, peeled, and sliced yams
1⅓ cups fresh orange juice
2 tbsp. orange zest
5 tbsp. brandy
2 tsp. salt
Freshly ground black pepper to taste
2 tsp. ground ginger
½ cup unsalted butter, melted
⅔ cup firmly packed light brown sugar
6 large egg yolks, lightly beaten

Topping

1⅓ cups firmly packed light brown sugar
1 cup unsalted butter, melted
2¼ cups toasted, coarsely chopped pecans
2 tsp. ground cinnamon

Heat oven to 350 degrees.

In a large mixing bowl, beat yams with an electric mixer until smooth. Mix in juice, zest, brandy, salt, pepper, ginger, melted butter, brown sugar, and egg yolks, beating until mixture is light and fluffy.

Butter a large, shallow casserole. Spoon yam mixture into casserole, smoothing top evenly.

For the Topping: In a medium bowl, mix the brown sugar, butter, pecans, and cinnamon until well blended. Spread evenly over the yam mixture.

Bake for 45 to 50 minutes or until golden brown and bubbly. Remove from oven and let stand 15 minutes before serving. Serves 8+.

Chef's Notes

About . . .
Though often considered interchangeable, sweet potatoes and yams are actually two different plants. Sweet potatoes are native to and grown in the Americas, while yams are cultivated primarily in tropical areas. The "yams" marketed in the United States are actually a type of sweet potato.

Forget those artificial marshmallows and reinvent your holiday yam dish with a smooth and creamy texture and a nutty, sweet crunch.

Quinoa-Stuffed Mushrooms

Quinoa and walnuts add a nutty, flavorful crunch to these smooth, woodsy mushrooms.

¼ cup quinoa
10-12 white or cremini mushrooms, 2" diameter, caps and stems wiped clean
2 tbsp. extra-virgin olive oil, divided
1 tbsp. finely minced garlic
⅓ cup chopped leek, white part only
¼ cup chicken broth or vegetable broth
1-2 tsp. fresh lemon juice
2 tbsp. toasted, finely chopped walnuts
2 tbsp. chopped fresh Italian (flat-leaf) parsley
Sea salt to taste

Chef's Notes

About . . .
Strictly speaking, mushrooms are not veggies but belong to a broad group called fungi.

In Season . . .
Look for mushrooms that are blemish free, without shiny spots or signs of decay. Store unwashed in a cloth or paper bag in the refrigerator. To clean, wipe with a paper towel or mushroom brush when ready to use.

Heat oven to 425 degrees.

Rinse the quinoa with cool water in a fine mesh strainer for 2 minutes until water runs clear. Allow quinoa to drain.

Separate mushroom caps from stems. Finely chop stems, measure out a generous ⅓ cup, and set aside. Brush the mushroom caps inside and out with 1 tbsp. of the olive oil. Arrange the caps open side up on a baking sheet or in a baking dish.

Heat remaining oil in a large skillet over medium heat. Add the garlic, leek, and reserved mushroom stems, sautéing until fragrant and tender, 3 to 4 minutes. Stir in the quinoa and broth and bring to a boil. Reduce the heat, cover, and simmer until all the liquid is absorbed and the quinoa is tender, 8 to 10 minutes. Stir in the lemon juice, walnuts, and parsley. Season to taste with salt.

Using a teaspoon, pack the stuffing inside the mushroom caps, mounding high. Roast until filled mushrooms are hot and fork tender, about 10 minutes. Serve hot or at room temperature. Serves 4+.

Grilled Portobello Sandwich

This hearty mushroom sandwich tastes just like a burger. Thick, meaty Portobello mushroom topped with roasted red peppers, grilled red onions, and slathered with garlic-lemon mayonnaise sits inside pita bread.

6 medium Portobello mushroom caps, cleaned, gills removed, and stemmed
1 large red onion, thickly sliced
1½ tbsp. extra-virgin olive oil
6 2-oz. whole-wheat pita breads
1 cup strips of roasted red peppers

Garlic-Lemon Mayonnaise

½ cup mayonnaise
3 large garlic cloves, finely minced
1 tbsp. fresh lemon juice
1 tbsp. capers, drained and coarsely chopped
Freshly ground black pepper

Chef's Notes

How to Do It . . .
The dark black gills inside the Portobello cap are strong and oftentimes bitter. Remove by gently scraping out with a teaspoon before using.

Heat gas, charcoal, or kitchen grill.

Place the Portobello caps and red onion slices directly on a hot grill and brush with the olive oil. Grill, turning once, until mushrooms are soft and onions are caramelized. Remove from the grill and set aside. Add the pita bread and grill on both sides.

For the Garlic-Lemon Mayonnaise: In a small bowl combine the mayonnaise, garlic, lemon juice, capers, and black pepper until well blended.

When ready to serve, open the grilled pita bread and spread with about 1 tbsp. of the mayo blend per sandwich. Top with a Portobello cap, peppers, and a red onion slice. Serves 6.

Roasted Roots with Cider

The sweetness of the cider really brings out the
natural flavors in these root veggies.

¼ cup cider vinegar
¼ cup apple cider
2 tbsp. extra-virgin olive oil
3 tbsp. unsalted butter, melted
1 tbsp. Dijon mustard
2 tbsp. finely chopped fresh rosemary
2 small turnips, trimmed, peeled, and
quartered lengthwise
4 small Yukon Gold or red potatoes, halved
1 medium sweet potato, peeled and cut into 2"
wedges
2 medium carrots, peeled and cut into 2" pieces
2 parsnips, peeled and cut into 2" pieces
Sea salt and freshly ground black pepper
to taste
2 tbsp. chopped fresh Italian (flat-leaf) parsley

Chef's Notes

In Season . . .
Don't know a turnip from a parsnip? The turnip is a
globe-shaped root vegetable that has reddish-purple
skin, crisp white flesh, and a sweet-hot flavor. A
parsnip is a fair-skinned cousin of a carrot . . . long,
fairly slender, and a tan/beige color.

Heat oven to 400 degrees.

In a large bowl, whisk together the vinegar, cider, oil,
butter, mustard, and rosemary until blended. Add the
turnips, potatoes, sweet potato, carrots, and parsnips,
tossing well to coat. Season with salt and pepper and
scatter the veggies in a single layer on a large parchment-paper-lined baking sheet.

Roast 45 to 50 minutes, turning veggies occasionally,
until they are tender and a light golden brown
around the edges. Toss with the parsley. Serve warm
or at room temperature. Serves 4+.

Carrot Vinaigrette

This vinaigrette has a beautiful color and sweet carrot flavor. Drizzle over corn dishes or toss with your favorite assorted greens.

½ cup chopped, peeled carrot
3 tbsp. white wine vinegar
½ cup + 2 tbsp. canola oil
Sea salt and freshly ground black pepper
to taste
1 tbsp. finely chopped fresh Italian
(flat-leaf) parsley

In a small saucepan of boiling water, cook carrot until very tender (about 10 minutes). Drain well. Pat carrot dry with paper towel.

In a blender, combine vinegar and warm, softened carrot. Blend until smooth, then add oil in a slow, steady stream until emulsified.

Season vinaigrette to taste with salt and pepper, then stir in parsley. Makes about 1 cup.

Chef's Notes

In Season . . .
Choose firm, clean, well-shaped carrots with bright orange-gold color. I prefer carrots with their tops still attached   they are likely to be fresher.

Sautéed Ramps

Serve these as a side dish to any roasted meat, fish, or
poultry dish or on top of polenta, rice, or pasta.

1 lb. ramps
1½ tbsp. extra-virgin olive oil
Sea salt and freshly ground black pepper
to taste

Chef's Notes

In Season . . .
Harvesting these wild leeks, or ramps, is a true rite of
spring, a sign that winter is over . . . that the fresh
foods of the spring season have once again arrived!

Trim and discard the greens from the ramps. Trim off
the root ends, leaving a bulb and about 3" of a pink-
ish stem. Remove any brown skin that covers the
outside of the bulbs.

In a large skillet, heat the oil over medium heat. Add
the ramps and cook, stirring frequently, until slightly
tender, about 4 or 5 minutes. Season with salt and
pepper and serve immediately. Serves 4+.

Baked Leeks

This versatile side dish is a refreshing change of pace from a potato gratin.

8 small leeks (about 1½ lb.)
2 large eggs, lightly beaten
5 oz. fresh goat cheese
⅓ cup plain, nonfat or low-fat yogurt
2 oz. freshly grated Parmesan cheese, divided
Sea salt and freshly ground black pepper to taste
1 oz. fresh breadcrumbs

Chef's Notes

In Season . . .
Select leeks with clean, white bottoms and crisp, fresh-looking tops. Small- to medium-size leeks are the most tender, with a mild, delicate (onion) flavor.

Heat oven to 350 degrees and butter a shallow baking dish.

Trim the leeks, cut a slit from the top to the bottom, and rinse well under cold water. Place the leeks in a large saucepan of water, bring to a boil, and simmer gently just until tender, about 6 minutes. Using a slotted spoon, remove and drain well. Allow to drain in a colander, then arrange leeks in the baking dish.

In a medium bowl, combine the eggs, goat cheese, yogurt, and *half* of the Parmesan cheese. Season well with salt and pepper.

Pour the cheese and yogurt mixture over the leeks. Mix the breadcrumbs and remaining Parmesan cheese together and sprinkle atop the leeks. Bake for 35 to 40 minutes or until the top is a crisp golden brown. Serves 4+.

In-Season Tomatoes

It's hard to improve on the flavor of vine-ripened, locally grown tomatoes, but I think this recipe does just that. Enjoy it often when tomatoes are in season!

6 medium tomatoes, cored or 10 red plum and
10 yellow plum tomatoes, cut into
½" slices
⅔ cup extra-virgin olive oil
¼ cup white wine vinegar
¼ cup finely chopped fresh Italian
(flat-leaf) parsley
¼ cup finely chopped scallions
1 large garlic clove, finely minced or pressed
1 tsp. sea salt
1 tsp. finely chopped fresh dill weed
1 tbsp. finely chopped fresh basil
¼ tsp. freshly ground black pepper

Arrange tomatoes on a large serving platter.

In a medium bowl, stir together the oil, vinegar, parsley, scallions, garlic, salt, dill weed, basil, and pepper. Mix well.

Pour dressing over tomatoes. Cover and let sit at room temperature for 1 hour, basting occasionally. Serves 6+.

Chef's Notes

In Season . . .
Store whole tomatoes stem end up at room temperature (to preserve their sweetness) away from direct sunlight.

Tomato Basil Coulis

There are so many ways to enjoy this . . . spooned atop freshly steamed asparagus, mixed in with crumbled goat cheese and spread atop whole grain crackers, or eaten directly from the blender!

2 tbsp. tomato paste
½ tsp. minced fresh yellow onion
¼ tsp. minced fresh garlic
¼ tsp. minced jalapeño pepper
1 tsp. extra-virgin olive oil
½ cup peeled, seeded, and chopped tomato
¼ cup chicken broth
¼ cup red wine vinegar
½ tsp. dried oregano, crushed
½ tsp. finely chopped fresh cilantro
¼ cup coarsely chopped fresh basil

In a large skillet over medium heat, sauté the tomato paste, onion, garlic, and jalapeño pepper in hot oil for 1 minute. Add the chopped tomato and broth; bring to a boil. Reduce heat and simmer, stirring occasionally, until thickened (about 10 minutes). Remove from heat and set aside to cool for 20 minutes.

Puree mixture in blender, stopping to scrape down sides of blender. Stir in the vinegar, oregano, cilantro, and basil. Cover coulis in a small serving bowl and chill until ready to use. Makes about 1 cup.

Chef's Notes

About . . .
A coulis refers to a thick puree or sauce.

How to Do It . . .
To peel a tomato, drop into a pot of boiling water and cook for 30 seconds to 1 minute. Immediately remove tomato with a slotted spoon and place into a bowl of ice water. When cool enough to handle, tomato skin should easily slip off using fingers or a sharp paring knife. Cut tomato in half and squeeze to remove the seeds.

Sweet Corn Succotash

There's no suffering with this succotash . . . only pure, fresh summer flavors.

1 medium yellow onion, diced
1 large garlic clove, minced
2 tbsp. extra-virgin olive oil
1 cup cooked fingerling potatoes, skin on, cut into bite-size pieces
1 cup green beans, trimmed, blanched, and cut into 1" pieces
1 cup shucked, blanched lima beans
3 scallions, cut into ½" slices
1 qt. corn kernels, freshly cut from the cob
3 tbsp. rice vinegar
1 cup cherry tomatoes, halved
½ cup torn basil leaves
Sea salt and freshly ground black pepper to taste

Sweat onion and garlic with olive oil in a large skillet over medium heat, cooking until translucent. Over medium-high heat, add the potatoes, both beans, and the scallions. Stir, warming mixture completely. Add corn kernels.

When corn becomes very hot, stir in the rice vinegar, cherry tomatoes, and basil. Remove from heat. Season to taste with salt and freshly ground black pepper. Serves 3+.

Chef's Notes

How to Do It . . .
Blanching is the process of plunging food into boiling water briefly, then into cold water to shock the food (this would shock you too!) and stop the cooking process.

In Season . . .
Lima beans, referred to as a shell bean, have to be shucked out of their rather tough pods. When buying, feel along the pod to make sure it contains plump beans, avoiding beans that are dried out or have dark pods.

Tuscan Warm Greens with Balsamic Vinaigrette

★

A delicious way to introduce your family and friends to kale and a tastier, more healthful version of that old-fashioned spinach-with-hot-bacon-dressing dish.

Balsamic Vinaigrette

¼ cup balsamic vinegar
¼ tsp. sweet paprika
1 large garlic clove, finely chopped
1 tsp. honey, your choice of flavor or color
¼ cup extra-virgin olive oil
¼ tsp. sea salt

Salad

1½ cups sliced white button mushrooms
2-3 cups lacinato or Tuscan kale, cleaned, discarding tough stems and center ribs, and torn into bite-size pieces
2 cups assorted baby greens, cleaned and torn into bite-size pieces
3 tbsp. pine nuts, toasted

For the Balsamic Vinaigrette: Combine the vinegar, paprika, garlic, honey, olive oil, and salt in a medium mixing bowl, whisking until well combined. Use immediately or store in a tightly covered container until ready to use.

For the Salad: Heat vinaigrette to boiling in a large sauté pan over medium heat. Cook mushrooms in vinaigrette for 2 minutes. Add kale, tossing and cooking until kale pieces just begin to wilt. Remove and toss mixture gently into a large bowl with the assorted baby greens. Serve immediately topped with toasted pine nuts. Serves 2+.

Chef's Notes

How to Do It . . .
To cook with kale, tear out and discard tough stems and center ribs. Use leaves whole or tear into bite-size pieces.

In Season . . .
Kale, affectionately referred to as a green with a bite, has a peppery flavor and holds most of its texture when cooked. Look for fresh, tender, deep-green leaves free of blemishes.

Mediterranean Vegetables with Tahini

Simple and delicious, this dish is a combination of sweetly roasted vegetables topped with a lemon-flavored sesame cream.

Vegetables

2 green or red bell peppers, seeded
and quartered
2 medium zucchini, halved lengthwise
2 small eggplants, halved lengthwise, sliced,
and degorged
1 fennel bulb, quartered
Extra-virgin olive oil
Sea salt and freshly ground black pepper
to taste
8 oz. feta cheese, crumbled

Tahini Cream

1 cup tahini
1 large garlic clove, pressed or finely minced
2 tbsp. extra-virgin olive oil
2 tbsp. fresh lemon juice
½ cup cold water
Sea salt and freshly ground black pepper
to taste

Heat oven to 425 degrees.

For the Vegetables: Brush the vegetables with the oil, place on a baking sheet, and turning once, roast just until browned, about 30 minutes.

Place the vegetables in a shallow pan and season with salt and pepper, then sprinkle with the feta cheese. Let cool.

For the Tahini Cream: Combine the tahini, garlic, oil, and lemon juice in a food processor or blender. Pulse to mix, then with the motor still running slowly pour in ½ cup cold water, blending until smooth. Season to taste with salt and freshly ground black pepper.

Serve the vegetables and cheese drizzled with the tahini cream on top. Serves 4+.

Chef's Notes

About . . .
Tahini is a thick paste made from ground sesame seeds.

Serve this dish with warm pita bread for dipping and eating.

How to Do It . . .
To degorge eggplants, sprinkle cut slices with salt and let the juices that form drain away in a colander. After 30 minutes or so, rinse well and pat dry. Degorged eggplants are less bitter.

In Season . . .
Fennel has been a Mediterranean favorite since Roman times. Look for firm, white bulbs with rigid, crisp stalks and feathery, bright green leaves.

Glazed Brussels Sprouts

A bright, refreshing sauce with citrus makes for a delicious
counterpoint to the assertive flavors of Brussels sprouts.

3 medium oranges
1 lb. fresh Brussels sprouts (about 4 cups)
1 tbsp. unsalted butter
2 tsp. cornstarch or arrowroot
¼ tsp. dried thyme, crushed
1 tbsp. Dijon mustard

Chef's Notes

About . . .
Blood oranges or navel oranges work well for this recipe.

Brussels sprouts tend to arouse strong emotions—people either love or hate them. The response probably hinges on the age of the sprouts they first experienced: young sprouts are sweet and delicate, but older ones have a strong cabbage flavor and odor and a coarse texture.

In Season . . .
Great-tasting Brussels sprouts are firm, compact, and fresh looking with a bright green color; they feel heavy for their size.

Finely shred a portion of the peel of one orange to make ½ tsp. zest; set aside. Halve the orange and squeeze to extract juice. Working over a bowl to catch the juice, peel and section the remaining 2 oranges; set aside. Combine the juices to get ⅓ cup, adding water if necessary.

Rinse the Brussels sprouts and halve any large sprouts. In a medium saucepan, cook sprouts uncovered in a small amount of boiling water for 10 to 12 minutes until tender. Drain and transfer to a serving bowl. Gently stir in orange sections; cover and keep warm.

In the same saucepan, melt the butter. Stir in the cornstarch and thyme. Add the orange zest, orange juice, and mustard. Cook and stir until thickened and bubbly, then cook for 1 additional minute, stirring continuously.

Top Brussels sprouts and fruit with sauce, tossing to combine. Serves 4+.

Cauliflower-Spinach Toss

Cauliflower is an often-neglected veggie, relegated most of the time to being smothered with cheese sauce. Wake up your taste buds with this veggie toss.

Toss

1 lb. spinach, cleaned and stemmed
½ medium-sized head cauliflower, broken into flowerets, then cut into ¼"-thick slices
1 large avocado
Fresh lemon juice
½ cup slivered almonds, toasted

Dressing

6 tbsp. extra-virgin olive oil
3 tbsp. white wine vinegar
1 large garlic clove, minced or pressed
½ tsp. sea salt
½ tsp. dried mustard
½ tsp. dried basil, crushed
¼ tsp. freshly ground black pepper
⅛ tsp. freshly grated nutmeg

For the Toss: Tear spinach into bite-size pieces. Place in a serving bowl with the cauliflower. Pit, peel, and slice avocado, dipping slices into lemon juice to coat; add to the spinach/cauliflower mixture.

For the Dressing: In a small bowl combine the oil, vinegar, garlic, salt, mustard, basil, pepper, and nutmeg; blend well.

Pour dressing over salad; add almonds and gently mix to coat thoroughly. Makes 5+ servings.

Chef's Notes

In Season . . .
When cauliflower shopping, choose firm, compact, creamy white (or bright purplish-green) heads with flowerets pressed tightly together. A yellow tinge and spreading flowerets indicate overmaturity. Any leaves should be crisp and bright green.

Broccoli, Cauliflower, and Carrots with Cheese Crumbs

Quick cooking helps these veggies maintain their crunch.

1½ bunches broccoli (about 1½ lb.)
1 large head cauliflower (about 2 lb.)
1 lb. carrots, peeled and cut into ¼" slices on the diagonal
1 tbsp. canola oil
4 tbsp. unsalted butter, divided
2 cups very coarse, dry breadcrumbs
½ cup freshly grated Parmesan cheese
½ tsp. cayenne
Sea salt to taste
Freshly ground black pepper to taste

Chef's Notes

Do Ahead Tip:
Vegetables may be blanched 1 day ahead, then chilled, covered, and refrigerated until needed.

In Season . . .
When picking broccoli, look for compact, dark clusters of tightly closed dark green florets. Avoid heads with yellowing florets and thick, woody stems.

Heat oven to 350 degrees.

Trim broccoli, reserving stems for another use, and cut florets into 1" pieces. Trim cauliflower and cut florets into 1" pieces.

In a large saucepan of boiling, salted water, cook broccoli, cauliflower, and carrots until crisp-tender, 2 to 5 minutes. Drain and shock in cold water to stop the cooking; drain again in a large colander.

In a large skillet heat oil and *2 tbsp.* of the butter over medium-high heat until foam begins to subside. Stirring, sauté breadcrumbs until golden. Stir in Parmesan and cayenne and salt to taste, stirring until crumbs are crisp.

In a large ovenproof skillet, melt remaining butter over medium heat. Toss the vegetables in the skillet with salt and pepper to taste. Sprinkle vegetables with breadcrumbs, tossing to combine. Bake uncovered for 10 minutes or just until heated through. Serves 6+.

Fresh Asparagus with Tomato Herb Concasse

*Fresh asparagus is best served in the simplest manner . . .
with a hint of something additional to highlight its spring flavors. In this
instance, a tomato herb concasse works perfectly.*

1 lb. assorted teardrop or cherry
tomatoes, halved
⅓ cup + ¼ cup extra-virgin olive oil, divided
2 tbsp. white wine or rice vinegar
1 tbsp. assorted coarsely chopped fresh herbs
½ tsp. sea salt
¼ tsp. freshly ground black pepper
1½ lb. asparagus spears
¾ lb. tender lettuce, cleaned and torn into
bite-size pieces
1 tbsp. minced fresh tarragon leaves

In a medium serving bowl, combine the tomatoes, ⁺⁺ *cup* of the olive oil, vinegar, assorted herbs, salt, and pepper. Cover and let sit at room temperature for 1 hour to allow flavors to blend.

Trim the ends of asparagus so that all spears are about 6" long. In a steamer or large covered sauté pan bring 1" of water to a boil. Steam the asparagus for about 1 ½ minutes, then shock the asparagus spears in ice water to stop the cooking. Drain well.

In a wide serving bowl, toss the asparagus and lettuce gently with the remaining olive oil and minced tarragon. Divide among individual serving plates. Top with a mound of the concasse. Makes 4 servings.

Chef's Notes

About . . .
"Concasse" refers to a mixture that's coarsely chopped or ground.

In Season . . .
Use chervil, savory, tarragon, parsley, chives, or other herbs of your choice.

Asparagus Spears with Citrus Ginger Dip

Often requested in my cooking classes that highlight how to cook with the seasons, this surprising way to enjoy asparagus is always a hit!

2 lb. asparagus

Citrus Ginger Dip

¾ cup mayonnaise, regular or reduced fat
¾ cup sour cream, regular or reduced fat
1 tbsp. apple cider vinegar
1 tbsp. fresh orange juice
1½ tsp. finely chopped orange zest
1 large garlic clove, pressed
1 tbsp. Dijon mustard
1½ tbsp. freshly grated ginger
1 tsp. soy sauce
½ tsp. granulated sugar
Sea salt and freshly ground black pepper to taste

Chef's Notes

About . . .
The choice of asparagus stalk thickness is more a matter of personal preference.

In Season . . .
Choose firm asparagus spears that are bright green almost their entire length, with tightly closed tips.

In a large sauté pan, bring 1" of water to a boil.

Snap tough ends off asparagus, then add asparagus to boiling water. Simmer uncovered until barely tender, 3 to 4 minutes. Drain and shock in ice water to stop the cooking. Drain again; cover and chill until serving time.

For the Citrus Ginger Dip: In a medium mixing bowl, combine the mayonnaise, sour cream, vinegar, orange juice and zest, garlic, mustard, ginger, soy sauce, sugar, and salt and pepper to taste. Serve with the asparagus spears as "dippers." Serves 6+.

Asparagus and Strawberries with Balsamic Vinaigrette

This recipe says, "Welcome, spring," and the combo of asparagus and strawberries shouts it!

1½ lb. asparagus
½ cup extra-virgin olive oil
4 large garlic cloves, peeled and flattened
¼ cup balsamic vinegar
1 tbsp. firmly packed light brown sugar
Sea salt to taste
Freshly ground black pepper to taste
1 head radicchio, thinly sliced
2 cups strawberries, cleaned, hulled, and thickly sliced

Chef's Notes

In Season . . .
Radicchio is a red-leafed, Italian chicory most often used as a salad green. It has a bite to its flavor and a color and crispness that's perfect for showcasing fresh asparagus and strawberries.

In a large sauté pan, bring 1" of water to a boil.

Snap tough ends off asparagus, then add asparagus to boiling water. Simmer uncovered until barely tender, 3 to 4 minutes. Drain and shock in ice water to stop the cooking. Drain again; cover and chill until serving time.

Heat oil in a small skillet over low heat. Add garlic and sauté until a light gold in color. Add vinegar and cook 2 minutes. Add sugar, stirring until dissolved. Remove garlic with a slotted spoon and discard; season mixture in skillet with salt and pepper.

Arrange radicchio on a large platter. Top with asparagus and strawberries. Spoon enough dressing from the skillet over the salad to lightly coat. Serves 4+.

Blueberry Coleslaw

This market kitchen specialty is served up during our Bluesberry Fest in July . . . and
is the perfect picnic "take along" the remainder of the summer season.

2 medium heads of red cabbage
1 medium head of green cabbage
4 ribs of celery, peeled
1 small red onion, halved, then julienned
4 cups mayonnaise
¼ cup balsamic vinegar
1 7-oz. can chipotle peppers in adobo sauce
2 cups salted, roasted peanuts
4 pt. fresh blueberries, cleaned

Coarsely shred cabbages and place into a large serving bowl. Dice celery and add that and julienned onion to the bowl with the cabbages. Toss to blend.

In a food processor blend the mayonnaise, vinegar, and chipotles in adobo sauce, stopping to scrape sides of work bowl. When mixture is well blended, scrape into serving bowl with cabbage mixture. Toss in peanuts and blueberries. Gently mix until all is evenly coated. Serves 8+.

Chef's Notes

In Season . . .
When choosing cabbages, pick firm heads that feel heavy for their size. Outer leaves should look fresh, have good color, and be free of blemishes.

Avocado-Lime Dip

Serve this fresh-tasting dip (that doesn't brown easily) with tortilla chips, alongside fresh organic vegetables, or spooned atop a taco or burrito.

2-3 large ripe avocados, peeled and pitted
6 tbsp. fresh lime juice
5 tbsp. sour cream
4 tbsp. freshly chopped cilantro leaves
2 tsp. ground coriander seeds
1 large garlic clove, finely minced
⅔ cup canola or corn oil
½ tsp. coarse sea salt
¼ tsp. freshly ground black pepper

In a food processor, combine the avocado, lime juice, sour cream, cilantro, ground coriander, and garlic. Blend well, stopping to scrape down sides of the work bowl. With machine running, add oil in a slow, steady stream through the feed tube until mixture is blended. Add salt and pepper. Makes about 3 cups.

Chef's Notes

About . . .
Nonfat or low-fat plain yogurt, as well as drained or silken tofu, may be substituted for the sour cream.

Opposite: Though avocado is a fruit, that shouldn't slow down the dipping action!

Avocado Club

A popular café menu item, this sandwich has the perfect elements to satisfy any club lovers cravings . . . crunchy and creamy and fresh.

2 slices refrigerated, firm tofu
½ tsp. hickory salt
½ large, firm ripe avocado, peeled and sliced
¼ cup alfalfa sprouts, rinsed and patted dry
2 slices fresh tomato
2 slices Swiss cheese
3 slices Seven Grain or Country Wheat bread from our bakery
Vegan mayonnaise, optional

Heat oven to 350 degrees.

Season tofu slices with hickory salt and bake on a parchment-lined baking sheet for 10 minutes until slightly crisp and dry.

To serve, layer the avocado, seasoned tofu, sprouts, tomato, and cheese between slices of bread—with one slice of bread in the middle and one at each end. Slather some mayonnaise on a slice or two of bread if desired. Serves 1.

Chef's Notes

About . . .
Vegans are the purists of the vegetarian world and have the most limited diet, refusing to eat any animal-derivative foods, including butter, cheese, eggs, and milk.

How to Do It . . .
To ripen hard avocados, store them in a loosely closed paper bag at room temperature.

In Season . . .
Avocados are best for eating when they yield to gentle pressure. Avoid avocados that look badly bruised or have dark, soft, sunken spots.

GLORIOUS GRAINS

If you stop to think about it, grains have always been an essential part of our diet, whether it's the oatmeal we eat for breakfast, the bread on the sandwich we grab for lunch, or the cookie we munch on for a snack. All of these are made from different grains.

Beyond the familiar there are enormous possibilities for grains. As with other foods, each grain is unique, having a character and distinctive flavor of its own. Some grains are strong flavored and assertive, others mellow. Some are sweet and rich tasting, while others are earthy. Some are a quick cook, others take more time.

The grain dishes in this chapter are not only versatile and varied, they're a marvelous source of nutrition. Besides the standard boil and simmer, enjoy recipes that toast, bake, marinate, sauté, and presoak grains to produce an assortment of textures and flavors. The recipes that follow offer tempting combinations of herbs and spices, creating great grain dishes. Enjoy them often!

Attractively presented Grains in a Lettuce Cup, this plated grain dish is even more tempting and inviting.

Roasted Butternut Squash Risotto

Risotto is typically made with short-grain Arborio rice with a constant stirring and slow addition of liquid for a chewy, creamy texture. Here we've added roasted butternut squash for extra richness.

Squash

1 medium butternut squash, peeled, halved, seeded, and cut into ½" cubes
2 tbsp. extra-virgin olive oil
Sea salt to taste
Freshly ground black pepper to taste
2 tsp. fresh thyme leaves

Risotto

2½-3 cups chicken or vegetable broth
2 tbsp. extra-virgin olive oil
½ cup finely chopped yellow onion
1 large garlic clove, minced
1 cup Arborio rice
⅓ cup dry white wine
1 tbsp. finely chopped fresh thyme
Freshly grated Parmesan cheese, optional

Heat oven to 400 degrees.

For the Squash: Place the squash in a baking pan, drizzle with the olive oil, season with salt and pepper, and toss with the thyme leaves to coat. Spread the squash in an even layer and roast for 35 minutes or until tender and golden brown around the edges. Remove pan from the oven and set aside while making risotto.

For the Risotto: In a medium saucepan, bring the broth to a boil over high heat. Reduce heat and keep broth cooking at a simmer.

In a 3-qt. saucepan, heat oil over medium heat and sauté onions until translucent. Add garlic and rice and sauté for 2 minutes until rice is well coated with oil.

Combine wine with hot broth. Add about 1 cup of the simmering broth mixture to the rice and cook, stirring, until liquid is absorbed. Continue cooking and stirring, adding more broth until rice has absorbed almost all of the broth before adding more. Rice should remain at a simmer. After rice has simmered for 15 minutes, taste a grain. It should be almost done, with only a small, firm center yet to be cooked through. Continue to cook for 4 minutes, stirring continuously until center is soft but not mushy.

Toss with thyme, roasted squash, and Parmesan cheese, if using. Serve immediately. Serves 4.

Chipotle Rice

A simple rice preparation with a kick!

1 tbsp. unsalted butter
1 tsp. finely chopped garlic
¼ cup water
1¾ cup chicken broth or vegetable broth
1-2 chipotle chilies in adobo sauce,
finely chopped
¼ tsp. ground cumin
1 cup long-grain white or brown rice

Chef's Notes

About . . .
Long-grain rice traditionally cooks up fluffier and drier than medium or short-grain rices.

In a 2-qt. saucepan melt the butter until sizzling. Add the garlic and cook over medium heat until garlic is softened. Do not allow garlic to turn brown, as it will become bitter. Add the water, broth, chipotle, and cumin. Continue cooking until broth comes to a boil. Add the rice. Reduce heat to low, cover, and cook until rice is tender (about 20 minutes for white, 40 minutes for brown).

Remove saucepan from heat and let stand for 5 minutes or until liquid is absorbed. Fluff rice with a fork. Makes 5+ servings.

Emerald Rice

Poblano peppers give this dish a richer flavor, but
milder Anaheim chilies may be substituted.

2 poblano peppers, roasted, peeled, seeded,
and chopped
1½ cups chopped green bell pepper
4 medium garlic cloves
2 cups fresh cilantro leaves
4 cups vegetable broth, divided
¾ cup diced white onion
1 tbsp. canola oil
2 cups basmati rice
Sea salt and freshly ground black pepper
to taste
Lime wedges for garnish, optional

Chef's Notes

About . . .
Basmati rice is a long-grained, fine-textured rice with
a nutlike texture and aroma.

Poblano—a blackish green, heart-shaped pasilla— is
a relatively mild pepper with just a touch of bitter-
ness; dried it's referred to as an ancho chili.

In a food processor, combine poblano peppers, bell
pepper, garlic, cilantro, and *2 cups* of the vegetable
broth. Puree until well blended.

In a 4-qt. saucepan over medium heat, sauté onion in
oil until translucent. Add rice, stirring until golden.
Add the pureed vegetables, remaining broth, salt,
and pepper; stir and bring mixture to a boil. Reduce
heat to medium low, cover, and simmer until rice is
cooked, about 25 minutes.

Remove from heat and allow to stand for 5 minutes.
Fluff rice mixture with a fork and serve immediately
with lime wedges, if desired. Serves 5+.

Smoked Tofu and Wild Rice

This market kitchen specialty is one of my personal lunch favorites.
Colorful, crunchy, and flavorful, it just makes you feel good eating it!

Dressing

1¼ cups fresh lemon juice
2 tbsp. toasted sesame oil
1½ tbsp. curry powder
¼ tsp. sea salt
¾ tsp. ground coriander
1¾ cups canola oil

Tofu/Wild Rice

2 cups wild rice blend
22 oz. refrigerated, firm smoked tofu
¾ cup diced yellow bell pepper
¾ cup diced red bell pepper
1 cup toasted pecan pieces
½ cup currants
⅓-½ cup Dressing

For the Dressing: In a medium bowl, whisk together the lemon juice, sesame oil, curry powder, salt, and coriander until well blended. Add canola oil in a slow, steady stream until mixture is emulsified. Cover and refrigerate until ready to use. Makes about 3 cups.

For the Tofu/Wild Rice: Boil or steam rice blend until tender. While rice is cooking, cut tofu into ¼" cubes.

In a large serving bowl, combine the cooked rice blend, tofu, peppers, pecan pieces, currants, and Dressing. Toss gently to blend well. Serves 4+.

Chef's Notes

About . . .
Wild rice blend is typically a combination of wild rice, long-grain brown rice, sweet brown rice, wehani (red rice), and occasionally other heirloom rices.

If you're in the mood for smoky, crunchy, and a hint of sweet, now is the perfect time to prepare this grain dish.

Cherry Walnut Rice

Sweet cherries add remarkable flavor to ordinary rice with this recipe. It's
a perfect rice side dish for a special occasion.

16-oz. package brown and wild rice mix,
substituting vegetable or chicken broth for the
cooking water
1 cup seeded and diced cucumber
½ cup diced red bell pepper
½ cup chopped water chestnuts or jicama
¼ cup chopped celery
⅛ cup chopped fresh Italian (flat-leaf) parsley
½ cup toasted, chopped walnuts
1 tbsp. freshly grated orange zest
2 tbsp. finely chopped yellow onion
1 small garlic clove, finely minced
1 lb. pitted, fresh sweet cherries, halved or
2 cups dried cherries

Prepare rice mix according to package directions, substituting broth for the cooking water.

While rice mix is cooking, in a large serving bowl combine the cucumber, pepper, water chestnuts/jicama, celery, parsley, walnuts, zest, onion, and garlic.

When rice mix has cooked, remove saucepan from heat and allow to cool for 15 minutes. Fluff mixture with a fork, and then toss into the serving bowl, adding the cherries.

With a large spatula, toss all ingredients gently but well to combine. Serve hot or at room temperature. Serves 4+.

Chef's Notes

About . . .
Wild rice is actually an aquatic grass seed grain, not true rice.

In Season . . .
Jicama has a crisp, sweet flavor. A large, bulbous root vegetable with a thin, brown skin and white, crunchy flesh, it is sometimes referred to as the Mexican potato.

Fruited Couscous

Sweet port gives this couscous dish added fruitiness and flavor as well as an inviting color.

¾ cup tawny port
½ cup balsamic vinegar
1 cup dried fruits, a blend of cranberries, apricots, pears, and currants, or your choice
8 oz. Israeli couscous
2 cups fresh orange juice
1 tsp. saffron
3 tbsp. unsalted butter
½ cup diced leeks, white part only
½ cup diced fennel bulb
¼ cup toasted, ground almonds
1 tbsp. finely chopped lemon zest
¼ cup fresh lemon juice
3 tbsp. chopped fresh basil
2 tbsp. chopped fresh purple basil, if available (or omit)
2 tbsp. chopped fresh mint
Freshly ground black pepper to taste

Heat the port and balsamic vinegar in a large sauté pan, simmering for 10 minutes to evaporate the liquid slightly, then add the dried fruits and plump over medium heat for 10 minutes. Set aside to cool.

Cook the couscous according to the package directions, substituting the orange juice for the water and adding the saffron.

In a large saucepan, melt the butter over high heat and sauté the leeks and fennel until lightly golden in color. Add the cooked couscous, stirring gently to combine. Add the almonds, zest, juice, basils, and mint. Season to taste with pepper.

Just before serving, toss in the port-plumped fruits (and any remaining liquid, if desired) and serve warm. Serves 5+.

Chef's Notes

About . . .
Israeli couscous resembles whole tapioca and is a relatively large, pearl-shaped grain.

In Season . . .
Purple basil is sold as opal basil, the leaves of which have a beautiful purple color.

Whole-Wheat Couscous Walnut Salad

Looking for a quick and easy dinner? This is it. Walnuts add just the right mix of texture and flavor to this delicious entrée salad.

8 oz. feta cheese, crumbled
8 oz. pitted Kalamata olives, coarsely chopped
1 bunch scallions, coarsely chopped
1 small garlic clove, pressed
Grated zest of 1 orange + the juice
½ cup very finely minced fresh Italian (flat-leaf) parsley
¾ cup extra-virgin olive oil
1 tbsp. red wine vinegar
10 oz. whole-wheat couscous
3-4 cups strips or large pieces of poached chicken, skinned and boned
8 oz. toasted, coarsely chopped walnuts

Chef's Notes

About . . .
Kalamata olives are an almond-shaped Greek olive with a rich, fruity flavor.

Couscous is technically a pasta, but we've included this recipe (and other couscous recipes) in the grains chapter.

In a medium serving bowl, combine the feta, olives, scallions, garlic, zest, juice, parsley, olive oil, and vinegar. Mix well and let stand at room temperature for 30 minutes to 1 hour.

Cook couscous according to package directions. Remove from heat and allow to stand for 5 minutes, then fluff with a fork.

Toss couscous in with the feta mixture. Add the poached chicken pieces, tossing gently to combine. Just before serving, sprinkle with walnuts. Makes 6+ servings.

Citrus Apricot Couscous

This fruit-flavored whole-wheat couscous dish is
perfect with freshly grilled salmon.

½ cup diced dried apricots
¼ cup fresh orange juice
1¼ cups vegetable broth, plus more if needed
1 cup whole-wheat couscous
2 tsp. ground cumin
Pinch cayenne pepper
1 tbsp. finely chopped orange zest
12 snow peas, strings removed
1 cup julienne red bell pepper
4 fresh mint sprigs for garnish, if desired

Chef's Notes

In Season . . .
An edible pea pod, snow peas are also referred to as
Chinese pea pod or sugar pea. Snow peas contain
tiny peas inside flat, tender pods 3" to 4" long. Look
for firm, crisp, bright green pods.

In a small bowl, combine the apricots and orange
juice and set aside for 20 minutes.

In a medium saucepan, bring *1¼ cups* of the vegetable
broth to a boil.

In a medium serving bowl, combine the couscous,
cumin, and cayenne. Add 1 cup of the boiling broth,
cover, and let stand for 10 minutes. Fluff the couscous with a fork and add more broth to loosen the
couscous if necessary. Stir in the apricots with any
juice and the zest.

Steam the snow peas and bell pepper strips for 2 minutes, just until fork tender.

To serve, mound the couscous on 4 or 5 individual
serving plates, topping with the snow peas, pepper
strips, and mint sprigs. Serves 4+.

Couscous Risotto with Shiitake Mushrooms

This recipe uses Israeli couscous instead of the traditional Arborio rice to make a risotto.

⅓ cup chopped shallots
1 tbsp. finely minced garlic
2 cups sliced shiitake mushrooms,
stems removed
2 tbsp. extra-virgin olive oil
2 cups Israeli couscous
½ cup dry white wine
4 cups vegetable broth, divided
1 tbsp. finely grated lemon zest
1 medium tomato, seeded and diced
¼ cup chopped fresh chives
½ cup freshly grated Romano cheese

Sauté the shallots, garlic, and shiitakes in olive oil in a 4-qt. saucepan until light golden. Add the couscous and sauté for 2 more minutes. Mix in the wine and *1 cup* of the broth, stirring occasionally until liquid is absorbed. Add remaining broth and continue to cook, stirring occasionally, until broth is almost completely absorbed, about 10 minutes. Stir in zest, tomato, chives and cheese. Serve immediately in warm bowls. Serves 4+.

Chef's Notes

About . . .
Israeli couscous is made from the same toasted semolina as regular couscous, but larger and round, about the size of whole peppercorns.

In Season . . .
Shallots are distinct small bulbs made up of cloves, like garlic, with a mild, delicate flavor and a tender texture.

Pasta and Porcini Millet Salad

Porcini mushrooms add an earthy flavor and heartiness to
this grain dish, making it perfect for an autumn lunch.

Salad

½ cup dried porcini mushrooms
8 cups water
⅓ cup millet
⅔ cup orzo pasta
1 cup frozen peas, thawed

Dressing

¼ cup canola or corn oil
2 tsp. finely chopped lemon zest
¼ cup fresh lemon juice
1 large garlic clove, pressed
½ tsp. sea salt
¼ tsp. sweet paprika
¼ tsp. freshly ground black pepper
1 cup chopped red bell pepper
1 tbsp. coarsely chopped fresh basil

Chef's Notes

About . . .
Millet, a cereal grass, is a staple grain for a third of
the world's population. Rich in protein, its bland flavor lends itself well as a background to other flavors.

Orzo is tiny, rice-shaped pasta, ideal for salads.

For the Salad: Soak the dried mushrooms for 15 minutes in enough hot water to cover. Drain; remove
and discard stems. Slice mushrooms and set aside.

In a large saucepan combine water, millet, and sliced
mushrooms. Bring to a boil; reduce heat. Cook
uncovered for 10 minutes. Stir in orzo pasta. Return
to boiling, then reduce heat and cook uncovered for
8 more minutes. Drain and rinse in a colander; drain
again, then transfer to a large serving bowl and add
peas.

For the Dressing: In a small bowl, whisk together the
oil, zest, juice, garlic, salt, paprika, and pepper.

Pour Dressing atop millet mixture, stir in the bell
pepper and basil, and toss gently to coat.

To allow flavors to blend, cover and chill for 2 to 24
hours, stirring occasionally. Makes 5+ servings.

Millet and Vegetables with Wasabi Lemon Dressing

Cultivated since ancient times, millet has a sweet cornlike flavor that works well in salads because it remains fluffy after cooking when the grains are pretoasted.

Dressing

1 tbsp. wasabi powder
1 tbsp. fresh lemon juice
1 tbsp. rice vinegar
6 tbsp. safflower oil
½ tsp. sea salt

Millet and Vegetables

1 cup millet, rinsed and drained
2 cups vegetable broth
1 tbsp. fresh thyme leaves
½ lb. fresh green beans, trimmed, blanched, and cut on the diagonal into ½" lengths
1 bunch scallions, thinly sliced
2 bunches radishes, cleaned and sliced into paper-thin rounds
2 tbsp. finely minced lemon zest
½ tsp. sea salt
1 tsp. freshly ground black pepper
½ cup toasted sliced almonds

For the Dressing: In a medium bowl, whisk the wasabi powder with the lemon juice and set aside for 10 minutes to allow flavors to blend. Add the vinegar, oil, and salt, whisking to emulsify. Set aside until ready to use.

For the Millet and Vegetables: Place a 4-qt. saucepan over medium heat. Add the millet and stir to keep the grains from sticking. Toast the millet just until fragrant and dry, stirring often. Slowly add the broth and thyme. Cover, reduce heat to medium low, and simmer about 20 minutes or until millet is tender and liquid is absorbed. Remove saucepan from heat and set aside covered for about 10 minutes. Place the millet in a large bowl and allow to continue cooling, fluffing with a fork to separate the grains.

Add the green beans, scallions, radishes, zest, salt and pepper; toss gently.

Toss the Dressing with the millet mixture. Adjust seasonings as needed. Sprinkle with almond slices. Serve at room temperature or chilled. Serves 6.

Chef's Notes

About . . .
Millet is a staple grain in many cultures throughout the world, but it is still little known in the United States—except for use as birdseed!

Although sometimes called Japanese horseradish, wasabi is unrelated to horseradish other than that they are both roots and have a pungent kick. From Asia, wasabi has a fierce bite and a sinus-clearing aroma and is often found ground or in the form of a paste.

How to Do It . . .
If you want to make this salad ahead, toss in the beans, scallions, radishes, and almonds at the last minute so they remain crisp.

Orange-Olive Bulgur Salad

What could be easier than a grain salad that requires no cooking? And the citrus flavors give our take on tabbouleh a whole new twist.

2 cups medium-grain bulgur
1 cup hot water
1 cup fresh orange juice
1 cup sliced pitted ripe olives, black or green
½ lb. tomatoes, seeded and diced
¼ cup sliced scallions
¾ cup sliced, seeded cucumbers
¼ cup finely chopped fresh Italian
(flat-leaf) parsley
1½ tsp. finely chopped fresh mint
⅛ cup fresh lemon juice
⅛ cup extra-virgin olive oil
½ tsp. sea salt
1 tsp. freshly grated orange zest
Clementine or tangerine slices, in season,
for garnish

Place bulgur in a medium bowl and cover with water and the orange juice. Let stand for 1 hour or until liquid is absorbed.

In a medium serving bowl, mix together the bulgur, olives, tomatoes, scallions, cucumbers, parsley, and mint.

In a small bowl, whisk together the juice, oil, salt, and zest. Toss this dressing into salad.

Chill for 1 hour or serve at room temperature. Garnish each serving with Clementine or tangerine slices, as available. Serves 6.

Chef's Notes

About . . .
Bulgur is made by steaming, drying, and crushing whole-wheat berries.

Bulgur with Corn, Garbanzo Beans, and Toasted Walnuts

Toasted walnuts and corn kernels add crunch and deliciously
complement the bulgur in this unique grain salad.

1 cup bulgur
1 cup hot water
2 tsp. cumin seeds
1½ tsp. fennel seeds
3 cups corn kernels
4 tbsp. fresh lime juice
1 tbsp. apple cider vinegar
1 tsp. sea salt
⅓ cup canola oil
4 jalapeños, roasted, peeled, seeded,
and finely chopped
1 cup finely chopped red onion
1 cup diced fennel bulb
½ cup chopped fresh cilantro
2 cups cooked garbanzo beans
1 cup toasted, chopped walnuts

Combine the bulgur and the cup of hot water in a large bowl; set aside for 1 hour until the liquid is absorbed.

Toast the cumin seeds and fennel seeds in a small skillet over medium heat until fragrant. Remove from heat to cool. Grind.

Combine the corn, lime juice, vinegar, salt, oil, jalapeños, onion, and diced fennel in a large serving bowl. Stir in the toasted spices and cilantro. Add the garbanzo beans to the corn mixture, then add the bulgur, stirring gently but well to combine.

Cover and set aside for 30 minutes to allow flavors to blend. Stir occasionally. Just before serving, stir in the walnuts. Serves 7+.

Chef's Notes

How to Do It . . .
Want the freshest flavor from your spices? Toasting the seeds then cooling and grinding (in a coffee or spice grinder reserved just for this purpose) is a chef's (not-so) secret weapon!

Wheat Berry Salad with Curry Vinaigrette

Wheat berries burst with flavor, and the roasted beets add striking color and texture contrast to this hearty grain dish.

Curry Vinaigrette

5 tbsp. fresh lemon juice
2 tbsp. red wine vinegar
1 tbsp. curry powder
1 tbsp. packed freshly grated ginger (about a 1" piece)
1 large garlic clove, minced or pressed
1 tsp. sea salt
Freshly ground black pepper to taste
½ cup extra-virgin olive oil

Wheat Berry Salad

8 cups water
1½ cups whole-grain wheat berries
3 tbsp. red wine vinegar
1 lb. red beets, washed, stems and roots cut off
1 tbsp. extra-virgin olive oil
Sea salt
Freshly ground black pepper
1 cup finely diced red onion
4 celery stalks, cut into ¼"-thick slices
½ cup dried cranberries or dried tart cherries
½ tsp. ground cinnamon
½ cup toasted, coarsely chopped pecans
Curry Vinaigrette

Chef's Notes

About . . .
Wheat berries are whole, unprocessed kernels of a hard, red winter wheat with short, rounded kernels.

For the Curry Vinaigrette: In a small bowl, whisk together the lemon juice, vinegar, curry powder, ginger, garlic, salt, and pepper. Add the oil in a slow, steady stream, whisking to blend and form an emulsion. Set aside until ready to use. Makes about 1 cup.

For the Wheat Berry Salad: In a large saucepan, combine 8 cups of water with the wheat berries and bring to a boil over high heat. Lower the heat to a simmer and cook uncovered for 35 minutes until the wheat berries are tender but still chewy. Drain the wheat berries in a colander, then place them into a large bowl. Pour the vinegar over the hot wheat berries and toss, coating evenly. Set aside to cool to room temperature.

Heat oven to 375 degrees. Halve the beets, cutting them into roughly the same size. Toss with the olive oil, sprinkle with salt and pepper, and place cut side down on a baking pan lined with foil. Roast for 30 to 35 minutes until soft when pierced with a fork.

When the beets are roasted, remove the pan from the oven and set aside just until the beets are cool enough to handle. Using a small paring knife or your fingers, peel the skin off the beets, and then cube the beets into ½" pieces. Set aside in a glass bowl until ready to use.

Toss the onion, celery, dried cranberries/cherries, and cinnamon into the bowl with the wheat berries. Pour the Curry Vinaigrette over the salad, tossing gently to combine. Just before serving, add the pecans and the beets. For best flavor, serve at room temperature. Makes 6+ servings.

The best way to test the wheat berries to see if they're done is to taste them!

Beets stain, so I'd advise wearing disposable gloves when cutting, peeling, and preparing.

Fresh ginger should have a smooth skin; wrinkled skin indicates that the root is dry and past its prime. It should have a fresh, spicy fragrance.

Introducing cooking school students to unexpected combinations of flavors and textures is always satisfying, and this salad with its wheat berries and curry vinaigrette is always the recipient of rave reviews.

Grains with Smoked Mozzarella and Parsley Salad

Hearty and rich with a meaty flavor, this grain dish
makes for a satisfying side or a full-flavored lunch.

Parsley Salad

3 cups packed fresh Italian (flat-leaf)
parsley leaves
2 tbsp. extra-virgin olive oil
1 tsp. fresh lemon juice
½ tsp. umeboshi (plum) vinegar

Wheat Berry/Barley Dish

1 cup whole-grain wheat berries
1 cup pearl barley
1 cup finely chopped red onion
2 large garlic cloves, pressed then mashed
with ½ tsp. sea salt
¼ cup balsamic vinegar
¼ cup extra-virgin olive oil
6 scallions, finely chopped
1½ cups corn kernels
½ lb. smoked mozzarella, cut into ¼" cubes
1 pt. cherry tomatoes, halved
½ cup chopped fresh chives
Freshly ground black pepper to taste
Parsley Salad

For the Parsley Salad: In a medium bowl, toss together the parsley, oil, lemon juice, and vinegar. Set aside until ready to serve.

For the Wheat Berry/Barley Dish: In a large pot of boiling water, stir the wheat berries and cook over medium-low heat for 20 minutes. Stir in barley and continue to cook grains over medium-low heat for an additional 35 minutes or until grains have a firm, chewy texture but taste done.

In a large bowl, stir together the onion, garlic paste, vinegar, and oil.

Drain grains in a colander and add to onion mixture. Toss well and allow to cool. Add scallions, corn, mozzarella, tomatoes, chives, and pepper. Toss well. Serve at room temperature with Parsley Salad alongside. Serves 5+.

Chef's Notes

About . . .
A hearty grain, (pearl) barley has had the bran removed and has been steamed.

Umeboshi vinegar adds a unique dimension to this salad. Sometimes referred to as plum vinegar, it is not true vinegar but the salty, slightly sour liquid left over from curing umeboshi (Japanese preserved plums).

Toasted Barley and Bean Tabbouleh

Once again we play with that basic Middle Eastern dish, tabbouleh, by adding barley and beans. You'll enjoy this delicious alternative.

½ cup hulled barley
6 cups water
½ cup bulgur
1¼ cups boiling water
½ cup chopped, seeded cucumber
½ cup chopped green bell pepper
⅓ cup chopped yellow onion
¼ cup fresh lemon juice
1 cup chopped plum tomatoes
2 cups cooked black beans
2 tbsp. chopped fresh cilantro
1 tbsp. extra-virgin olive oil
2 large garlic cloves, pressed
½ tsp. sea salt
¼ tsp. freshly ground black pepper

Chef's Notes

About . . .
Bulgur is cracked wheat that has been hulled and parboiled.

Hulled or whole-grain barley has had only the outer husk removed and is the most nutritious form of the grain.

In a large skillet, toast barley over medium heat, stirring occasionally, until light golden brown.

In a 4-qt. saucepan combine the toasted barley with the 6 cups of water. Cook over high heat until mixture comes to a full boil. Reduce heat to medium, then simmer until barley is tender, about 35 minutes. Rinse with cold water and drain well.

While barley is cooking, combine bulgur and the 1¼ cups boiling water in a medium bowl. Let stand at least 30 minutes. Drain, rinsing with cold water, then draining again.

In a large serving bowl, combine the barley, bulgur, cucumber, pepper, onion, lemon juice, tomatoes, black beans, cilantro, oil, garlic, salt, and pepper. Stir gently to combine.

Cover and refrigerate at least 2 hours to allow flavors to blend. Serves 6+.

Wilted Greens with Quinoa

The quick preparation and the combination of grains and greens yields satisfying results. Enjoy this dish warm.

1 cup quinoa
1½ cups water
½ cup strips sun-dried tomatoes (not oil packed)
1½ lb. red or green Swiss chard or kale
4 tbsp. extra-virgin olive oil
2 large garlic cloves, thinly sliced
4 tbsp. red wine vinegar
Sea salt and freshly ground black pepper to taste

Chef's Notes

In Season . . .
Swiss chard is actually a type of beet that develops lush leaves rather than a flashy root. Look for bunches with fresh, glossy leaves and heavy white or red stems.

Rinse the quinoa with cold water for several minutes; drain.

Heat a large nonstick skillet over medium-high heat. Add the quinoa and stir until it is no longer moist and is beginning to turn a golden brown. Add the 1½ cups of water and bring to a boil. Reduce heat to medium low; cover and simmer until water is absorbed and grains are dry, about 12 minutes. Remove from heat; uncover and allow to cool.

While quinoa is cooling, reconstitute sun-dried tomatoes by placing them in a small bowl and covering them with boiling water. Let stand until tomatoes are soft, about 15 minutes. Drain.

Trim tough stems from greens and discard. Cut leaves crosswise into ½"-wide strips. Rinse under cold water to remove any grit; drain well. Place greens in a large saucepan and toss over medium-high heat just until wilted and tender. Transfer to a strainer and drain, wiping saucepan dry.

Add the oil and garlic to the dried saucepan. Stir over medium-high heat for 1 minute. Add the greens, quinoa, and sun-dried tomatoes and stir until heated through. Stir in the vinegar, season with salt and pepper, and serve immediately. Serves 4+.

Grains in a Lettuce Cup

An inviting presentation sure to attract the attention of even nonadventurous eaters . . . One taste and they'll be hooked.

Vinaigrette
2 tbsp. honey
½ cup fresh lemon juice
⅓ cup grapeseed oil
1 tsp. finely grated lemon zest
1 tsp. sea salt
¼ tsp. freshly ground black pepper

Grains
2 cups quinoa
1 cup amaranth
3 cups water
2 medium carrots, peeled then cut into wide
strips with a vegetable peeler
1 cup wedged pitted ripe green olives
3 tbsp. snipped fresh chives
3 tbsp. coarsely chopped fresh dill weed
Boston or Bibb lettuce leaves for "cups"

For the Vinaigrette: In a medium bowl whisk together the honey, lemon juice, oil, zest, and salt and pepper until well blended. Set aside until ready to use. Makes about 1 cup.

For the Grains: Rinse the quinoa with cold water for several minutes. Cook quinoa and amaranth in a large skillet just until grains are toasted. Add water and bring to a boil. Cover and simmer over medium heat for 10 minutes or until quinoa is cooked and has absorbed the water. Set aside to cool.

Gently combine the cooled grain mixture with carrots, olives, chives, dill, and vinaigrette. Place individual portions in lettuce cups and serve. Serves 6+.

Chef's Notes

About . . .
Quinoa is the seedlike fruit of a broad-leafed plant that reaches 5 feet high. A traditional food of the Andes, cooked quinoa has a nutty flavor and fluffy texture. It is higher in protein (containing the most complete protein) and contains more amino acids than any other grain. Always rinse the quinoa before cooking to remove the outer coating, which contains bitter saponin.

Amaranth has a nutty, slightly spicy flavor and a sticky, glutinous texture.

Fruited Grains

Delicious as an entrée or side salad, this versatile grain
dish is made with a triple hit of grains. It feeds a crowd or makes for
great leftovers if less than a crowd is all you're feeding!

4 cups water
¼ tsp. sea salt
1 cup wheat berries, rinsed
1 cup pearl barley, rinsed
1 cup millet, rinsed
¼ cup fresh lemon juice
½ cup extra-virgin olive oil
Freshly ground black pepper
2 tsp. freshly grated orange zest
6 scallions, coarsely chopped
½ cup chopped fresh Italian (flat-leaf) parsley
⅓ cup chopped fresh spearmint
⅓ cup dried tart cherries
2 cups sliced fresh fruit and/or seasonal berries
(Pears, blueberries, or raspberries are delicious
additions depending on the season.)

Chef's Notes

In Season . . .
I prefer spearmint for its refreshing taste and a flavor
that doesn't overpower, but your favorite fresh mint
will do as well.

In a large saucepan, bring the 4 cups of water and salt
to a boil. Add the wheat berries. Reduce heat to low,
cover, and simmer 30 minutes. Add the barley, cover,
and simmer 20 more minutes.

Meanwhile, in a medium-size dry skillet toast the
millet over medium-high heat, shaking pan and stirring just until the grains darken and "pop."

After the wheat berry/barley mixture has cooked,
add the toasted millet. Cover and simmer until all
the grains are tender and the water is absorbed, 12 to
15 minutes. Remove from heat, fluff grains with a
fork, and allow to cool.

In a small bowl, whisk together the lemon juice and
oil, then season to taste with freshly ground black
pepper.

In a large serving bowl, combine the cooked grains,
zest, scallions, parsley, mint, and dried cherries, tossing gently to combine. Pour juice/oil mixture over
grain mixture, tossing well to combine.

Cover and refrigerate for at least 1 hour and up to 12
hours to allow the flavors time to blend. Just before
serving, top with fresh fruit. Serves 8+.

Mediterranean Barley

This dish is typical of the heart-healthy Mediterranean diet.

2 tbsp. extra-virgin olive oil
1 large garlic clove, pressed
1 cup sliced fennel bulb
6 scallions, coarsely chopped
1 cup quick-cooking barley
½ cup seedless raisins
2 cups cooked garbanzo beans
1¾ cups vegetable broth
½ tsp. sea salt
½ tsp. ground allspice
¼ tsp. coarsely ground black pepper
½ cup chopped feathery fennel tops
1 cup chopped fresh Italian (flat-leaf) parsley

Heat oil and garlic in a large nonstick skillet until garlic turns golden in color. Add fennel and scallions. Stirring occasionally, cover and cook over medium heat until veggies are tender.

Increase heat to medium high. Stir in barley, raisins, beans, broth, salt, allspice, and black pepper. Cook until mixture comes to a boil, and then reduce heat to low and cover and cook until barley is tender, about 12 minutes.

Stir in fennel tops and parsley. Serve immediately. Serves 4+.

Chef's Notes

About . . .
Some think allspice is a blend because it tastes like a combination of cinnamon, nutmeg, and cloves. Allspice is, in fact, one spice—a dark brown, dried, pea-size berry of the evergreen pimento tree.

In Season . . .
It's fun to use all of the fennel—the crisp bulb and the feathery tops, also known as the fronds. (Great info to impress your friends!)

BEAN THERE, DONE THAT!

All manner of beans have been enjoyed world-wide for thousands of years. Some of their nutritional "bean-afits" are that they are high in dietary fiber and complex carbs and are an excellent source of protein.

Need to get it on the table in a hurry? Canned beans are the route to nutritious fast food. In general, beans double in volume after soaking and cooking. (Two cups of dried beans, for example, yield 4 to 5 cups of freshly cooked beans.) Rinse canned beans well in a colander before using; this helps limit the amount of sodium.

Beans from the dried state are not difficult, but require some advance preparation. If you leave your beans uncovered during cooking, they'll be firmer than those covered during cooking. Add salt and anything acidic (such as lemon juice, tomatoes, or vinegar) near the end of the bean cooking time since adding these things at the beginning of the cooking time keeps the beans from softening.

Each bean's color, variety, flavor, and texture will differ slightly, but don't shy away from using a different bean than one called for in these recipes. Follow your own tastes and/or bean selection so you won't get bored saying, "Bean there, done that!"

The question is: How much beer have these Drunken Beans really had? Once you taste them you'll know the answer: Just enough!

Black-Eyed-Pea Salad

Cumin and hot pepper sauce add complex, peppery flavors to this bean salad.

Salad

2 15-oz. cans black-eyed peas,
rinsed and drained
⅓ cup sliced scallions
⅓ cup thinly sliced celery
⅓ cup coarsely chopped green bell pepper
⅓ cup chopped fresh Italian (flat-leaf) parsley
⅓ cup thinly sliced radishes

Dressing

2 tbsp. extra-virgin olive oil
1 tbsp. fresh lemon juice
¼ tsp. sea salt
½ tsp. ground cumin
¼ tsp. hot pepper sauce

Chef's Notes

About . . .
The black-eyed pea is a small, beige bean with a black circular "eye" at its inner curve. These legumes are particularly popular in the southern United States.

For the Salad: Combine the black-eyed peas, scallions, celery, bell pepper, parsley, and radishes in a medium serving bowl.

For the Dressing: In a small bowl, whisk together the oil, lemon juice, salt, cumin, and hot pepper sauce. Pour over salad, tossing gently to combine.

Cover and refrigerate for 1 to 2 hours to allow flavors to blend. Stir occasionally. Serves 4+.

Adzuki Beans and Vegetables

Dark brown miso brings out the flavor of the garlic, ginger, and vegetables in this savory bean dish.

2 tsp. toasted sesame oil
1 cup finely chopped yellow onion
2-4 large garlic cloves, pressed
1 cup diced carrot
1 cup diced turnip
1 tsp. freshly grated ginger
1 cup + 2 tbsp. vegetable broth, divided
3 cups cooked adzuki beans
1-2 tbsp. dark red miso, or to taste
2 tbsp. coarsely chopped fresh cilantro leaves
Cooked rice or other cooked grain
of your choice

In a large skillet over medium heat, heat sesame oil. Sauté onion until translucent. Stir in garlic, carrot, turnip, and ginger; sauté for 2 minutes. Add *1 cup* of the broth and all the beans. Bring to a simmer, cover, and reduce heat. Cook just until the vegetables are tender, about 10 minutes.

In a small bowl, whisk together the miso and remaining vegetable broth to a smooth paste. Stir into bean mixture. Heat briefly, being careful not to boil. Toss in the cilantro, then serve atop rice/grain. Serves 4+.

Chef's Notes

About . . .
Adzuki beans are a small, dried, russet-colored bean with a sweet flavor.

How to Do It . . .
For 3 cups cooked beans, cook 1 cup presoaked beans (measured before soaking) in 4 cups of water for 1 hour or until firm but cooked through.

Smother Your Own Beans in Our Barbecue Sauce

Baked beans are only as good as the sauce they're smothered in. We invite
you to smother away with our savory, spicy, simmered barbecue sauce . . .

1¾ cup + 1 tbsp. ketchup
4 oz. firmly packed light brown sugar
2 cups cider vinegar
¼ cup blackstrap molasses
2½ tbsp. Worcestershire sauce
1½ tsp. sea salt
¾ tsp. hickory salt
1 tbsp. freshly ground black pepper
¼ tsp. cayenne pepper

In a 5-qt. saucepan combine the ketchup, brown sugar, vinegar, molasses, Worcestershire sauce, salts, and peppers. Bring to a boil, reduce heat, and simmer over medium-low heat for 45 minutes or until thickened, stirring often to prevent scorching. Makes about 5 cups.

Chef's Notes

How to Do It . . .
We like to combine cooked kidney, pinto, navy, and lima beans with some sautéed onion and chopped, crisp cooked bacon. Toss in a deep baking dish with some of our barbecue sauce for 35 minutes at 325 degrees . . . *Voila!* Baked beans our way.

Buckaroo Beans

Although the name is reminiscent of a cowboy campfire, we invite you to enjoy this spicy-sweet baked bean dish with or without your cowboy hat and chaps!

1 cup coarsely chopped yellow onion
½ cup coarsely chopped green bell pepper
¾ cup coarsely chopped red bell pepper
3 tbsp. canola oil
20 oz. diced, canned tomatoes
26-28 oz. canned kidney beans,
rinsed and drained
12 oz. tomato sauce
⅓ cup Barbados molasses
½ cup of our own barbecue sauce (see Smother
Your Own Beans)
2 tbsp. fair trade, dark-roast brewed coffee
3 tbsp. hot sauce
1½ tsp. dried basil, crumbled
1½ tsp. dried oregano, crumbled
1½ tsp. dried thyme, crumbled
½ cup firmly packed light brown sugar
1 tsp. freshly ground black pepper
1 tsp. sea salt

Heat oven to 350 degrees.

In a medium saucepan, sauté the onion and peppers in the oil until crisp-tender, stirring often.

In a large bowl, combine the onion/pepper mixture with the tomatoes, beans, tomato sauce, molasses, barbecue sauce, coffee, hot sauce, basil, oregano, thyme, brown sugar, pepper, and salt.

Toss mixture into a deep baking dish and bake for 45 minutes to 1 hour or until beans are bubbly in the middle. Remove from oven and serve warm. Serves 5+.

Chef's Notes

About . . .
Barbados molasses is a pleasant-tasting unsulphured molasses that comes from the first boiling of the sugar syrup.

Chili Bean Salad

You'll be amazed by how easily you can throw together this bean salad—
complete with a complexity of flavors and textures.

Dressing

¼ cup red wine vinegar
2 tbsp. extra-virgin olive oil
1 tsp. chili powder
1 tsp. ground cumin
1 tsp. dried oregano, crushed
¼ tsp. freshly ground black pepper

Salad

15-oz. can garbanzo beans, rinsed and drained
15-oz. can kidney beans, rinsed and drained
15-oz. can pinto beans, rinsed and drained
2 cups corn kernels, fresh (if in season)
or frozen
1½ cups coarsely chopped green or
red bell pepper
½ cup chopped scallions
⅓ cup chopped fresh cilantro
4-oz. can diced green chilies or ½ cup finely
diced fresh hot chilies

For the Dressing: In a small bowl, whisk together the vinegar, oil, chili powder, cumin, oregano, and pepper. Set aside until ready to use.

For the Salad: In a large serving bowl, mix the beans, corn, pepper, scallions, cilantro, and chilies with the Dressing. Cover and chill for at least 1 hour or up to 12 hours, stirring occasionally, allowing flavors time to blend. Serves 6+.

Chef's Notes

About . . .
A garbanzo by any other name is a chickpea or ceci.

Black Bean Nachos

A café favorite when you're in the mood for something spicy, hearty, and fun!

4 cups blue corn and yellow corn tortilla chips
1 cup canned black beans, rinsed and drained
½ cup (your favorite) salsa, mild, spicy, or chunky, plus more for serving
2 cups shredded Monterey Jack cheese
½ cup strips of roasted red bell peppers
4 tbsp. sliced fresh jalapeño peppers

Chef's Notes

About . . .
Black beans are also known as turtle beans and have a black skin, cream-colored flesh, and a sweet flavor.

Heat oven to 425 degrees.

Arrange tortilla chips in a single layer, overlapping slightly, on an 11" or 12" ovenproof platter.

In a medium saucepan, combine the black beans with the ½ cup of salsa. Cook, stirring gently over low heat, just until heated through. Remove saucepan from heat and spoon mixture atop chips.

Sprinkle cheese, roasted peppers, and jalapeño peppers over bean mixture. Bake for 5 to 8 minutes or until cheese is melted. Serve immediately with additional salsa for dipping. Makes 4+ servings.

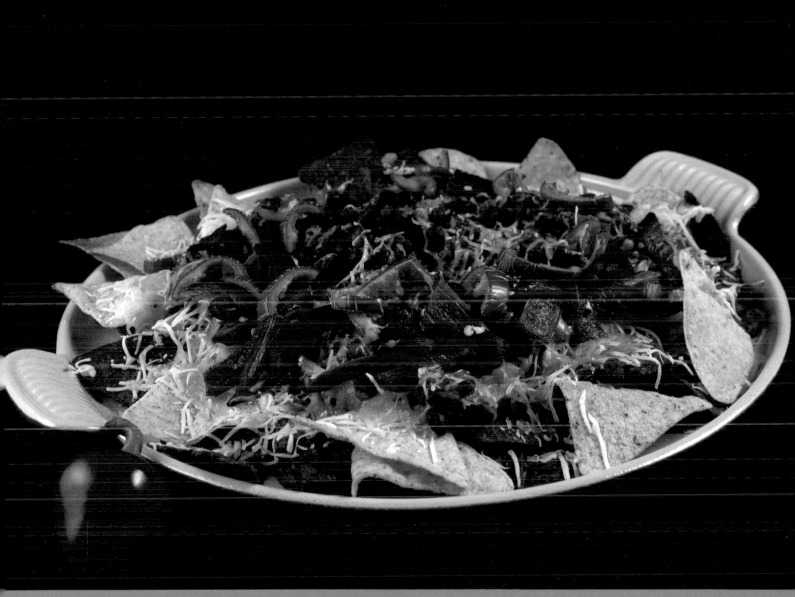

Toss that artificial cheese dip away, and enjoy these nachos instead—with real flavor, heat, and texture.

Three-Bean Salad with Jicama

This salad is surprisingly light and full of pleasing textures. The pinto, black, and red beans take on the sweetness of the orange in the vinaigrette, combined with the heat of the chilies. The crunchy jicama adds a fresh flavor.

Golden Vinaigrette

1 tsp. finely minced orange zest
5 tbsp. fresh orange juice
4 tbsp. golden balsamic vinegar
1 large garlic clove, pressed
1 tsp. cumin seed, toasted and ground
1 tsp. sea salt
2 tbsp. extra-virgin olive oil
1/8 tsp. cayenne pepper

Bean Salad

1/2 cup diced red onion
Splash of champagne vinegar
1 1/4 cups cooked pinto beans
1 1/4 cups cooked black beans
1 1/4 cups cooked red beans
1/2 cup diced jicama
2 jalapeños, seeded and finely diced
Sea salt to taste
2 tbsp. coarsely chopped fresh cilantro

For the Golden Vinaigrette: In a small bowl, whisk together the zest, juice, vinegar, garlic, cumin, salt, oil, and cayenne pepper. Set aside until ready to use. Makes about 1/2 cup.

For the Bean Salad: Bring a small saucepan of water to a boil and drop the onion in it for 30 seconds. Drain well and toss the blanched onion with a splash of champagne vinegar.

Toss the warm, cooked beans immediately with the Golden Vinaigrette, then add the onion, jicama, and jalapeños. Add salt to taste. Sprinkle in the cilantro and serve at room temperature. Serves 5+.

Chef's Notes

About . . .
Pinto beans (Spanish for "painted") have reddish brown streaks on a background of pale pink. Red beans are a dark red, medium-size bean that are most commonly used for making chili con carne.

How to Do It . . .
Beans vary in cooking time, so be sure to cook them separately to avoid under- or overcooking each type. (Presoaked) pinto beans take roughly 40 minutes to cook; black beans and red beans (presoaked) take roughly 25 minutes each to cook.

Zest is the outermost skin of citrus fruit, removed with the aid of a zester, grater, paring knife, or vegetable peeler. Only the colored portion of the skin (and not the white pith) is considered the zest. The aromatic oils in citrus zest are what add so much flavor to food.

Balsamic Three-Bean Salad

Easy to put together, low in fat, and delicious
on a picnic or a potluck buffet table.

1¼ cups cooked pinto beans
1 cup cooked great northern beans
1¼ cups cooked black beans
¾ cup chopped red bell pepper
1 cup chopped yellow bell pepper
1 cup chopped roasted red bell peppers
20 cherry tomatoes, halved
3 tbsp. chopped fresh Italian (flat-leaf) parsley
12 tbsp. balsamic vinegar
2 tbsp. Worcestershire sauce
2 tsp. granulated sugar
2 tsp. dried basil leaves, crushed
3 large cloves garlic, pressed

In a large bowl, combine beans, peppers, and tomatoes.

In a small bowl, combine the parsley, vinegar, Worcestershire sauce, sugar, basil, and garlic; blend well to combine. Pour over bean mixture; toss gently to coat.

Cover and let stand at room temperature for 30 minutes or refrigerate for 2 hours to allow flavors to blend. Makes 5+ servings.

Drunken Beans

This vegetarian version is lighter than its traditional Mexican counterpart.
Chipotle chilies provide the smoky flavor that bacon gives in the original dish.

2 tsp. corn oil or canola oil
1 cup chopped white onion
2 medium ripe tomatoes, cored and
coarsely chopped
4 large garlic cloves, minced
2 cups pinto beans, soaked overnight
and drained
12-oz. bottle dark beer
4 cups vegetable broth, plus additional
as necessary
½ tsp. ground cinnamon
1-2 chipotle chilies in adobo sauce, diced
Sea salt and freshly ground black pepper
to taste
Fresh cilantro for garnish

Heat oil in a large sauté pan. Add onions, cooking and stirring until translucent. Add the tomatoes and garlic and cook until garlic begins to turn a golden brown.

Add the presoaked beans, beer, broth, cinnamon, and chipotle. Simmer for 1 hour or until beans are tender, adding more broth as necessary to keep mixture from drying out.

Season with salt and pepper and garnish with fresh cilantro when ready to serve. Serves 4+.

Chef's Notes

About . . .
My dark beer of preference for this recipe is a stout . . . made with dark-roasted barley, which gives it a deep, dark color and a bittersweet flavor.

Garbanzo Beans with Brown Rice

Red beans and rice is the most common of bean dishes. Here we've put our spin on it with a variation of beans and a heartier rice.

2 tsp. canola oil
1 cup coarsely chopped yellow onion
2 large garlic cloves, minced or pressed
1½ cups coarsely chopped red bell pepper
1 tbsp. chopped fresh Italian (flat–leaf) parsley
2 cups cooked garbanzo beans
2 8-oz. cans tomato sauce
½ tsp. dried oregano, crushed
½ tsp. dried basil, crushed
½ tsp. freshly ground black pepper
2 cups hot cooked brown rice
½ cup shredded extra-sharp Cheddar cheese
1 tbsp. freshly grated Parmesan cheese

Add oil to a large skillet and place over medium heat until hot. Add the onion, garlic, pepper, and parsley and sauté until tender, stirring often. Add garbanzo beans, tomato sauce, oregano, basil, and black pepper. Cover, reduce heat, and simmer for 30 minutes. Remove from heat and gently stir in the brown rice.

In a small bowl, combine the cheeses and stir to blend. Serve beans and rice while still hot, topped with the cheeses. Makes 4+ servings.

Chef's Notes

How to Do It . . .
As a general rule, you can expect 1 cup of uncooked grain (in this case, rice) to expand to 3 cups during cooking.

Garbanzo Bean and Rice Salad

A lemony, creamy dressing adds a change of pace to this bean salad—
and the crunchy vegetables and fruit add unique textures and flavors.

Dressing

16 oz. lemon nonfat or low-fat yogurt
2 tsp. Dijon mustard
2 tbsp. finely chopped fresh chives
1 large garlic clove, pressed

Salad

3 cups cooked long-grain brown rice
¾ cup finely chopped celery
¾ cup finely chopped carrots
½ cup seedless raisins
2 cups cooked garbanzo beans
1½ cups chunks of fresh pineapple, chilled

For the Dressing: In a small bowl whisk together the yogurt, mustard, chives, and garlic until well blended.

For the Salad: In a large serving bowl, combine the rice, celery, carrots, raisins, and beans. Pour dressing over salad, tossing gently to coat. Refrigerate covered until well chilled.

Just before serving, toss salad mixture with chilled pineapple chunks. Makes 5+ servings.

Chorizo and Three-Bean Salad with Choice of Dressings

There's a lot of flavors going on in this salad—a range of spicy, delicate, and fresh with a bite, plus your choice of 2 zesty dressings.

2 fresh chorizo sausages, sliced ¼" thick
1 cup cooked cranberry or pink beans
1 cup cooked garbanzo beans
1 cup cooked black beans
3 scallions, thinly sliced
1 cup finely diced red onion
2 large garlic cloves, pressed
2 small jalapeño peppers, seeded and finely diced
6-oz. jar marinated artichoke hearts, drained and quartered
⅓ cup (Your Choice) Dressing
1 tbsp. chopped fresh cilantro leaves
Sea salt and freshly ground black pepper to taste

Brown chorizos over medium heat in a large nonstick skillet. Drain and set aside to cool.

In a large serving bowl, combine the beans, scallions, onion, garlic, jalapeños, artichoke hearts, and chorizo. Add ⅓ cup of Dressing and gently toss to evenly coat. Add the cilantro and season with salt and pepper.

Refrigerate covered for 1 to 4 hours to allow the flavors to blend. Serve chilled or at room temperature. Makes 8 to 10 servings.

Chef's Notes

About . . .
Loaded with garlic and spices, chorizo is a spicy sausage used in Spanish and Caribbean cooking. Our chicken chorizo offers the same authentic flavor as the traditional pork version.

Veggies in Your Dressing

(This is a sweet, tart, spicy dressing.)
1 cup extra-virgin olive oil
3 ripe plum tomatoes, cored and quartered lengthwise
1 large garlic clove, minced
½ tsp. chopped fresh thyme leaves
1 tsp. chipotle chili in adobo sauce, diced
¼ cup balsamic vinegar

Heat oil in a large skillet over medium-high heat. Add the tomatoes and cook, stirring until softened. Add the garlic, thyme, diced chipotle, and vinegar and cook, stirring for 4 more minutes. Set aside to cool.

Transfer to a blender and puree until smooth. Use immediately or cover and refrigerate up to one week. Makes about 1½ cups.

Chipotle Chili Dressing

3 tbsp. sherry vinegar
3 tbsp. fresh lime juice
1 tbsp. + 1½ tsp. canola oil
¾ tsp. dried oregano, crushed
1 chipotle chili in adobo sauce, diced

In a blender, combine the vinegar, juice, oil, oregano, and chipotle, pureeing until smooth. Use immediately or cover and refrigerate up to one week. Makes about ½ cup.

White-Bean-and-Garlic Hummus

As a delicious change, try this atop pizza with sun-dried
tomatoes and a sprinkling of cheese.

4 large garlic cloves, minced
1 tbsp. extra-virgin olive oil
1½ tsp. ground cumin
2 tsp. coarsely chopped fresh sage
1 cup cooked white beans
1 tsp. finely grated lemon zest
¼ cup fresh lemon juice
2 tbsp. water
1 tsp. sea salt
¼ tsp. freshly ground black pepper

In a small sauté pan, cook the garlic in oil over medium heat just until golden. Add the cumin and sage and sauté for 1 minute. Transfer mixture to a medium bowl. Add the beans, zest, juice, water, salt, and pepper.

Mash by hand with 2 forks or a potato masher until mixture is smooth but still retains some texture. Makes about 1½ cups.

Chef's Notes

About . . .
Delicious served with pita bread and sun-dried tomatoes.

How to Do It . . .
Adjust seasonings according to your tastes. If you like, add more lemon zest, additional salt and pepper, or even cayenne pepper for some zing!

White Bean Salad with Spinach

The addition of olives, sun-dried tomatoes, and spinach is our variation on an Italian theme.

Balsamic Vinaigrette

¼ cup red wine vinegar
¼ cup golden balsamic vinegar
1 tsp. sea salt
¼ tsp. freshly ground black pepper
1½ cups extra-virgin olive oil

Salad

1½ cups dried navy beans, rinsed and picked over
¼ cup extra-virgin olive oil
1 cup finely chopped yellow onion
4 cups firmly packed spinach, washed, drained, and stems removed
½ cup chopped oil-packed sun-dried tomatoes, well drained
½ lb. fresh mozzarella cheese, cut into ½" cubes
½ cup pitted black olives, such as Kalamata or niçoise
1 cup Balsamic Vinaigrette
Sea salt and freshly ground black pepper to taste

Chef's Notes

About . . .
Navy beans are a small white legume also known as Yankee beans, so named because the United States Navy has served these beans as a staple food since the mid-1800s.

Niçoise olives are a small, oval olive ranging in color from purple brown to brown black with a rich, nutty, mellow flavor.

For the Vinaigrette: In a small bowl whisk together the vinegars, salt, and pepper. Gradually whisk in the oil in a slow, steady stream until emulsified. Makes about 2 cups.

For the Salad: Quick soak the beans by placing them in a large saucepan with water to cover by 3". Bring to a boil. Reduce heat and simmer uncovered 45 minutes. Remove from heat, drain, and rinse.

Return the soaked beans to the saucepan and add enough fresh water to cover by 3". Bring to a boil, lower heat, and simmer uncovered for 45 minutes to 1 hour, or until beans are tender but still firm. Drain and rinse the beans thoroughly. Set aside to cool.

In a large skillet, heat the olive oil over medium heat. Add the onion, cooking and stirring until golden brown, about 8 minutes.

In a large serving bowl, combine the beans, onion, spinach, sun-dried tomatoes, mozzarella, and olives with 1 cup of the Balsamic Vinaigrette just until combined. Season with salt and pepper as needed and serve immediately. (Best served at room temperature.) Serves 6+.

Greens, Beans, and Tomato Gratin

We use a white bean for this gratin, but any one of
your favorite variety from our bulk department will do.

1 large bunch leafy greens or a mixture of kale,
chard, or beet greens (about 1¾ lb.)
2 tbsp. extra-virgin olive oil
2 large garlic cloves, pressed
2 cups cooked white beans
2 medium tomatoes, peeled, seeded,
and chopped
½ cup vegetable broth
½ tsp. dried thyme or 1½ tsp. finely chopped
fresh thyme leaves
1 tsp. sea salt
½ tsp. freshly ground black pepper
1½ cups crumbled crackers

Heat oven to 350 degrees. Grease a 10" oval gratin or baking dish.

Remove tough stems from greens and rinse well. Stack greens and cut into thin strips.

In a 5-qt. saucepan, heat oil over medium-high heat. Add garlic and stir briefly just to flavor the oil. Add greens and cook until tender, tossing often, about 10 minutes. Remove from heat.

Add beans, tomatoes, broth, thyme, salt, and pepper and mix well. Spoon into prepared gratin dish, spreading evenly. Sprinkle crumbs over top of greens mixture. Bake until hot, about 35 to 40 minutes. Serves 4+.

Chef's Notes

About . . .
White beans is a generic term applied to a bean that falls into the categories of marrow beans, great northern, navy beans, or pea beans.

How to Do It . . .
Vary your cracker crumb top based on how you'll serve this dish. I often use a whole-grain cracker when I want a hearty, satisfying side.

To peel tomatoes, blanch by dipping in boiling water for 30 seconds. Rinse in cold water to cool. Slide tip of knife under skin and strip off skin, then cut out core from stem end and proceed with recipe.

Opposite: Nutritious, satisfying comfort food . . . perfect on a cold winter night. Enjoy with slices of our bakery's fresh bread and the crunch of pears for dessert.

Baked Beans with Seitan

Forget the pork and beans and enjoy our vegetarian version instead.

1½ cups dried navy beans, soaked overnight
and drained
2 tbsp. canola oil
1 cup diced yellow onion
2 large garlic cloves, minced or pressed
⅔ cup ketchup
⅓ cup molasses
¼ cup firmly packed dark brown sugar
3 tbsp. vegetarian Worcestershire sauce
½ tsp. salt
⅓ lb. seitan, diced

Chef's Notes

About . . .
Seitan is a protein-rich food made from wheat gluten with a firm, chewy, meatlike texture and a neutral flavor.

Place beans in a large saucepan, adding water to cover. Bring to a simmer and cook uncovered over medium-low heat until tender, about 1 hour. Drain the beans, discarding the liquid.

Heat oven to 350 degrees.

In a large ovenproof casserole, heat the oil over medium heat. Add the onion and cook until the onion becomes translucent, stirring continuously. Add the garlic and cook for an additional 2 minutes, continuing to stir. Mix in the ketchup, molasses, brown sugar, Worcestershire sauce, and salt. Stirring gently but frequently, cook over low heat for 3 minutes. Stir in the beans and seitan until combined.

Cover the casserole and transfer to the oven, baking for 40 minutes and stirring occasionally. Remove from heat and serve while still hot. Serves 6+.

Cannellini Bean Salad

Avocado adds an unexpected creaminess and color to this fresh-tasting bean salad.

2 tbsp. extra-virgin olive oil
¼ tsp. sea salt
¼ tsp. freshly ground black pepper
2 large garlic cloves, pressed or minced
¾ cup diced red bell pepper
½ cup diced avocado
½ cup minced fresh cilantro
¼ cup fresh lime juice
4 cups cooked cannellini beans

In a small bowl, whisk together the oil, salt, pepper, and garlic to blend.

In a large serving bowl, combine the bell pepper, avocado, cilantro, lime juice, and cannellini beans. Add oil mixture, tossing gently to combine.

Serve at once or cover and chill for 1 hour. Makes 4+ servings.

Chef's Notes

About . . .
Cannellini is a large, white Italian kidney bean.

White Beans and Radicchio

In this recipe, we pair roasted leafy greens with
sage-scented white beans and tomatoes, a favorite Tuscan dish.

4 tsp. extra-virgin olive oil, divided
1 lb. (about 2 medium heads) radicchio
½ tsp. sea salt
¼ tsp. freshly ground black pepper
½ cup chopped yellow onion
1 tbsp. minced or pressed garlic
4 cups cooked cannellini or other white beans
14.5-oz. can diced tomatoes
2 tbsp. minced fresh Italian (flat-leaf) parsley
1 tbsp. minced fresh sage leaves or 1 tsp. dried
sage, crushed

Chef's Notes

In Season . . .
Radicchio is a red-leafed Italian chicory with tender
but firm leaves and a slightly bitter flavor.

Heat oven to 425 degrees. Grease baking dish with *1 tsp.* of the olive oil; set aside.

Discard outer leaves of radicchio; cut each head through the core into 4 wedges. Arrange wedges in a single layer in the prepared baking dish. Brush with *2 tsp.* of the olive oil. Sprinkle with ½ tsp. salt and ¼ tsp. freshly ground black pepper. Bake until radicchio is tender, 10 to 15 minutes, turning after 7 minutes.

While radicchio is baking, heat remaining olive oil in a large nonstick skillet over medium-high heat. Add the onion and cook until translucent, stirring occasionally. Add garlic and continue cooking and stirring for 1 minute.

Combine beans, tomatoes, parsley, and sage with onion and garlic and cook, stirring gently, until heated through.

To serve, arrange radicchio on an oval serving platter. Spoon warm bean mixture into center and serve hot. Makes 5+ servings.

Warm Beans with Herbed Tomatoes and Goat Cheese

A simple dish delicious served as the main attraction with a side of grilled fish or beef.

1½ cups seeded and chopped tomatoes
¼ cup snipped fresh basil
¼ cup snipped fresh oregano
2 scallions, sliced
1 large garlic clove, pressed
½ tsp. sea salt
¼ tsp. freshly ground black pepper
2 cups cooked small red beans or kidney beans
2 cups cooked great northern beans or navy beans
¼ cup vegetable broth
1 cup semisoft goat cheese, crumbled
Baguette slices

Chef's Notes

About . . .
Kidney beans are a firm, medium-size bean with a dark skin and cream-colored flesh.

Great northern beans are large, white beans with a delicate, distinctive flavor.

In a medium bowl, combine the tomatoes, basil, oregano, scallions, garlic, salt, and pepper. Cover and let stand at room temperature for 30 minutes to allow flavors to blend.

In a medium saucepan, combine the beans and broth. Bring to a boil, then reduce heat. Cover and simmer just until heated through.

To serve, toss warm bean mixture with tomato mixture. Sprinkle with cheese. Serve warm with slices of a freshly made baguette from our bakery department. Makes 4+ servings.

Jamaican Jerk Lentils

Use any of the three main types of lentils for this recipe: French (with a grayish brown exterior), red (without the seed coat and of a smaller, rounder size), or yellow.

1 tbsp. peanut oil
1 cup coarsely chopped yellow onion
3 cups sliced carrots
3 medium leeks, white part only, sliced
2 large garlic cloves, finely chopped
3 cups chicken broth
½ cup fresh orange juice
1½ cups dried lentils, sorted and rinsed
½ cup seedless raisins
1 tbsp. celery flakes
1 tsp. ground coriander
¾ tsp. ground cardamom
½ tsp. sea salt
½ tsp. freshly ground black pepper
1 tsp. ground cinnamon
28 oz. crushed tomatoes, undrained
8 cups cooked couscous, regular or whole wheat

Heat oil in a large saucepan over medium heat. Stirring occasionally, cook onion, carrots, leeks, and garlic in oil until onion and leeks are crisp-tender.

Add the broth, orange juice, lentils, raisins, celery flakes, coriander, cardamom, sea salt, pepper, cinnamon, and tomatoes. Heat to boiling, stirring occasionally.

Reduce heat, cover, and simmer 40 minutes, stirring occasionally, until lentils and carrots are tender. Serve over couscous in wide bowls. Serves 6+.

Chef's Notes

About . . .
A member of the ginger family, cardamom is an aromatic spice native to India, though it grows in many other tropical areas. It has a pungent aroma and a warm, spicy-sweet flavor and is widely used in Scandinavian and East Indian cooking. Be frugal with it—a little goes a long way!

Greek Lentil Salad

Bulgur and lentils combine with fresh tomatoes, the crunch of cucumbers, and red onion tossed with a refreshing lemony vinaigrette . . . just the right main or side dish for your next Greek festival or toga party!

Greek-Style Vinaigrette

⅓ cup extra-virgin olive oil
3 tbsp. red wine vinegar
1 tsp. granulated sugar
1 tbsp. fresh lemon juice
1 tsp. Dijon mustard
½ tsp. dried oregano, crushed

Lentil Salad

3½ cups water, divided
¾ cup bulgur
¼ tsp. sea salt
¾ cup dry lentils
1 medium tomato, cut into thin wedges
1 small cucumber, quartered lengthwise and sliced
¼ cup chopped red onion
⅓ cup pitted sliced Kalamata olives or ripe olives
½ cup crumbled feta cheese

Chef's Notes

About . . .
Lentils are a member of the legume family and provide an excellent source of vegetable protein. Cooked lentils have a beanlike texture and a mild, nutty flavor, and they're a quick cook since they don't require any presoaking.

For the Greek-Style Vinaigrette: In a small bowl, whisk together the oil, vinegar, sugar, lemon juice, mustard, and oregano until well blended. Makes about ½ cup.

For the Lentil Salad: In a medium saucepan bring *1 ½ cups* water to a boil. Remove from heat, then stir in bulgur and salt. Cover and let stand for 30 minutes. Drain thoroughly, pressing bulgur in a sieve or colander to remove excess water.

While bulgur is draining, rinse lentils. In another medium saucepan combine 2 cups water and the lentils. Bring to a boil, reduce heat, then cover and simmer for 20 minutes or until tender; drain. Rinse with cold water; drain again.

In a large serving bowl, combine the bulgur, cooked lentils, tomato, cucumber, onion, and olives. Toss mixture with Greek-Style Vinaigrette until well combined.

Cover and chill for at least 4 hours or overnight to allow flavors to blend. Just before serving, stir in feta cheese. Makes 4 servings.

Curried Lentils

Fresh and ground ginger combine with curry in this
recipe to wake lentils with their bright, unique flavors.

1¾ cups water
¾ cup lentils, rinsed and drained
½ cup coarsely chopped carrots
½ cup coarsely chopped yellow onion
⅓ cup coarsely chopped celery
2 tsp. curry powder
½ tsp. freshly grated ginger
⅛ tsp. ground ginger
1 small garlic clove, minced or pressed
¼ tsp. sea salt
½ cup plain low-fat or nonfat yogurt
½ cup chopped fresh tomato
1 tbsp. snipped fresh Italian (flat-leaf) parsley

In a medium saucepan combine the 1¾ cups water
with the lentils, carrots, onion, celery, curry powder,
gingers, garlic, and salt. Bring to a boil; reduce heat.
Simmer covered for 20 to 25 minutes or until lentils
are tender and liquid is absorbed.

In a small bowl, stir together the yogurt, tomato, and
parsley. Serve the yogurt mixture as a side with the
curried lentils. Makes 3+ servings.

Chef's Notes

About . . .
Curry powder is a pulverized blend of up to 20 spices,
herbs, and seeds. Most commonly used are cardamom, chilies, cinnamon, cloves, coriander, cumin,
fennel seed, fenugreek, mace, nutmeg, ground peppers, sesame and poppy seeds, saffron, tamarind, and
turmeric.

THE MAIN EVENT: MEAT DISHES AND THE GREAT BEYOND (PLANT-BASED DISHES)

Many a chef has built her (or his) reputation on succulent entrées containing meat, poultry, or a plant-based protein cooked to perfection. Knowledgeable shopping and skillful cooking can give you as a home cook results that earn equally high accolades.

Main dishes are still the centerpiece of a meal and of a table, and this chapter contains centerpiece recipes at their finest—clean, vibrantly flavored food, healthful and absolutely satisfying. There are weeknight standbys—Open-Faced Turkey Burgers—mains that are special enough for company—Coriander-Rubbed Lamb Rack—and those that are just plain fun to eat—Tofu Ginger! So, whether you're looking to expand your carnivore consciousness or your virtuous vegetarian vendetta . . . these recipes are winners at the *real* test: taste!

Chicken cooked to perfection with a bright lemon glaze. Cold chicken doesn't get any tastier than this Cold Lemon Chicken!

Coriander-Rubbed Lamb Rack

Our café serves this mouth-watering lamb rack with
roasted tomatoes and scallions atop freshly minted couscous.

2 medium tomatoes, cored and cut into
large pieces
3 scallions, trimmed and sliced into 1" pieces
1 tsp. extra-virgin olive oil
1 tsp. kosher salt
7 or 8 bone, whole lamb rack, cut in half
Sea salt to taste
Freshly ground black pepper to taste
1 tbsp. ground coriander

Chef's Notes

How to Do It . . .
Most agree that lamb tastes best when cooked medium rare to medium—still pink and juicy inside.

Heat oven to 450 degrees.

Toss tomatoes and scallions with olive oil and kosher salt in a medium bowl. Set aside.

Trim any additional fat off lamb rack as needed. Sprinkle with salt and pepper to taste, then rub ground coriander into both sides of lamb rack.

Place tomato/scallion mixture in roasting pan alongside lamb. Roast in oven for 20 minutes for medium rare to medium. Adjust roasting time according to your preference for doneness. Serves 2.

Wild-Mushroom-Crusted Beef Tenderloin

Medallions of grass-fed, organic beef tenderloin crusted with dried wild mushrooms, flavored with a garlic-compound butter, and served atop horseradish potato pancakes in our cafés . . . a dinner menu favorite.

Garlic-Compound Butter

1 large garlic bulb
1 tbsp. extra-virgin olive oil
¼ cup unsalted butter, cold

Tenderloin

8 oz. beef tenderloin, cut into 2 4-oz. medallions
4 tsp. ground, dried shiitake mushrooms
Sea salt
Freshly ground black pepper
Canola oil as needed

Chef's Notes

About . . .
A grass-fed cow must eat only herbaceous plants and/or mother's milk its whole life and is never fattened with grain. Organic beef is raised on only organic feed with no antibiotics, hormones, or animal byproducts.

Heat oven to 350 degrees.

For the Garlic-Compound Butter: Slice top ½" off garlic bulb, then place bulb atop a large piece of foil. Drizzle with oil, enclose in foil, and roast for 1 hour in hot oven. When garlic is tender, remove from oven and allow to cool for 15 minutes. Squeeze garlic paste out of each clove into a small mixing bowl; allow to cool completely.

Using an electric mixer, whip butter until light and fluffy then fold in the garlic paste. Cover and refrigerate overnight or until ready to use.

For the Tenderloin: Coat both sides of each medallion with 1 tsp. of ground mushrooms and a sprinkling of salt and pepper. Set aside.

Heat no more than 1 tsp. canola oil in a small skillet until hot, then sauté medallions until desired doneness, turning once. Serve immediately with a dab of the Garlic-Compound Butter to soften atop the beef. Serves 2.

Cherry Chipotle Barbecue Sauce over Ribs Fallin' off the Bone

These ribs are moist and tender, yet relatively quick and easy. They slow roast in a low oven, then are finished on a charcoal grill for flavor and sauce slathering!

Ribs

1 large yellow onion, sliced
3½ lb. baby back ribs
12-oz. bottle of local specialty beer
Sea salt to taste
Freshly ground black pepper to taste

Cherry Chipotle Barbecue Sauce

2 cups fresh in-season or frozen sweet cherries, pitted and chopped
1 cup chicken broth
⅔ cup ketchup
¼ cup cider vinegar
2 tbsp. minced canned chipotle chilies in adobo sauce
1 tbsp. dried thyme, crushed
¾ tsp. ground allspice

Chef's Notes

About . . .
Baby back ribs come from the back of the pig, about as high on the hog as it gets. They're smaller and typically leaner than spare ribs.

How to Do It . . .
Ask our meat department to remove the membrane from the back of the ribs, or do it yourself at home. Take a small, *dull* knife and *carefully* pry the tip of the knife between the membrane and bone at the edge of the ribs in the center of the slab. Lift to separate the membrane from the bone, then grab the membrane with your fingers and pull it off and discard.

Be sure to measure frozen cherries while still frozen, then thaw, draining juices before using.

Heat oven to 325 degrees.

For the Ribs: Spread the onion slices evenly on a large baking pan and place the ribs, bone side down, on top of the onions. Pour the beer over the ribs, season with salt and pepper, and cover with foil. Bake for 2 hours. While ribs are roasting, prepare the Sauce.

For the Cherry Chipotle Barbecue Sauce: In a medium saucepan, combine the cherries, broth, ketchup, vinegar, chipotle chilies, thyme, and allspice. Bring to a boil over medium-high heat, then simmer and cook until the sauce is reduced by about half, about 15 minutes. Remove from heat and set aside until ready to use.

Prepare a charcoal grill to medium heat. Brush both sides of the ribs with 2 cups of the sauce and place them meat side down over the coals. Grill for 15 minutes or until slightly charred, basting several times. Turn the ribs and baste the cooked side liberally with additional sauce. Close the lid of the grill and cook the ribs 10 minutes longer, basting often. Cut the slabs into individual ribs, pile high on a large platter, and serve hot from the grill. Serves 4+.

Rib-Eye Roast with an Espresso Crust

This company special entrée requires little attention once it's in the oven and is perfect with roasted vegetables and a wild rice blend.

1 beef rib-eye roast, 5-6 lbs.

Espresso Crust

1 tbsp. freshly ground espresso beans
1 tbsp. firmly packed light brown sugar
1 tsp. sea salt
1 tsp. coarsely ground black pepper

Balsamic Glaze

1 cup balsamic vinegar
1 cup beef broth
$\frac{1}{4}$ tsp. coarsely ground black pepper
$\frac{1}{4}$ cup unsalted butter, room temperature
4 tsp. unbleached, all-purpose flour

Chef's Notes

About . . .
Have our meat department cut you the perfect rib-eye roast . . . and savor those natural flavors!

How to Do It . . .
The suggested cooking times are merely a guide—the only accurate measure for doneness is a meat thermometer. Begin checking after 75 percent of the suggested time has passed.

Heat oven to 350 degrees. Place roast in a shallow roasting pan.

For the Espresso Crust: Combine crust ingredients in a small bowl; cover and set aside until ready to use.

For the Balsamic Glaze: In a small saucepan, bring the vinegar to a boil and cook over medium heat until reduced to $\frac{1}{4}$ cup (this will take 15 to 25 minutes). Add the broth and pepper to the reduced balsamic.

Make a paste with the butter and flour in a small bowl. Slowly whisk the butter paste into the vinegar reduction and broth until smooth. Bring to a boil, then reduce heat and simmer for 1 minute, stirring constantly. Remove from heat and keep warm.

Press Espresso Crust evenly onto roast and place on a rack in oven. Roast uncovered for $1\frac{3}{4}$ to 2 hours for medium rare and $2\frac{1}{2}$ hours for medium doneness. Remove roast when a thermometer registers 135 degrees for medium rare, 150 degrees for medium. (Once out of the oven, the roast's internal temperature will continue to rise by about 10 degrees.) Transfer meat to a carving board, tent loosely with foil, and allow to stand for 20 minutes.

When ready to serve, carve roast into thin slices and serve with a drizzle of the Balsamic Glaze. Makes 6+ servings.

It's hard to improve on the perfect cut of grass-fed, organic beef . . . but somehow this espresso crust and balsamic glaze does just that!

Horseradish Mustard Sauce for Steaks or Grilled Tofu

This is a creamy, spicy condiment and a favorite from the cooking school. Use more or less horseradish or substitute a sweet, spicy mustard to vary the basic sauce.

4 tbsp. prepared horseradish
2 tbsp. Dijon mustard, regular or extra sharp
½ cup buttermilk
2 tbsp. sour cream
2 tsp. freshly ground white pepper
1 tsp. coarse sea salt
2 tsp. finely chopped fresh rosemary

In a small bowl combine the horseradish, mustard, buttermilk, sour cream, pepper, salt, and rosemary, blending well. Cover and refrigerate until ready to use. Leftovers keep for 10 days in the refrigerator. Makes about 2 cups.

Chef's Notes

About . . .
Perfect to slather atop hot grilled steaks or tofu.

How to Do It . . .
Grass-fed beef is leaner and cooks faster than regular steaks, so cook lean beef for about half the time of regular, then let your steak rest for 5 to 10 minutes before serving to improve the texture and juiciness.

Bison Stroganoff

Bison, with its sweet, rich flavor, does a stand-in for
beef in our version of this classic comfort food.

6 tbsp. unsalted butter, divided
2 medium leeks, white part only, chopped
3 garlic cloves, finely minced
1½ cups white button, shiitake, or cremini
mushrooms, quartered
1½ tbsp. unbleached, all-purpose flour
1½ cups beef broth
3 tbsp. tomato paste
½ cup sour cream, low fat or regular
2½ lb. bison sirloin steak, cut into 2¼" strips
1½ lb. wide noodles, cooked

Chef's Notes

About . . .
Bison meat is surprisingly tender, with a taste resembling beef. It is extremely lean, so use caution and do not overcook.

Melt *2 tbsp.* of the butter in a large sauté pan and sauté the leeks until tender. Add garlic and mushrooms and sauté until mushrooms release their juices and are softened. Remove from heat and set aside.

Melt *2 tbsp. of the butter* in a medium saucepan then add the flour, whisking until smooth. Add the broth and tomato paste and continue to whisk until mixture is hot and thickened; stir in the sour cream and continue to cook just until heated through.

Melt remaining butter in a large skillet and quickly sauté the bison. Combine all ingredients and spoon atop hot, cooked noodles. Makes 4+ servings.

Bison Delmonico

A café dinner favorite. Our chefs are mindful that bison tastes best when grilled to rare or medium (still pink in the center). Overcooking toughens this lean meat.

4 8-oz. bison rib-eye steaks

Cajun Seasoning

1 tsp. sweet paprika
1 tsp. onion powder
1 tsp. garlic powder
1 tsp. cayenne pepper
1 tsp. basil leaves, crushed
½ tsp. thyme leaves, crushed
Freshly ground black pepper
Sea salt

Chef's Notes

How to Do It . . .
Bison basics: as a *general* rule, for a 1½"-thick steak, cook 8 to 10 minutes for rare, 10 to 12 minutes for medium.

For the Cajun Seasoning: Combine the paprika, onion powder, garlic powder, cayenne pepper, basil, thyme, black pepper, and salt in a small bowl, whisking to combine. Pour into a spice jar and seal tightly. Shake before using.

Work the Cajun Seasoning into the meat of the bison. Let stand for 10 minutes to allow seasoning to soften and flavor the meat.

Sear on a hot grill or sauté in a hot skillet until done as desired, turning every 2 minutes. Serve hot. Serves 4.

Pork Tenderloin with Herbed Breadcrumb Crust

This simple and appealing pork dish will soon
become one of your at-home favorites.

6 cups fresh breadcrumbs made from one of
our loaves of bakery-fresh artisan bread
⅔ cup chopped fresh Italian (flat-leaf) parsley
2 tbsp. chopped fresh rosemary
1¾ tsp. crumbled bay leaves
¼ tsp. sea salt
⅛ tsp. freshly ground black pepper
3 lb. pork tenderloin
2 large eggs, lightly beaten
4 tbsp. unsalted butter, divided
2 tbsp. extra-virgin olive oil, divided

Chef's Notes

About . . .
Our meat department sells 100 percent natural pork,
with no artificial ingredients, no antibiotics or growth
stimulants (we like to say, "Our meat and seafood
don't do drugs!"), and no water or phosphates added.

How to Do It . . .
Pork today is lean so it must be cooked more quickly and is best when cooked medium or still on the
pink side.

Heat oven to 375 degrees.

In a large bowl, mix together the crumbs, parsley,
rosemary, and bay leaves to blend. Season with the
salt and pepper.

Sprinkle pork lightly with salt and pepper. Dip pork
into eggs, then into crumb mixture, coating completely.

Melt *2 tbsp.* of the butter and combine with *1 tbsp.* of
the oil in a large skillet over medium-high heat. Add
half the pork, cooking until golden on all sides. Place
on oven rack in a large roasting pan. After carefully
wiping out skillet with paper towels, repeat with
remaining butter, oil, and pork.

Roast pork until crust is golden and a thermometer
inserted into center registers 155 degrees, about 20
minutes. Transfer to a cutting board. Let stand 10
minutes before carving. Makes 6+ servings.

Chicken with Sun-Dried Tomato Sauce

Chicken is one of America's most popular foods—topping beef and pork in consumption. This easy-to-assemble dish once again shows its versatility.

½ cup chicken broth
¼ cup coarsely chopped sun-dried tomatoes
(not oil packed)
½ cup sliced white button mushrooms
2 tbsp. chopped scallions
2 garlic cloves, pressed
2 tbsp. dry red wine
1 tsp. extra-virgin olive oil
3 large skinned and boned split chicken
breasts, cut into strips or chunks
½ cup milk, skim or 2 percent
2 tsp. cornstarch or arrowroot
1 tbsp. chopped fresh basil
2 cups hot, cooked fettuccine, rice, or couscous

Chef's Notes

About . . .
Look for natural or organic chicken, fed an all-veg-etable diet of natural grains, no antibiotics adminis-tered, and humanely raised.

Heat chicken broth in a small saucepan; stir in toma-toes and remove from heat. Set aside to steep for 30 minutes.

In a large skillet, cook mushrooms, scallions, and gar-lic in wine over medium heat, stirring occasionally, until mushrooms are tender. Remove mixture from skillet and set aside.

Add oil to skillet and cook chicken over medium heat until light golden in color. Add tomato mixture. Boil, then reduce heat to a simmer and cover, cook-ing chicken an additional 5 minutes or until it is completely cooked. Reserving the tomato mixture, remove chicken pieces from skillet to a platter and keep warm.

In a small bowl, mix together the milk, cornstarch/arrowroot, and basil; stir into tomato mixture in skillet. Heat to boiling, stirring constantly. After stirring at a boil for 1 minute, add mushroom mixture; heat through. Serve with chicken over fettuccine, rice, or couscous. Serves 4 generously.

Spicy Chicken with Black-Bean Puree

Served with a side of warmed flour tortillas, freshly steamed brown rice, and your favorite salsa, this chicken dish will wake up your taste buds.

2 skinned and boned split chicken breasts
2 tsp. fajita seasoning
1 tsp. extra-virgin olive oil
½ cup coarsely chopped yellow onion
2 garlic cloves, pressed
15-oz. can black beans, undrained
10-oz. can diced tomatoes with green chilies
¼ tsp. cayenne pepper
½ tsp. ground cumin
2 tbsp. chopped fresh cilantro
1 tbsp. fresh lime juice
Shredded Monterey Jack cheese

Rub chicken with fajita seasoning. In a large skillet, cook in hot oil over medium heat until cooked through. Remove chicken from skillet to a large plate and keep warm.

Sauté onion and garlic in reserved drippings in skillet until onion is tender.

Drain beans, *reserving 2 tbsp.* of the liquid; rinse and drain beans again.

In a food processor, pulse the onion mixture, beans, reserved liquid, tomatoes, cayenne, cumin, cilantro, and lime juice until smooth, stopping to scrape down sides of work bowl as needed. Pour mixture into a small saucepan and stirring, cook over medium heat until hot. Spoon atop chicken on individual serving plates and sprinkle with cheese. Serves 4.

Cold Lemon Chicken

Inspired by lemon chicken, a Chinese restaurant favorite, this heavenly, slightly tart dish is a market kitchen favorite meant to be enjoyed cold.

Lemon Sauce

4 tbsp. fresh lemon juice
1½ tbsp. peanut oil
¼ cup freshly grated ginger
1 tbsp. granulated sugar
½ tsp. sea salt
¾ tsp. pure lemon extract

Chicken with Garnishes

2¼ lb. skinned and boned split chicken breasts
Peanut oil
Sea salt to taste
Freshly ground black pepper to taste
⅓ cup dried wild mushrooms, reconstituted
¼ cup julienne red bell pepper
¼ cup julienne green bell pepper
2 lemons, zested

Chef's Notes

How to Do It . . .
Reconstitute mushrooms by soaking in hot water for 30 minutes. Drain, pat dry, then proceed with recipe.

For the Lemon Sauce: In a small bowl, whisk together the sauce ingredients and set aside.

For the Chicken with Garnishes: Cut chicken into large strips, brushing lightly with oil and sprinkling with salt and pepper. Mark and cook on hot grill, brushing generously with Lemon Sauce. When chicken is cooked through, remove from grill and place in a large serving bowl to cool.

If any Lemon Sauce remains, place in a small saucepan and bring to a boil; simmer for 5 minutes then cool before using. Pour atop chicken.

Drain mushrooms and julienne. Serve chicken topped with julienned peppers and mushrooms and sprinkled with lemon zest. Serves 3+.

Italian Turkey with Polenta

★

This quick and easy weeknight dish makes use of convenient cooked (cornmeal) polenta in a tube on our grocery shelves.

½ lb. ground turkey meat
1 garlic clove, pressed
1 bay leaf
¼ tsp. red pepper flakes
15 oz. diced tomatoes with basil
1 tsp. dried Italian herbs
16 oz. tube polenta
¼ cup freshly grated Parmesan cheese

In a skillet cook ground turkey with garlic, bay leaf, and pepper flakes. Add tomatoes and herbs and simmer until liquid is reduced slightly.

Slice polenta and place in 4 wide soup bowls. Remove bay leaf from sauce and spoon Italian turkey mixture atop polenta. Sprinkle each portion with part of the Parmesan cheese and serve immediately. Serves 4.

Chef's Notes

About . . .
Use a purchased blend of Italian herbs or make your own by combining basil, oregano, garlic salt, and ground fennel.

Open-Faced Turkey Burgers

Delicious on one of our bakery's whole-wheat hamburger buns or
placed between 2 slices of our Signature Seven Grain Bread.

2 cups crushed herbed croutons
⅓ cup chicken broth, divided
1 lb. lean ground turkey
8 oz. whole-berry cranberry sauce

In a large bowl combine the croutons and *half* of the broth; mix well. Add remaining broth and turkey, stirring until well mixed. Shape mixture into 4 to 6 flat oval patties, about ½" thick.

Broil or grill about 15 minutes or until no longer pink in the center, turning only once.

Served topped with cranberry sauce. Makes 4 to 6.

Chef's Notes

How to Do It . . .
Crushing croutons: Buy a bag of seasonal croutons, place the desired amount in a Ziplock bag, and seal. Then, using a rolling pin, crush!

Buffalo-Sauced Quorn Taco

From our café, two white-corn tortillas grilled and filled with vegetarian Quorn patties, diced tomato, romaine lettuce, and a zesty buffalo sauce.

Buffalo Sauce

½ cup unsalted butter
½ cup hot sauce

Quorn Taco

4 Quorn patties
4 6" corn tortillas
2 cups shredded Romaine lettuce
1 cup medium diced tomato
¼ cup Buffalo Sauce
¼ cup shredded red cabbage

Chef's Notes

About . . .
Quorn has a meatlike texture but is from a plant-based source. The principle ingredient in all Quorn products is mycoprotein ("myco" is Greek for "fungi").

Heat oven to 350 degrees.

For the Buffalo Sauce: Combine butter and hot sauce in a small saucepan over low heat, mixing well until butter is melted.

For the Quorn Taco: Warm the Quorn patties in the oven for 15 minutes. Once warmed slice into thirds.

Heat the corn tortillas in a sauté pan at low heat until warmed. On 2 plates, place the heated corn tortillas side by side. Equally divide the shredded Romaine atop the tortillas, followed with the Quorn patty slices. Top with the diced tomato and Buffalo Sauce. Fold gently and garnish with the shredded red cabbage. Serves 4.

TVP Chili

You won't miss the meat in our kitchen's own vegetarian chili . . . loaded
with flavor and perfect with a large square of cornbread from our bakery.

½ cup extra-virgin olive oil
1½ cups coarsely chopped yellow onion
1 cup coarsely chopped green bell pepper
1 tbsp. finely chopped garlic
3 cups Texturized Vegetable Protein (TVP)
2 cups cooked black beans
2 cups corn kernels, fresh in season or frozen
24 oz. diced tomatoes with juice
6 oz. tomato paste
2 cups water
2 tbsp. chili powder
1 tbsp. ground cumin
¼ cup granulated sugar
2 tsp. freshly ground black pepper
1 tsp. sea salt

Heat oil in a large saucepan over medium heat until
hot. Sauté onion, peppers, garlic, and TVP until
onions are soft. Add the beans, corn, tomatoes,
tomato paste, water, chili powder, cumin, sugar, pepper, and salt. Stir well to combine.

Let mixture simmer for 35 minutes, then serve.
Serves 6+.

Chef's Notes

About . . .
TVP (Texturized Vegetable Protein) is a byproduct
of soy and is sold in our bulk department in granules,
flakes, or chunks.

Farmer's Market Couscous-Tempeh Dinner

Especially in the summer, our produce departments are an adventure in what's local right now. The organic farmers that grow specialty, seasonal, and heirloom produce just for you keep the selection varied and bursting with "just picked" flavors.

Tempeh

4 oz. tempeh, cut into strips
1 tbsp. extra-virgin olive oil
2 tbsp. balsamic vinegar
1 tsp. fresh thyme leaves
⅛ tsp. sea salt
A few grinds fresh black pepper

Couscous Dinner

2 tbsp. extra-virgin olive oil
2 garlic cloves, minced
8 oz. Brussels sprouts, blanched and halved
1 cup thin strips of carrot
1 medium red bell pepper, seeded and sliced
1 medium yellow squash, sliced
2 oz. shiitake mushrooms, stemmed and sliced
½ cup halved, sliced red onion, blanched
3 scallions, thinly sliced
¼ cup vegetable broth
1 tbsp. honey
2 tsp. cornstarch or arrowroot
3½ cups cooked whole-wheat couscous

For the Tempeh: Marinate the tempeh in the oil, vinegar, thyme, salt, and pepper in a baking dish for 1 hour.

For the Couscous Dinner: Heat *1 tbsp.* of the olive oil in a large sauté pan. Sauté garlic 1 minute, then stir in Brussels sprouts, carrot, pepper, squash, and additional 1 tbsp. oil; sauté 3 minutes. Add mushrooms, onions, and scallions; sauté just until vegetables are crisp-tender.

In a small bowl whisk together the broth and honey until blended; whisk in the cornstarch/arrowroot until dissolved. Stir mixture into sauté pan, cooking over medium heat until thickened. Add tempeh, stirring gently until heated through.

When ready to serve, spoon the vegetable/tempeh mixture over the couscous. Makes 3+ servings.

Chef's Notes

About . . .
Tempeh, with its hearty texture, is made by splitting, cooking, and fermenting soybeans. It is available refrigerated in a variety of flavor profiles.

Tempeh and Potato-Garlic Ragout

Tender chunks of tempeh and potatoes simmer in an aromatic, garlic-spiced tomato sauce. This makes a hearty, one-dish meal.

2 large russet potatoes, skin scrubbed, cut into small (½") dice
3 tbsp. extra-virgin olive oil
6 garlic cloves, pressed
¼ tsp. crushed red pepper flakes
8 oz. tempeh, steamed then cut into small (½") dice
16-oz. can diced tomatoes
½ tsp. sea salt
Freshly ground black pepper to taste
¼ cup water
¼ cup finely chopped fresh Italian (flat-leaf) parsley

Chef's Notes

About . . .
Ragout means "to stimulate the appetite" and is a thick, rich, well-seasoned stew.

How to Do It . . .
Steam the tempeh in a vegetable steamer covered for 20 minutes. Remove tempeh and allow to cool just slightly before proceeding with recipe.

Place the potatoes in a large skillet, adding about ½" water. Cover and cook over medium heat until tender when gently pierced. Drain in a colander and set aside until ready to use.

Wipe the skillet clean. Pour the oil in the skillet and heat over medium heat. Add the garlic, pepper flakes, and tempeh and cook 1 minute.

Mix in the tomatoes, salt, pepper, and water. Cover and simmer 5 minutes; remove lid and check the thickness of the sauce. If watery, cook uncovered a few additional minutes. Add potatoes to the pan and reheat mixture until hot. Stir in parsley just before serving. Serves 3.

Vegetable-and-Tofu-Stuffed Peppers

Cooking classes featuring soy ideas are always sellouts, and
these peppers are one of the reasons!

Cheese Crumb Topping

¼ cup soft breadcrumbs
¼ cup shredded cheddar cheese
1 tbsp. snipped fresh Italian (flat-leaf) parsley

Stuffed Peppers

4 medium green, red, yellow, or orange
bell peppers
8 oz. refrigerated, firm tofu
Nonstick cooking spray
1 cup finely chopped broccoli
½ cup finely chopped carrots
⅓ cup sliced scallions
1 garlic clove, minced
½ cup chopped tomato
½ cup corn kernels, fresh in season or frozen
½ tsp. dried basil, crushed
½ tsp. dried thyme, crushed
2 cups spaghetti sauce, warmed

Chef's Notes

About . . .
Tofu, also known as soybean curd, is a custard-like
white cake made from curdled soy milk, the liquid
extracted from ground, cooked soybeans.

Heat oven to 350 degrees.

For the Cheese Crumb Topping: In a small bowl, toss together the crumbs, cheese, and parsley. Set aside until ready to use.

For the Stuffed Peppers: Cut tops from the peppers and discard stems, seeds, and membranes. Chop tops to make ¾ cup of peppers and set aside. Cook peppers in simmering water for 5 minutes; drain well.

Drain tofu and crumble into small pieces.

Spray a large nonstick skillet with cooking spray. Cook the chopped pepper, broccoli, carrots, scallions, and garlic over medium heat until crisp-tender. Stir in tomato, corn, basil, and thyme; remove from heat. Gently stir in tofu.

Place peppers cut side up in a large baking dish. Spoon tofu mixture into peppers, then sprinkle with Cheese Crumb Topping. Bake loosely covered with foil for 35 minutes until peppers and filling are hot. Serve in wide individual bowls topped with hot spaghetti sauce. Serves 4+.

Tofu Ginger

Tofu gets the royal taste treatment . . . crisped then slathered
and baked with a unique, spicy ginger sauce.

Ginger Sauce

18 oz. tomato sauce
1⅛ cups granulated sugar
¼ cup finely chopped fresh ginger
½ tsp. freshly ground black pepper
⅔ cup tamari

Tofu

3 or 4 16-oz. packs of firm, refrigerated
tofu, drained
Cornstarch to coat
Canola oil/olive oil blend as needed for frying
Slivers of fresh ginger, optional

Chef's Notes

About . . .
Tamari, also made from soybeans, is similar to but
thicker than soy sauce, with a distinctively mellow
flavor and dark color.

How to Do It . . .
If you keep the oil hot, your tofu will absorb almost
no oil and will be infused with the true flavors you
want, that of the sauce!

For the Ginger Sauce: Combine ingredients in a
large saucepan, stirring to blend well. Bring to a boil,
then reduce heat to low and simmer for 2 to 3 hours
or until mixture is reduced and slightly thickened,
and sugar has completely dissolved.

For the Tofu: Cut tofu by first carefully cutting tofu
cakes horizontally through the middle, then slice
into sticks as thick or as thin as you like. Coat in
cornstarch, covering well and shaking off excess. Fry
in *hot* oil until crisp, allowing to drain on cooling
rack set atop paper-towel-lined trays.

Heat oven to 325 degrees. Place tofu in single layers
in a baking pan, spooning Ginger Sauce on top. Bake
uncovered for 30 to 45 minutes or until the tofu just
begins to puff. Remove from heat and toss in some
slivers of fresh ginger if desired. Serve hot, room temperature, or cold. Serves 8+.

Opposite: There's a great deal of satisfaction in
the ability to stack these sauced tofu sticks, but
the satisfaction really comes from eating them!

Baked Thai Tofu

This method of baking marinated tofu gives it a crispy coating and intensifies all the flavors in the "sauce." Another cooking class soy favorite!

Marinade

2 tbsp. tamari
1 tbsp. toasted sesame oil
1 tbsp. peanut oil
½ tsp. freshly grated ginger
1 garlic clove, pressed
¼ tsp. crushed red pepper flakes
1 lb. extrafirm, pressed tofu, cut into ¾" cubes
1 medium red bell pepper, cut into thin strips

Sauce

1 tbsp. smooth peanut butter
2 tbsp. fresh lime juice
1 scallion, very thinly sliced
2 tsp. finely chopped fresh basil
2 tsp. finely chopped fresh mint

Chef's Notes

How to Do It . . .
By pressing the tofu you remove some of the excess water, allowing the flavors to be better absorbed. Take a large plate and line it with paper towels; place drained tofu atop paper towels, then cover with additional paper towels and another large plate. Refrigerate at least 30 minutes and as long as overnight. When ready to use, discard paper towels and remove tofu. Cut and proceed with recipe.

Heat oven to 450 degrees.

For the Marinade: In a large bowl, whisk together the tamari, sesame and peanut oils, ginger, garlic, and red pepper flakes until combined. Toss in the tofu and red pepper strips to coat them evenly with the Marinade. Let stand covered at room temperature for 30 minutes.

Place the tofu mixture with Marinade in a single layer in a large baking dish. Bake 15 minutes, turning once with a spatula after 8 minutes.

For the Sauce: In a medium bowl, whisk together the peanut butter, lime juice, scallion, basil, and mint until well combined. Remove the tofu from the oven and spoon on the Sauce, tossing the ingredients together until well coated. Return the dish to the oven and bake for 10 minutes.

Remove from the oven and allow to sit for 12 minutes so the flavors have a chance to blend and the tofu cools down slightly. Serves 2+.

FISH: THE ORIGINAL FAST FOOD (AND SOME OTHER SEAFOOD, TOO!)

One of the easiest and most impressive entrées or the perfect answer to dinner in a hurry, fish symbolizes light, delicious, and, yes, elegant dining.

If fish were shaped like blocks, cooking times would be easy to calculate. Most whole or fillets of fish have irregular shapes. A general rule to keep in mind for pan-frying or poaching is 8 to 10 minutes of cooking per inch of thickness. Don't overcook it!

In the past, recipes have recommended cooking fish until it flakes easily when prodded in the thickest portion with a fork. ("Flaking" means that the fish's flesh slides apart.) In the cooking school, however, I tell my students that cooking to this stage is usually a touch too much since fish will continue to cook internally when removed from the heat. A much better method is to cook the fish until the flesh inside is slightly opaque. If you follow this simple rule, the fish will flake (yet still be mouth-wateringly moist) when it arrives at the table.

As fish cooks, its translucent flesh changes to opaque white (or pink in the case of salmon). Near the end of the estimated cooking time, take this doneness test: cut a slit in the center of the thickest part of the fish. When the flesh inside is just slightly opaque and has lost its wet look, take the fish off the heat. Yes, this will take some getting used to—but you'll be rewarded with sensational results.

Once you acquire a knack for the ease of cooking fish, you'll enjoy the versatility of this Pesto Tilapia with Smoked Tomato Relish as well as the other selections in this chapter.

Potato-Crusted Trout

The sweet, mild flavor of trout is enhanced by a horseradish potato crust and killer balsamic onions. A popular café entrée, it is served with fresh spinach, cherry tomatoes, and roasted garlic puree warmed quickly in olive oil.

Trout

2 medium red-skin potatoes
2 tsp. prepared horseradish
1 tsp. mayonnaise
1 tsp. sour cream
½ tsp. drained capers, coarsely chopped
Sea salt to taste
Freshly ground black pepper to taste
4 4-oz. split rainbow trout fillets
Extra-virgin olive oil
Greens, for plating

Balsamic Onions

1 large red onion, halved then thinly sliced
1¼ cups balsamic vinegar

Chef's Notes

About . . .
Rainbow trout is the most popular and best known of the freshwater trout species. It has firm-textured flesh and a mild, sweet flavor.

How to Do It . . .
To roast garlic, trim the top inch off the garlic bulb, exposing the cloves underneath the papery skin. Pour 2 tbsp. olive oil over bulb and wrap in foil. Bake in a 375-degree oven for 1 hour. Allow to cool slightly, then squeeze garlic paste from roasted cloves.

Freshly wilted greens are a quick, nutritious "extra." Take 2 to 3 cups of washed greens (such as kale, collards, spinach), tear into bite-size pieces, and quickly sauté in a hot skillet *just until* slightly wilted.

Heat oven to 350 degrees.

For the Trout: Shred the potatoes. In a large bowl combine the shredded potatoes, horseradish, mayonnaise, sour cream, capers, and salt and pepper to taste. Coat trout with potato mixture on meat side of fillets. Set aside.

Heat oil in a medium ovenproof skillet. When skillet is hot, sauté trout until golden brown on potato-crusted bottom; flip fillets and place skillet in oven about 5 minutes or until trout is cooked through.

For the Balsamic Onions: In a medium saucepan combine the onion slices with the balsamic vinegar. Cook, stirring occasionally, until onions are very soft and balsamic is reduced to a thick glaze that clings to the onions.

Plate the crusted trout with a mixture of some wilted, warmed greens and a scoop of balsamic onions. Serves 2.

Roasted Herbed Halibut with Relish

The tomato relish enhances the sweet, moist flavors of the roasted halibut.

Tomato Caper Relish

2 tsp. finely chopped shallots
2 tbsp. extra-virgin olive oil
2 medium tomatoes, chopped
½ cup finely diced fennel bulb
1 tbsp. balsamic vinegar
¼ tsp. freshly ground black pepper
1 tsp. chopped fresh cilantro
2 tsp. drained, finely chopped capers

Herbed Halibut

Sea salt to taste
Freshly ground black pepper to taste
4 6-oz. halibut fillets
4 tbsp. extra-virgin olive oil
2 tsp. finely chopped shallots
2 tbsp. finely chopped fresh cilantro
2 tsp. fresh lime juice

Chef's Notes

How to Do It . . .
Marinating the halibut for 30 minutes infuses the fish with additional layers of flavor.

For the Tomato Caper Relish: In a medium bowl combine the shallots, oil, tomatoes, fennel, vinegar, pepper, cilantro, and capers. Mix well. Set aside for 1 hour to allow flavors to blend.

For the Herbed Halibut: Lightly salt and pepper the fish. In a small bowl, mix the oil, shallots, cilantro, and juice. Spread all the marinade over the fish. Cover and marinate in a glass dish in the refrigerator for 30 minutes.

Heat oven to 400 degrees. Bake the fish with the marinade for 10 minutes or until done. Remove to individual serving plates and top with Tomato Caper Relish. Makes 4 servings.

Pumpkin-Seed-Encrusted Halibut

This café dinner entrée is typically served atop spiced scalloped sweet potatoes, spinach, and a side of cranberry chutney . . . a collection of fall's finest flavors.

½ cup unbleached, all-purpose flour
2 large eggs
½ cup water
4 oz. green pumpkin seeds, roasted then coarsely chopped
2 oz. breadcrumbs
4 5-oz. halibut fillet pieces
½ cup canola oil

Chef's Notes

About . . .
The meat from halibut is white, firm, and mild flavored.

Heat oven to 350 degrees.

Set up wide bowls for breading. One bowl should contain flour, one bowl the eggs whisked with water to combine, and the third the pumpkin seeds mixed with the breadcrumbs.

Bread the halibut by dipping first into the flour, then the egg wash and coat with the seed/crumb mixture.

Heat the oil in a large (preferably cast-iron) oven-proof skillet. Place the breaded halibut in pan, turning every 30 seconds until all sides are golden brown. Place in oven for 7 to 10 minutes or until done. Serves 4.

Halibut Fillets with Pine-Nut-Parmesan Crust

Pine nuts and Parmesan add richness to the crust of this cooking school favorite.

4 tbsp. pine nuts, chopped
2 tbsp. freshly grated Parmesan cheese
1 garlic clove, pressed
2 tsp. chopped fresh herb blend (mixture of basil, marjoram, mint, and sage)
1/8 tsp. cayenne pepper
2 tsp. extra-virgin olive oil
2 6-oz. halibut fillets
Sea salt to taste

Chef's Notes

About . . .
Pine nuts have a thin shell with ivory-colored nut meat and vary in flavor from light and delicate to pungent. Store in the refrigerator or freezer to keep from becoming rancid.

How to Do It . . .
If the topping looks like it's going to burn before the fish is cooked, reduce the oven temperature to 375 degrees.

As fish fillets taper, it's best to tuck the thin ends under, allowing for a more even thickness and cooking time.

Heat oven to 425 degrees. Line a small baking sheet with parchment paper or lightly brush a pan with oil.

In a small bowl, gently mix the chopped pine nuts, Parmesan, garlic, herbs, cayenne, and olive oil.

Season the halibut with a sprinkling of salt. Carefully pat the nut/cheese topping over the surface of each fillet, pressing lightly to stick.

Set the fillets on the prepared pan and bake until the topping is golden brown and the fish is cooked all the way through when poked with a thin knife or skewer, 12 to 15 minutes. Serve immediately. Serves 2.

Spiced Halibut

Incredibly easy to prepare, this is a delicious Middle Eastern twist on a moist fish . . . and perfect atop a tabbouleh salad or freshly cooked spinach or kale.

4 6-oz. halibut fillets
1 tbsp. extra-virgin olive oil
¼ tsp. ground cumin
¼ tsp. sweet or hot paprika
¼ tsp. ground cinnamon
Sea salt to taste

Heat oven to broil and lightly oil a baking sheet.

Brush tops of halibut fillets with oil. In a small bowl, combine the cumin, paprika, cinnamon, and salt; sprinkle evenly over halibut.

Broil about 4" from heat without turning until golden on top, about 3 minutes.

Reduce oven heat to 450 degrees. Roast halibut just until cooked through, about 4 minutes. Makes 4 servings.

Salmon with Spiced Pinot Noir Sauce

The spicy, rich, complex flavors of Pinot Noir wine
complement these sweet salmon fillets.

4 6-oz. center-cut skinless salmon fillets
Sea salt
1½ cups Pinot Noir wine
2 tbsp. coarsely ground black pepper
2 tbsp. finely grated fresh ginger
2 tbsp. minced garlic
3 tbsp. cold unsalted butter, cut into pieces

Chef's Notes

In Season . . .
Serve with a simple salad of fresh, assorted organic greens, toasted almonds, sun-dried tomatoes, orange slices, and a light drizzle of vinegar and olive oil.

Pat salmon dry and season lightly with salt. Heat a 12" nonstick skillet over medium-high heat until hot, then quickly sear the salmon on both sides just until golden.

Add the wine, pepper, ginger, and garlic and cook salmon at a bare simmer, turning pieces over once, just until cooked through.

With a slotted spatula transfer salmon to warm plates and keep lightly covered.

Boil the cooking liquid until syrupy and reduced to about ¼ cup. Remove skillet from heat and whisk in butter until blended. Season sauce with additional salt and pour over salmon. Serves 4.

Lemon Miso Salmon

Cooked udon noodles sprinkled with toasted sesame oil and
sesame seeds complement this Asian favorite from our café.

5 6-oz. skinless salmon fillets
4 oz. drained capers
1 oz. white (golden) miso
1 cup dry white wine
1 oz. butter, cut into small pieces

Chef's Notes

About . . .
Capers, the flower bud of a bush native to the
Mediterranean and parts of Asia, have a pungent fla-
vor that goes well with fish.

Heat oven to 375 degrees.

Place salmon in a ceramic dish with capers. In a separate small bowl, combine miso with white wine
until thoroughly combined. Add butter, then pour
mixture over salmon.

Cover and bake for 12 to 15 minutes or until salmon
is cooked. Serve in bowls with miso/wine sauce.
Serves 4+.

Roast Salmon with Thai Coconut Sauce

★

The impact of this bold sauce is a fantastic match to the
salmon, which has its own rich flavor.

Thai Coconut Sauce

2 tbsp. finely minced fresh ginger
1 cup unsweetened coconut milk
2 tbsp. dry white wine
1 tsp. cornstarch or arrowroot
2 tsp. Asian chili sauce
1 tsp. curry powder
½ tsp. sea salt
¼ cup chopped fresh cilantro, divided

Roast Salmon

4 8-oz. pieces salmon fillet (not the tail
section), skinned
1 lime, cut into wedges

Chef's Notes

About . . .
Coconut milk is made by combining equal parts
water and shredded, fresh coconut meat, simmered
then strained.

Heat oven to 325 degrees. Line a baking sheet with foil.

For the Thai Coconut Sauce: In a small bowl combine the ginger, coconut milk, wine, cornstarch/arrowroot, chili sauce, curry powder, salt, and *2 tbsp.* of the cilantro. Mix well.

For the Roast Salmon: Place the salmon on the prepared baking sheet, leaving room between each piece. Bake for 18 to 20 minutes or until done.

Stir the sauce, dissolving any cornstarch that has settled to the bottom, and pour into a saucepan. Bring to a boil over medium-high heat and boil rapidly for 1 minute. Taste and adjust seasonings if necessary.

Transfer the salmon to serving plates and spoon the sauce over the top. Garnish with the reserved cilantro and serve at once, accompanied by lime wedges. Serves 4.

Ohio Peach Salmon

Ohio peaches flavor salmon and are served with organic brown rice and roasted asparagus. Can't you just hear our café menu calling out, "Summer is here!"

4 6-oz. pieces skinless salmon
3 peaches, pitted and sliced
1 pt. peach nectar

Chef's Notes

In Season . . .
To be savored only in season, a ripe, intensely flavored peach should give slightly to gentle palm pressure, and the juices should drip down your chin. Underripe peaches should never be refrigerated—they become mealy.

Heat oven to 400 degrees.

Place salmon in a large ovenproof skillet or baking dish. Top with sliced peaches and nectar. Bake for 12 to 15 minutes or until salmon is cooked.

Serve immediately, spooning peaches and juices atop salmon. Makes 4 servings.

Poached Salmon with Spiced Fruit Salsa

This Copper River Salmon, served cold, quickly becomes the hit of the picnic!

Salmon

1-2 cups water
1 cup dry white wine
½ cup fresh green celery leaves
4 sprigs fresh curly parsley
1 medium carrot, cut into 4 pieces
4 black peppercorns
1 4-lb. side Copper River Salmon

Spiced Fruit Salsa

4 cups seasonal fresh fruit assortment (apricots, peaches, nectarines, seedless watermelon), cleaned and cubed into bite-size pieces
2-4 tbsp. fresh orange juice
1 tbsp. ground cinnamon
1 tsp. freshly ground black pepper

For the Salmon: Place the water, wine, celery leaves, parsley, carrot, and peppercorns into a very large sauté pan or fish poacher and bring to a boil over medium heat. Reduce the heat to a simmer, then add the salmon. Poach uncovered just until cooked through, 9 to 10 minutes per inch. Gently remove the fish from the poaching liquid and set aside to cool.

For the Spiced Fruit Salsa: In a serving bowl combine the fruit, juice, cinnamon, and pepper, tossing gently to blend.

To serve, slice the salmon and enjoy with salsa on the side. Serves 6+.

Chef's Notes

About . . .
Choose ecofriendly fish, rated by its abundance and the ecological impact of its fishing or farm-raised methods.

How to Do It . . .
Fresh orange juice in this salsa keeps any of the seasonal stone fruits (those fruits with pits) from blackening.

In Season . . .
This recipe takes advantage of the spectacular color and sweet flavors of wild Alaskan salmon seasonally available from the Copper River.

Salmon Burgers with Honey Barbecue Sauce

Each component of this recipe is easy to make—and the sweet flavors of salmon are complemented well by the sauce.

Honey Barbecue Sauce

⅓ cup honey
⅓ cup ketchup
1½ tsp. cider vinegar
1 tsp. prepared horseradish
¼ tsp. minced fresh garlic
⅛ tsp. crushed red pepper flakes, if desired

Patties

1½ cups whole-grain bread cubes,
½" in size
¾ tsp. finely grated lemon zest
1 tbsp. fresh lemon juice
1 large egg white
14¾-oz. can pink salmon, well drained, skin
and large bones discarded, flaked
¼ cup mayonnaise
2 tbsp. chopped fresh dill
1 medium tomato, cored and sliced
½ medium cucumber, thinly sliced
2 tbsp. Honey Barbecue Sauce

For the Honey Barbecue Sauce: In a small bowl combine the honey, ketchup, vinegar, horseradish, garlic, and red pepper flakes until well blended. Set aside.

For the Patties: Place bread cubes, zest, lemon juice, and egg white in a medium bowl; blend well. Add the salmon and mix well. Shape into 4 or 5 flat, oval-shaped patties about ½" thick. Broil or grill patties for 10 to 15 minutes or until lightly browned, turning once.

In a small bowl, combine mayonnaise and dill; blend well. Spread mayonnaise mixture over patties. Top with tomato and cucumber slices and Honey Barbecue Sauce. Makes 4 or 5 patties.

Chef's Notes

About . . .
Our made-from-scratch Country Wheat bread is perfect for the bread cubes.

How to Do It . . .
Be sure to use fresh bread to make the cubes, not dry, bagged croutons. The salmon patties will be easier to shape and will retain their shape while cooking.

Macadamia-Nut-Encrusted Salmon

Although this dish stands alone, our café chefs enjoy serving it with an apricot-infused hollandaise sauce, and in the cooking school we serve it with a Thai red curry sauce.

½ lb. macadamia nuts
1 cup unbleached, all-purpose flour
2 large eggs
½ cup water
¾ cup breadcrumbs
4 5-oz. skinless, boneless salmon fillets
Canola oil as needed for cooking

Chef's Notes

About . . .
Macadamia nuts are a buttery-rich, slightly sweet nut arriving mainly from Hawaii; store refrigerated or freeze to prevent rancidity.

Heat oven to 350 degrees.

In a food processor, pulse the macadamia nuts into small pieces.

In three separate shallow bowls build your breading stations. Place flour in one bowl, the combined eggs and water in another. Combine the chopped macadamia nuts and breadcrumbs in a third bowl.

Dredge the salmon in flour, then egg wash, and finally the nut/crumb mixture.

Place oil in a nonstick, ovenproof sauté pan and heat to medium. Sauté salmon until golden brown, about 1 minute. Turn salmon and place pan in oven and finish cooking for 12 minutes or just until salmon is done. Serve immediately. Serves 4.

Grouper with Roasted Ratatouille

*It's hard to decide whether the best catch in this dish is the fresh,
seasonal grouper or the sensational ratatouille.*

1 lb. eggplant, peeled and cut into 1" pieces
1 medium red bell pepper, cut into 1" pieces
1 medium yellow bell pepper, cut into 1" pieces
1 medium zucchini, quartered lengthwise then
cut into 1" pieces
1 medium yellow squash, quartered lengthwise
then cut into 1" pieces
1 cup chopped yellow onion
2 garlic cloves, minced or pressed
3 tbsp. extra-virgin olive oil
2 tsp. finely chopped fresh rosemary
½ tsp. sea salt
2 8-oz. grouper fillets, cut into 1½" pieces
½ cup seeded, diced plum tomatoes
1 tbsp. balsamic vinegar
½ tsp. freshly ground black pepper
½ lb. fresh spinach leaves, stemmed

Heat oven to 400 degrees.

In a large roasting pan, combine the eggplant, peppers, zucchini, yellow squash, onion, and garlic. Coat with the olive oil and sprinkle with the rosemary and salt, tossing gently to combine. Roast the vegetables for 25 minutes or until tender, stirring occasionally.

Add the grouper fillets and bake for an additional 12 to 15 minutes or until done. Remove from oven and add the tomato, vinegar, and pepper, tossing gently to combine.

Arrange spinach on individual, wide serving bowls. Spoon fish mixture over spinach and serve. Makes 6 servings.

Chef's Notes

About . . .
The word "ratatouille" is a French term referring to a stew mix of summer vegetables and herbs.

Grouper has a lean, firm flesh that is perfect for a wide variety of cooking methods.

Toasted-Almond-Topped Fish

*This recipe is versatile and works well with just about any
of your favorite fresh fish selections.*

1 lb. fish fillets or steaks (your choice of
grouper, cod, tilapia, red snapper,
halibut, or other)
¼ cup buttermilk
½ cup fine dry breadcrumbs
2 tbsp. coarsely chopped fresh Italian
(flat-leaf) parsley
½ tsp. dry mustard
¼ tsp. sea salt
⅛ tsp. freshly ground black pepper
½ cup sliced almonds, coarsely chopped
2 tbsp. unsalted butter, melted
Thin cucumber slices

Chef's Notes

How to Do It . . .
To measure thickness of fish fillets or steaks, place a
ruler against the thickest part of the fish. Use this
measurement to calculate the estimated cooking
time.

Heat oven to 475 degrees. Grease a shallow baking
pan.

Cut fish into 4 serving-size pieces. Pat dry with paper
towels, then measure thickness of fish to determine
cooking time.

Pour buttermilk into a shallow pan. In another shallow pan combine breadcrumbs, parsley, dry mustard,
salt, and pepper. Dip fish into buttermilk, then roll in
crumb mixture. Place coated fish in greased pan.

Sprinkle fish with coarsely chopped almonds. Drizzle
melted butter over fish and bake until golden and
fish is done, allowing 4 to 5 minutes for each ½" of
thickness.

Transfer fish to serving plates and garnish with fresh
cucumber slices. Serves 4.

Pecan-Encrusted Atlantic Cod

Our café chefs love to encrust their fish—adding texture and flavor while helping maintain moistness. This cod is served on a bed of organic brown rice with steamed asparagus.

½ lb. pecan pieces
⅛ cup Cajun seasoning
3-4 large eggs, lightly beaten
¼ cup water
1 cup unbleached, all-purpose flour
4 6-oz. portions cod
A few tbsp. of extra-virgin olive oil to sauté fish

Chef's Notes

About . . .
Cod's mild-flavored meat is white, lean, firm, and very versatile.

You can purchase ready-made Cajun seasoning in the spice aisle or make your own. See the Blackened Sea Scallops recipe in this chapter for our café Cajun Seasoning recipe.

How to Do It . . .
When you dredge, you lightly coat food to be fried. This coating (usually flour, cornmeal, or breadcrumbs) helps brown the food.

In a food processor, grind pecans to a medium-fine texture. Do not puree. Remove and place in a shallow pan. Stir in Cajun seasoning. In another shallow pan combine eggs and water, blending well. Place flour in a third shallow pan to complete your breading stations.

Dredge fish in flour, shaking off excess. Dip in egg wash, then dredge in pecan mixture. Sauté quickly in oil in a hot skillet until topping is golden and fish is cooked. Serves 4.

Tuna in Herbed Citrus Butter

The flavors of meaty tuna slathered with seasoned butter then roasted to a medium rare complement each other perfectly!

5 tbsp. unsalted butter
½ tsp. lemon juice
¼ tsp. finely chopped fresh tarragon
¼ tsp. chopped fresh dill
¼ tsp. chopped fresh chives
¼ cup dry white wine
4 6-oz. yellowfin tuna steaks, cut ¾" thick
Sea salt to taste
Freshly ground black pepper to taste
1 tbsp. or more minced fresh Italian (flat-leaf) parsley
1 tbsp. or more diced tomato

Heat oven to 425 degrees.

In a small saucepan, melt the butter and add the lemon juice, tarragon, dill, and chives. Sauté for 30 seconds, then add the wine and simmer for 1 additional minute.

Measure the thickness of the tuna, then place it on a baking sheet and sprinkle with salt and pepper. Pour the herbed butter over the tuna and bake for 6 to 8 minutes per inch of thickness for a lightly pink inside. Makes 4 servings.

Serving this dish is the perfect way to appreciate the glories of fresh tuna.

Peppered Yellowfin Tuna

This café entrée is perfect served over a bed of whole-wheat linguine with olive oil and garlic sauce.

4 6-oz. portions yellowfin tuna
Mélange of peppercorns (white, green, pink, black), coarsely crushed
4 oz. extra-virgin olive oil
4 oz. blue cheese, crumbled

Chef's Notes

How to Do It . . .
To some, eating fish rare is difficult . . . but two things are most important: know and trust your seafood source (our seafood department is available to answer your questions and concerns) and don't overcook great tuna—if it's dry you might as well have opened a can!

Dredge tuna in crushed peppercorns.

Heat oil in a medium-sized sauté pan on medium-high heat. Add tuna and sauté 2 minutes on each side.

Serve rare, thinly sliced, topped with blue cheese crumbles. Serves 4.

Black-Bean-Encrusted Tuna

A spicy, surprising coating on a moist, flavorful, meaty fish.

25-oz. can black beans, rinsed and drained
2 oz. wasabi powder
⅛ cup water
4 6-oz. tuna steaks
¼ cup Dijon mustard
¼ cup honey

Heat oven to 350 degrees.

Spread drained black beans on a baking sheet and dry in oven for 30 minutes.

In a small bowl, whisk together wasabi powder and water; set aside.

Pan-sear tuna in a hot skillet for 20 seconds on each side. Remove tuna from skillet and rub equal amounts of wasabi, Dijon, and honey onto tuna, coating all sides well.

Using the bottom of a heavy skillet, crush beans. Dredge tuna in beans until completely coated. Sauté tuna in hot skillet for 2 to 3 minutes on each side. Serve medium rare. Serves 4.

Sautéed Tilapia with Warm Dressing

The low-fat flesh of tilapia is white (occasionally with a pink tinge), sweet, and fine textured. It's the perfect fish for almost any preparation.

1½-2 lb. tilapia fillets, cut into pieces
Unbleached, all-purpose flour seasoned with sea salt and ground black pepper for dredging
½ cup + 2 tbsp. extra-virgin olive oil, divided
2 tbsp. minced shallot
2 cups minced, peeled, seeded tomatoes
½ cup fresh lemon juice
2 tbsp. granulated sugar
1 tbsp. chopped fresh basil leaves
¼ cup dry white wine
1 lb. fresh spinach, stemmed
¼ cup minced scallions
¼ cup lightly toasted sliced almonds

Chef's Notes

About . . .
Shallots, used often in fish dishes, are prized for their mild onion flavor that enhances without overpowering.

Dredge tilapia in flour, shaking off excess. In a large skillet, heat *2 tbsp.* of the olive oil over medium-high heat until hot but not smoking; sauté tilapia in batches until golden, turning often. Transfer fillets to a cooling rack set atop a baking sheet to drain. Discard oil.

In the skillet, heat remaining ½ cup olive oil; add shallot and cook, stirring, over medium-low heat until softened. Add tomatoes, lemon juice, sugar, and basil and cook mixture over medium heat for 1 to 2 minutes. Add wine and bring mixture to a boil; boil dressing for 3 minutes.

To serve, arrange spinach on plates and top with tilapia fillets. Spoon warm dressing over salads. Garnish with scallions and almonds. Serves 4+.

Pesto Tilapia with Smoked Tomato Relish

A few simple prep steps and a simple assembly and the rewards—a fish dish with bold flavors—are perfect for every day or company. Use your favorite prepared pesto or try our Herb Pesto for delicious results!

Herb Pesto

½ cup loosely packed fresh basil leaves
½ cup loosely packed fresh Italian (flat-leaf) parsley leaves
3 tbsp. fresh oregano leaves
3 tbsp. fresh thyme leaves
1 tbsp. finely chopped fresh rosemary
3 tbsp. coarsely chopped walnuts
2 tbsp. white (golden) miso
¼ cup extra-virgin olive oil
Freshly ground black pepper to taste

Tilapia

½ cup prepared pesto or Herb Pesto
4 6-oz. tilapia fillets
1 cup breadcrumbs

Relish

1 cup prepared salsa
2 plum tomatoes, finely diced
2 tbsp. ketchup
1 tsp. liquid smoke

For the Herb Pesto: In a food processor, combine the basil, parsley, oregano, thyme, and rosemary, pulsing briefly just to begin to chop leaves. Add the walnuts and miso and pulse until herbs are finely chopped, stopping to scrape down sides of work bowl. With motor running, add oil in a thin, steady stream until mixture forms a thick, coarse paste. Season with pepper. Leftovers may be stored in the refrigerator for 1 or 2 days. Makes about ¾ cup.

Heat oven to 400 degrees.

For the Tilapia: In a baking pan, spread 2 tsp. of the Herb Pesto or other prepared pesto over each fillet. Sprinkle breadcrumbs evenly atop pesto. Bake for 8 to 10 minutes or until fillets are cooked.

For the Relish: In a small bowl combine the salsa, tomatoes, ketchup, and liquid smoke.

Serve each fillet topped with 1 to 2 tbsp. of the Relish. Makes 4 servings.

Chef's Notes

How to Do It . . .
If you want to take a little more time with this fish dish and make your own pesto, this Herb Pesto recipe from the cooking school is divine. I prefer this pesto, made not just with basil but with a blend of fresh herbs. Miso, used here in place of Parmesan, gives this version its zing.

The taste of fresh rosemary can overpower if it's not handled well, so be sure to finely chop before adding to the food processor. By doing this, the rosemary will enhance the flavor of the pesto instead of taking over!

Crispy Fish with a Yogurt Dill Sauce

Cornmeal adds texture, crunch, and flavor . . . and the yogurt dill sauce is easily thrown together while the fish is roasting.

Yogurt Dill Sauce

½ cup plain, fat-free yogurt
½ cup lemon fat-free or low-fat yogurt
1 tsp. finely grated lemon zest
1 tsp. dried dill weed
⅛ tsp. hot pepper sauce

Crispy Fish

Nonstick cooking spray
1 lb. tilapia, mahi mahi, or halibut fillets,
½"-¾" thick
¼ cup cornmeal
½ tsp. dried thyme, crushed
¼ tsp. finely grated lemon zest
¼ tsp. freshly ground black pepper
1 large egg white
2 tbsp. water
¼ cup fine, dry breadcrumbs
2 tbsp. toasted wheat germ
1 tbsp. finely chopped fresh Italian
(flat-leaf) parsley
½ tsp. sweet paprika

For the Yogurt Dill Sauce: In a small bowl combine the yogurts, zest, dill, and hot pepper sauce until well blended. Set aside.

Heat oven to 450 degrees. Lightly spray baking dish.

For the Crispy Fish: Cut fish into 4 serving-size pieces.

In a shallow bowl combine the cornmeal, thyme, zest, and pepper. In another bowl beat together the egg white and water until well combined. In a third bowl combine crumbs, wheat germ, parsley, and paprika.

Dredge the fish into the cornmeal mixture, shaking off any excess. Dip in the egg white mixture, then coat with the crumb mixture. Place in baking dish, tucking under any thin edges.

Bake for 4 to 6 minutes per ½" thickness of fish until cooked. Serve with Yogurt Dill Sauce. Serves 4.

Black Sea Bass with Sun-Dried Tomato Tapenade

The pungent flavors of the thick tapenade hold up well to the
firm, moderately fatty texture of black sea bass.

20 sun-dried tomato halves (not oil packed)
Boiling water to cover
32 kalamata olives, pitted
8 tbsp. chopped red onion
8 tbsp. chopped fresh basil
4 tbsp. chopped fresh Italian (flat-leaf) parsley
4 garlic cloves, peeled
8 tsp. red wine vinegar
4 tsp. extra-virgin olive oil
Sea salt to taste
Freshly ground black pepper to taste
4 6-oz. black sea bass fillets

Chef's Notes

About . . .
Black sea bass is a true bass, but oftentimes sea bass is
a term used to describe any of a variety of saltwater
fish.

In a small bowl combine the sun-dried tomatoes and
boiling water to cover. Let stand for 30 minutes to
soften tomatoes. Drain, reserving 1 cup of the liquid.

Transfer tomatoes to a food processor with the olives,
onion, basil, parsley, and garlic cloves and pulse to
finely chop. Add the vinegar, oil, and *½ cup* of the
reserved liquid and blend until a moist paste forms,
stopping to scrape down sides of work bowl. Add
more of the soaking liquid if paste appears too thick.
Season with salt and pepper and set aside.

Sprinkle bass with salt and pepper. Grill, broil, or
pan-fry fish until opaque in the center. Transfer to
plates and top with spoonfuls of the tapenade mixture. Serve immediately. Serves 4.

Shrimp in Green Tea

This dish, with its delicate green tea infusion, is best suited to being served with freshly steamed plain rice that allows for the showcasing of the Asian flavor profile.

1 tbsp. green tea leaves
1 cup boiling water
1½ tbsp. canola oil
1 lb. large shrimp, peeled and deveined, tail shell left on if desired
1 tbsp. dry sherry or sake
Steamed white rice, such as basmati or jasmine

Chef's Notes

About . . .
Green tea is produced from tea leaves that are steamed and dried but not fermented.

Sake is a Japanese wine made from fermented rice.

Place the tea leaves in a glass measuring cup and pour the boiling water atop the tea leaves. Allow to steep for 15 minutes.

Heat the oil in a large skillet until very hot. Add the shrimp and sherry/sake and cook over high heat for 1 minute, stirring. Add the tea infusion and about ⅓ of the tea leaves, cooking for 1 additional minute.

Using a slotted spoon, remove the shrimp from the skillet and place on a warm serving platter. Reduce the cooking liquid in the skillet to about ¾ cup. When reduced, spoon over shrimp and serve at once with rice. Serves 3+.

The presentation of this dish is a simple labor of love, and the recipe itself presents a sampling of how delicate flavors can enhance without masking sensational seafood.

Crab Cakes with Mustard Crème Fraîche

Our customers can't get enough of crab cakes. From café menus to market kitchen to go, from catering events to the cooking school, we do crab cakes exceptionally well. This version is enhanced with creamy avocado and served with a spicy, rich accompaniment.

Cakes

2 lb. crab meat
3 cups Panko crumbs
1 lb. ripe avocados, diced then smashed
1 cup finely diced red bell pepper
1 cup finely diced yellow bell pepper
½ cup finely diced red onion
1 large egg + 1 egg white, beaten to blend
½ cup mayonnaise
¼ tsp. cayenne pepper
¼ cup thinly sliced chives
Butter and olive oil for frying

Mustard Crème Fraîche

1 cup crème fraîche
½ cup whole-grain mustard
½ cup apple juice
Sea salt to taste
Freshly ground black pepper to taste

For the Cakes: In a large bowl, mix crab, Panko crumbs, avocados, peppers, onion, egg blend, mayonnaise, cayenne pepper, and chives. Scoop and shape into 8 to 10 cakes. Set aside.

For the Mustard Crème Fraîche: In a medium mixing bowl combine the crème fraîche, mustard, apple juice, sea salt, and pepper, blending until well combined.

Turning once, sauté crab cakes in butter/oil mixture in a hot skillet until lightly browned on both sides and hot. Serve immediately with a few tablespoonfuls of the Mustard Crème Fraîche. Serves 5+.

Chef's Notes

About . . .
Look for crème fraîche in our dairy/cheese department. This matured, thickened cream has a slightly tangy flavor and a rich, velvety texture.

Panko crumbs, often referred to as Japanese breadcrumbs, are coarser than those normally used. Their texture creates crunch.

Blackened Sea Scallops

Our café often accompanies its plated Blackened Sea Scallops with steamed fresh kale and a lemon-butter sauce.

Cajun Seasoning

1 oz. garlic powder
1 oz. ground black pepper
1 oz. granulated onion
1 oz. ground cumin
1½ oz. sweet paprika
1½ oz. sea salt
¼ oz. cayenne pepper
½ oz. dried thyme
½ oz. dried oregano
¼ oz. ground white pepper

Lemon-Butter Sauce

Juice from 2 large lemons (about 8 tbsp.)
¼ cup white wine
1 tbsp. chopped fresh flat leaf (Italian) parsley
3 tbsp. butter, cut into pieces

Blackened Scallops

10 sea scallops
½ cup Cajun seasoning
¼ cup extra-virgin olive oil

For the Cajun Seasoning: In a medium bowl, mix all ingredients well to blend. Store in a glass jar with a tight-fitting lid.

For the Lemon-Butter Sauce: Add lemon juice and white wine to a small sauté pan. Cook over medium-high heat until mixture is reduced by a third. Add chopped parsley and butter in pieces. Remove from heat and whisk until butter is completely melted. Set aside.

For the Blackened Scallops: Pull muscle from scallops. Rinse and pat dry.

Dredge scallops in Cajun Seasoning. Add oil to a large sauté pan and just as oil reaches the smoke point, add the scallops. Sauté each side 2 to 3 minutes or until done to your likeness. Serve with Lemon-Butter Sauce. Serves 2.

Chef's Notes

How to Do It . . .
Sometimes you really need a kitchen scale for more accurate measurement of ingredients. Look for one that is in ounce increments and goes up to 1 pound, with a removable tray or flat surface.

Why settle for just mac and cheese when you can add a touch of fresh greens and a bit of spice with this Spinach Mac and Cheese with a Kick!

PLAYFUL PASTA

Pasta's popularity is easy to understand.

Pasta can be fun: from whimsical corkscrews to straightforward tubes.

Pasta can be creative: from soba noodles to slurp, to transparent cellophane noodles to savor.

Pasta can be dressed with a wide variety of sauces from rich and zesty to light and delicate.

Put on that big pot of water and start the boiling! This chapter is filled with ideas to get you started, complete with special combinations to fill your kitchen with alluring aromas and establish your reputation as an innovative cook, naturally.

Some of these recipes require some preplanning while others take only minutes to prepare, and most taste best when served immediately. For the quick, easy selections have everyone seated around the dinner table for some pre-pasta conversation as the pasta goes into the boiling water. No one will mind waiting briefly—and you'll love it when they applaud your virtuoso pasta performance!

Let the boiling begin . . .

Backyard Macaroni

Our market kitchen doesn't require that you eat this in your backyard . . . in fact, they invite you to enjoy it anywhere.

Backyard Macaroni Dressing

1½ cups mayonnaise
¼ cup sweet pickle juice (from jar of sweet pickles)
1½ tsp. celery seed
¼ tsp. sea salt

Salad

1 lb. elbow pasta
7 large hard-boiled eggs, peeled
16½ oz. pickle chips
¼ lb. roasted red bell pepper
1½ cups thinly sliced celery
¾ cup diced white onion
½ tsp. freshly ground black pepper
1 cup Backyard Macaroni Dressing

Chef's Notes

How to Do It . . .
The cooking time for pasta varies with the pasta size and shape, but the doneness test is the same for all: boil it al dente. Literally, this Italian term means "to the tooth"—tender but firm to bite—and that's the way pasta tastes best.

For the Backyard Macaroni Dressing: In a large bowl, combine the mayonnaise, juice, celery seed, and salt, mixing to blend well. Cover and refrigerate until ready to use.

For the Salad: Cook elbow macaroni until done but still firm to the bite. Drain, rinse with cold water to stop the cooking, then drain again.

Coarsely chop eggs and pickle chips. Thinly slice roasted red bell pepper.

In a large serving bowl, combine the pasta, eggs, pickle chips, bell pepper, celery, onion, and black pepper. Toss gently with the Dressing until well coated. Serve or cover and chill until ready to enjoy. Makes 6+ servings.

Spinach Mac and Cheese with a Kick

A creamy macaroni and cheese with a sprinkling of spinach and
a surprise—a flavorful, can't-get-enough-of-it kick!

½ lb. short, bite-size pasta
2 tbsp. extra-virgin olive oil, divided
2 tbsp. unsalted butter
1½ cups diced yellow onion
3 garlic cloves, minced
2 cups milk, whole or 2 percent
2 cups heavy (whipping) cream
1 tsp. sea salt
2 generous cups shredded cheddar cheese
½ cup freshly grated Parmesan cheese
10 oz. fresh spinach, stemmed, washed, and
torn into bite-size pieces
2 tbsp. chopped fresh marjoram leaves
2 tbsp. hot pepper sauce
1 tsp. freshly ground black pepper
Sprinkle of sweet paprika

Chef's Notes

How to Do It . . .
You want the cheese mixture to surround every curve
and groove of the pasta, so shape matters. Choose
tubular pasta, shells, or bow ties for this recipe.

Heat oven to 350 degrees. Lightly butter a 13x9"
baking dish.

Bring a large pot of water to a boil and stirring, cook
pasta until al dente. Drain in a colander and transfer
to a large bowl, adding *1 tbsp.* of the olive oil and
tossing well to coat.

In a large skillet over medium heat, melt the butter
with the remaining olive oil. Add the onion and
cook, stirring, until translucent. Add the garlic and
cook for 1 minute, stirring constantly so the garlic
doesn't brown. Add the milk, cream, and salt.
Reduce the heat to low and simmer, stirring occasionally, until the sauce is reduced by half and coats
the back of a spoon, about 20 minutes.

Remove the sauce from the heat and add the cheddar, Parmesan, spinach, marjoram, hot sauce, and
pepper. Stir until the cheeses melt and the spinach is
wilted. Pour into the bowl with the pasta, tossing
gently to coat well.

Transfer the pasta to a prepared baking dish, being
sure to scrape all the sauce out of the bowl! Bake for
40 minutes or until the sauce is bubbling around the
edges and the pasta is a light golden brown on top.
Remove from oven and let rest for 10 minutes before
serving. Sprinkle lightly with paprika and serve
warm. Serves 6+.

Orzo with Spicy Broccoli, Cauliflower, and Raisins

Broccoli and cauliflower, slightly spiced and combined with the sweet
crunch of raisins, make for a unique, flavorful pasta dish.

¾ cup orzo
2 tsp. extra-virgin olive oil
1 cup chopped yellow onion
1 garlic clove, pressed
3½ cups broccoli florets
3 cups cauliflower florets
¼ tsp. red pepper flakes
½ cup dry white wine
¼ cup seedless raisins
¼ tsp. sea salt
Freshly ground black pepper
½ cup coarsely grated sharp
cheddar cheese

Cook orzo until done; drain and set aside.

In a large nonstick skillet, heat oil over medium heat and sauté onion and garlic until the onion begins to soften. Add the broccoli, cauliflower, pepper flakes, wine, raisins, salt, and ground pepper. Cover pan; reduce heat and simmer until the vegetables are tender, about 10 minutes.

When vegetable mixture is done, combine with cooked orzo in a large serving bowl. Add the grated cheese, gently stirring to combine. Makes 4+ servings.

Chef's Notes

About . . .
Orzo is tiny durum wheat pasta that resembles rice.

Sesame Chicken Oriental Salad

▼

Once your cutting and assembling is complete,
this is an easy, satisfying noodle dish.

1 bunch scallions, trimmed and cut
into 2" pieces
1 whole skinned and boned chicken breast,
sliced crosswise into 3"x¼" strips
3 tbsp. toasted sesame oil, divided
½ cup water
⅓ cup creamy peanut butter
2 tbsp. soy sauce
¼ tsp. crushed red pepper flakes
8 oz. soba or udon noodles, cooked
3 large carrots, diagonally sliced then blanched
just until crisp-tender
½ lb. snow pea pods, stringed, halved on the
diagonal, then blanched just until crisp-tender
1 tbsp. toasted sesame seeds

Chef's Notes

About . . .
Udon noodles are a thick, slightly chewy Japanese
wheat noodle.

How to Do It . . .
To toast sesame seeds, place in a small skillet; shaking the pan, heat just until seeds are fragrant and
turn a light golden color.

Slit scallions ¾" deep at ends. Place in a large bowl of
ice water for up to 30 minutes to curl ends, then
drain and pat dry on paper towels.

Toss chicken with *1 tbsp.* of the sesame oil. Cook
chicken covered in a large nonstick skillet over
medium heat just until cooked through. Remove
from heat and cool slightly. Place chicken in a bowl
and refrigerate covered until ready to use.

In a large bowl, whisk together the water and peanut
butter until smooth. Add the soy sauce, *1 tbsp.* of the
sesame oil, and the red pepper flakes. Toss the
cooked noodles with the peanut butter mixture until
evenly coated. Place noodles in a large, low serving
bowl.

Toss carrots and snow peas with the remaining
sesame oil. Arrange the chicken, carrots, snow peas,
and scallions atop the noodles. Sprinkle with the
toasted sesame seeds. Toss lightly before serving.
Makes 5+ servings.

A playful pasta dish with Asian flavors, just waiting to be slurped and enjoyed.

Soba Noodles with Cilantro Sauce

This delicate dish with Asian flavors showcases soba noodles.

Noodles

8 oz. soba noodles
1 cup seeded, ¼" slices cucumber
1 cup ¼" strips red bell pepper
¾ cup (1"x¼") strips peeled carrot
1 tbsp. toasted sesame seeds
2 tbsp. jalapeño slices, optional

Sauce

⅓ cup packed fresh cilantro leaves
1½ tsp. granulated sugar
½ tsp. sea salt
1 tsp. finely chopped fresh garlic
1 tsp. finely chopped fresh ginger
2 tsp. Dijon mustard
2 tbsp. rice vinegar
3 tbsp. peanut oil

For the Noodles: Cook noodles as directed on package; rinse with cold water and drain well.

In a large bowl combine the cooked noodles, cucumber, pepper, carrot, sesame seeds, and jalapeño slices, if using.

For the Sauce: In a food processor or blender, combine the cilantro, sugar, salt, garlic, ginger, mustard, and vinegar. Process until well blended, stopping to scrape down sides of work bowl. Continue processing while adding oil in a slow, steady stream until well blended.

Pour Sauce over noodle mixture, tossing gently to coat. Serves 4.

Chef's Notes

About . . .
Soba, a Japanese buckwheat noodle, has a nutty flavor and a great nutritional profile (they're high in protein and fiber).

Asian Noodle Salad

Chilling this salad allows the flavors of the dressing to be absorbed by the tofu and noodles. A favorite in the cooking school.

Salad

2 medium carrots, cut into matchstick pieces
1 package udon or soba noodles
1 cup firm, refrigerated tofu, drained, pressed, and cubed
4 scallions, thinly sliced

Dressing

1 tbsp. toasted hot-pepper sesame oil
1 tbsp. toasted sesame oil
2 tbsp. umeboshi plum vinegar
¼ cup tahini
3 garlic cloves, minced or pressed
2 tbsp. vegetable broth

Chef's Notes

About . . .
Tahini is a thick paste made from ground sesame seeds.

Umeboshi plum vinegar is a byproduct of the pickling of Japanese plums.

For the Salad: Blanch carrots briefly in boiling water, then shock in ice water to stop cooking and set color. Drain well.

Cook noodles according to package directions; rinse and drain.

In a large serving bowl, combine carrots, noodles, tofu, and scallions.

For the Dressing: In a small bowl mix together the oils, vinegar, tahini, garlic, and vegetable broth until well blended.

Toss Dressing with the noodle salad, blending well. Serve chilled. Makes 5+ servings.

Linguine with Spicy Lentil Sauce

Combining pasta and beans is an economical way to get a balanced meal in one bowl.

7-8 tbsp. extra-virgin olive oil, divided
1 cup finely chopped celery
2 carrots, peeled and finely chopped
2 cups coarsely chopped yellow onion
2 garlic cloves, coarsely chopped
1-2 fresh jalapeño peppers, seeded
and chopped
1 tsp. sea salt
½ tsp. crushed red pepper flakes
1½ cups lentils
5 cups water
1½ lb. linguine, freshly cooked
1 tsp. finely minced lemon zest
½ cup coarsely chopped fresh Italian
(flat-leaf) parsley

Heat 6 *tbsp.* of the olive oil in a large saucepan. Add the celery, carrots, onion, and garlic. Sauté over medium-high heat, stirring occasionally, until vegetables are soft and just beginning to turn golden brown, about 12 minutes.

Add the jalapeños, salt, and pepper flakes. Continue to sauté, allowing the vegetables to brown while watching carefully and stirring often so they don't burn.

Add the lentils and water and bring to a boil, then lower the heat, cover, and simmer until the lentils are soft but not falling apart, about 20 minutes.

Add the cooked linguine to the lentil sauce with the remaining olive oil. Fold in the lemon zest and parsley, toss gently but well to coat, and serve immediately. Serves 6+.

Chef's Notes

About . . .
Linguine are long, narrow, flat noodles, sometimes referred to as flat spaghetti.

How to Do It . . .
Browning the vegetables in olive oil, a technique used often in Italian cooking, increases the depth of flavor—a useful tip for vegetarian cooking.

Mediterranean Linguine

Flavors of the Mediterranean abound in this tuna-tomato-sauced pasta dish.

½ lb. linguine
¼ cup extra-virgin olive oil
2 tsp. minced garlic
½ tsp. crushed red pepper flakes
½ tsp. fennel seeds
2 5-oz. cans tuna packed in oil, drained
½ tsp. sea salt
1½ lb. ripe tomatoes, peeled, seeded, and
coarsely chopped; juices reserved
1 tsp. lemon zest
2 tbsp. finely chopped Italian (flat–leaf) parsley

Chef's Notes

About . . .
Fennel seeds have a sweet, delicate, aniselike aroma and flavor.

How to Do It . . .
Using the pasta water as needed adds some flavor and starch to the dish.

Cook the pasta in a large pot of boiling water until almost al dente. Drain, reserving some of the pasta water.

In a large skillet, heat olive oil over medium-high heat. Add the garlic, red pepper flakes, and fennel seeds and cook just until garlic is golden.

Add the tuna and salt; raise the heat to high and cook until the tuna begins to sizzle. Be careful not to break the fish apart too much. Add the tomatoes and their juices and bring mixture to a boil, then simmer over medium heat until tomatoes are softened, 2 to 3 minutes. Stir in the lemon zest.

Add the linguine to the sauce and cook over medium-low heat for 1 minute. Add the pasta water 1 tbsp. at a time if the pasta seems too dry. Serve immediately, garnished with the fresh parsley. Serves 2+.

Ravioli with Vegetable Sauce

Freshly cooked veggies add color and crunch to this comfort-food pasta dish.

9 oz. refrigerated cheese ravioli
2 tbsp. unsalted butter
1 cup frozen cut green beans, thawed, or fresh
in-season green beans, trimmed and halved
½ cup thinly sliced carrots
1 cup thickly sliced fresh white button or
cremini mushrooms
1 cup milk, whole or 2 percent
1 tbsp. unbleached, all-purpose flour
1 tbsp. chopped fresh basil leaves
¼ tsp. sea salt
⅛ tsp. freshly ground black pepper
¼ cup sour cream

Chef's Notes

How to Do It . . .
Some prefer this dish as is, with its simple flavors. If you'd like to spice things up, sauté some sliced hot peppers with the beans and carrots or toss some hot pepper sauce into the sauce mixture.

Cook ravioli to desired doneness as directed on package. Drain, rinse with hot water, and keep warm.

Melt butter in a large skillet over medium heat. Add green beans and carrots and cook until crisp-tender, stirring continuously. Add mushrooms and sauté until tender.

In a small bowl, whisk together the milk, flour, basil, salt, and pepper. Blend well. Add to the vegetables and cook until mixture thickens and boils, stirring constantly.

Stir in the sour cream; heat thoroughly. Serve over hot ravioli. Makes 2+ servings.

Fresh Spinach Bacon Sauce

With the inclusion of spinach and whipped ricotta cheese, this sauce ends
up having a sweet, smooth flavor. Enjoy on your favorite pasta.

½ cup diced bacon
1 cup chopped yellow onion
1 tbsp. minced garlic
8 cups fresh spinach, stemmed, cleaned, and
torn into bite-size pieces
½ cup dry white wine
½ cup chicken broth
¾ cup ricotta cheese
¼ cup freshly grated Parmesan cheese
¼ tsp. freshly grated nutmeg
⅛ tsp. cayenne pepper
Sea salt to taste

Sauté bacon in a large skillet until crisp and lightly golden. Add onion, garlic, and spinach; cook until onions soften and spinach begins to wilt. Remove from skillet to a bowl and set aside.

Deglaze skillet with the wine and chicken broth over medium heat, stirring and scraping to remove every last tasty particle.

In a food processor, blend ricotta cheese until "whipped." Add spinach mixture, deglazed pan juices, Parmesan, nutmeg, pepper, and salt. Pulse once or twice to combine, then toss with hot pasta. Makes 2 cups of sauce.

Chef's Notes

How to Do It . . .
Deglazing is done by heating a small amount of liquid in the bottom of the skillet and stirring to loosen browned bits of food that were cooked onto the bottom. These bits add extra flavor to the final dish and are simply too good to scrub away in the kitchen sink!

Marinated Tomato and Basil Sauce
with Garlic Breadcrumbs

When tomatoes are fresh, local, and drip-down-your-chin juicy,
this is the perfect pasta sauce to make!

Garlic Breadcrumbs
Garlic
Extra-virgin olive oil
Bakery bread

Sauce
1½ lb. tomatoes, cored, cut in half
crosswise, and seeded
¼ cup extra-virgin olive oil
4 garlic cloves, finely chopped
⅓ cup coarsely chopped fresh basil
½ tsp. sea salt
¼ tsp. freshly ground black pepper
½ cup Garlic Breadcrumbs
Freshly grated Parmesan cheese

Chef's Notes

About . . .
It's not necessary to peel the tomatoes for this sauce
recipe because they're just heated through and not
cooked long enough to lose their skins.

How to Do It . . .
Adding unexpected texture and garlic flavor, the
crispy Garlic Breadcrumbs are not an exact science
of a recipe. I make mine with our bakery's baguette or
Pain au Levain bread. This simple recipe leaves the
garlic decision to you, so use as much or as little as
you'd like.

Heat oven to 325 degrees.

For the Garlic Breadcrumbs: Peel and finely chop the
garlic and add to the olive oil.

Thinly slice the bread and brush it on one side with
the garlic oil. Lay the brushed slices on a baking
sheet and toast for about 10 minutes, until they are
crisp and golden. Set aside to cool.

Break up the slices, then grind them in a food processor, leaving the texture a little coarse.

For the Sauce: Cut the tomatoes into large pieces
and toss in a medium bowl with the olive oil, garlic,
basil, sea salt, and black pepper. Set aside covered to
marinate for 30 minutes.

Transfer the tomatoes to a large sauté pan and quickly warm them over medium heat. (Be sure not to
cook them or their skins will separate.)

Toss with pasta of your choice and sprinkle generously with the crumbs, serving with freshly grated
Parmesan cheese. Serves 4+.

Lemon Pesto Sauce

This bright, citrus-flavored pesto is perfect to
toss with hot pasta of your choosing.

¼ cup blanched whole almonds
2 large garlic cloves, quartered
3 cups loosely packed fresh basil leaves
½ cup extra-virgin olive oil
¼ cup freshly grated Parmesan cheese
3 tbsp. fresh lemon juice

Chef's Notes

How to Do It . . .
As a general rule, 1 cup of pesto is enough for ½ lb.
cooked pasta.

In a food processor or blender, cover and process almonds until finely chopped. Add the garlic; process just until blended. Add the basil leaves and pulse to chop.

With the machine running, slowly add oil in a thin, steady stream, processing until the mixture is combined and slightly chunky. Add the cheese and lemon juice. Blend just until combined. Makes 1 cup.

Turkey Meatball Sauce

For those who prefer their meatballs made from ground turkey, this flavorful sauce is easy to put together and if you make extra, freezes well.

12 oz. ground turkey
4 oz. turkey sausage, casings removed, crumbled
4 tbsp. freshly grated Parmesan cheese
2 tbsp. finely chopped Italian (flat-leaf) parsley
4 garlic cloves, minced, divided
2 tsp. chopped fresh thyme
¾ tsp. sea salt
½ tsp. freshly ground black pepper
2 tsp. extra-virgin olive oil
1 cup coarsely chopped yellow onion
28-oz. can crushed tomatoes
Sea salt to taste
Freshly ground black pepper to taste

In a medium bowl, mix together the turkey, sausage, cheese, parsley, *half* of the garlic, thyme, salt, and pepper. Form mixture into 1" meatballs, making about 1 dozen.

Heat oil in a large nonstick skillet over medium heat. Add onion and sauté until softened. Add remaining garlic, stirring 1 minute. Add tomatoes and bring mixture to a boil. Reduce heat to medium and simmer until sauce thickens slightly, about 12 minutes. Season with salt and pepper.

Add meatballs to sauce. Reduce heat to medium low, cover, and simmer until meatballs are cooked through, about 15 minutes. Serve with your favorite pasta. Makes about 4 cups of sauce.

Anything-but-Boring Tomato Sauce

What could sound more ho-hum than pasta with baked tomato sauce?
Yet this extremely simple pasta dish will surprise you with its fresh
flavors and inspire you to make it again (and again).

2 tbsp. extra-virgin olive oil, plus more for
brushing pan
1 lb. very ripe cherry tomatoes, halved
(preferably red and yellow)
⅓ cup plain dry breadcrumbs
¼ cup freshly grated Parmigiano-
Reggiano cheese
3 tbsp. freshly grated Romano cheese
2 garlic cloves, pressed
Sea salt to taste
Freshly ground black pepper to taste
¼ cup loosely packed fresh basil leaves, torn
into bite-size pieces

Chef's Notes

How to Do It . . .
Time the boiling of the pasta so it finishes cooking
about the time the tomatoes are ready to come out of
the oven.

Heat oven to 400 degrees. Lightly brush a 13x9" baking dish with olive oil.

Place tomatoes cut side up in the dish.

In a small bowl, combine breadcrumbs, cheeses, and garlic and toss with a fork to mix well. Sprinkle the breadcrumb mixture over the tomatoes, making sure that each side is well covered. Sprinkle with salt and pepper. Bake until the tomatoes are cooked through and starting to brown on top, about 20 minutes.

When the tomatoes are done, add the basil and stir to mix everything well to make a "sauce." Toss your just-cooked pasta with the remaining olive oil and transfer to a large serving bowl with the hot Anything-but-Boring sauce; toss to coat and serve immediately. Makes enough sauce to cover about 1 lb. of pasta.

A quick roast of fresh, organic cherry tomatoes makes for a seasonal tomato sauce bursting with flavors.

Rich Squash Sauce

*Fall flavors with a hint of freshly grated nutmeg make
for a silky, smooth, satisfying sauce.*

¼ cup unsalted butter
1 leek, cleaned and diced
1 celery rib, diced
3 lb. peeled, seeded, chopped butternut squash
or pumpkin
1¾ cup chicken broth or vegetable broth
½ tsp. sea salt
½ tsp. freshly ground black pepper
¾ tsp. freshly grated nutmeg
⅔ cup half-and-half or heavy
(whipping) cream
½ cup freshly grated Parmesan cheese

Chef's Notes

How to Do It . . .
Nutmeg graters and grinders are small tools used to
turn a whole nutmeg seed into a coarse powder,
yielding a delicately warm, spicy-sweet aroma and
flavor that shines compared to already ground nutmeg.

Melt the butter in a large saucepan over medium
heat; add leek and celery and sauté until tender. Add
the squash; sauté 3 minutes. Add the broth and bring
to a boil. Cover, reduce heat, and simmer for 25 minutes or until tender. Add salt, pepper, and nutmeg.

Let cool slightly, then process squash mixture in a
blender until smooth.

Return to saucepan; stir in half-and-half or heavy
cream and cook over low heat until blended and
heated through, stirring often. Serve over freshly
cooked pasta and top with the cheese when serving.
Makes 5+ servings.

Artichoke and Mushroom Sauce

Artichokes and citrus blend well together, and mushrooms
add earthy overtones to this change-of-pace sauce.

2 tbsp. extra-virgin olive oil
8 oz. white button, cremini, or shiitake
mushrooms, thinly sliced
2 garlic cloves, pressed
1 tsp. dried oregano, crushed
9 oz. artichoke hearts, drained and thinly sliced
1½ cups chicken broth or vegetable broth
2 tsp. fresh lemon juice
1 tsp. finely grated lemon zest
¼ tsp. crushed red pepper flakes
5 tbsp. unsalted butter, room temperature
1½ tbsp. chopped fresh Italian
(flat-leaf) parsley
¾ cup freshly grated Asiago cheese

Heat oil in a large skillet over medium heat. Sauté the mushrooms, garlic, and oregano until golden. Add the artichokes and sauté 4 minutes. Stir in the broth, juice, zest, and crushed pepper flakes, cooking until slightly thickened, about 5 minutes. Add butter, whisking just until melted.

When ready to serve, add your cooked pasta and the parsley. Toss until pasta is coated and heated through. Add the Asiago cheese and toss to coat. Serve immediately. Makes 3+ servings.

Chef's Notes

About . . .
Asiago is a semifirm Italian cheese with a rich, nutty flavor often referred to as "poor man's Parmesan."

In Season . . .
Shiitake mushrooms have a full-bodied flavor. Their stems are extremely tough and not edible but add wonderful flavor to stocks and sauces.

Greek Pasta Sauce

This quick, easy pasta sauce is a festival of Greek flavors that will soon become a part of your weeknight cooking repertoire.

2 tsp. Greek extra-virgin olive oil
½ cup chopped kale
½ cup chopped red bell pepper
½ cup chopped fresh tomatoes, in season, or canned, undrained plum tomatoes
1 tbsp. minced fresh garlic
¼ tsp. dried basil, crushed
Dash red pepper flakes
¾ cup crumbled feta cheese
3 tbsp. chopped fresh Italian (flat-leaf) parsley
¼ tsp. freshly ground black pepper
¼ tsp. sea salt

Heat oil in a large nonstick skillet over medium-high heat. Add the kale, bell pepper, tomatoes, garlic, basil, and red pepper flakes and cook until softened, stirring frequently. Add feta cheese and cook just until cheese begins to soften and melt. Add parsley, black pepper, and salt. Stir and toss immediately with hot cooked pasta of your choice. Makes 4+ servings.

Chef's Notes

About . . .
Greek olive oil gives this sauce a peppery, full-bodied flavor.

QUENCH YOUR THIRST

Your beverage should be more than just a way to quench that thirst.

Our fair trade organic coffees and teas give you an opportunity to feel good about what you're drinking . . . an eco-friendly way to give back and help ensure that others get a fair price for their work efforts, something we all expect and oftentimes take for granted. Our smoothies should nourish and satisfy you, and our hot drinks—Mulled Wine with Citrus or White Hot Chocolate—should warm you and perk your appetite or provide a sweet ending to a satisfying meal. Our juice bar specialties should just make you smile . . . the names, Beet Me Up, Scotty or Pulp Friction, and the presentation (Sunrise, Sunset) are sensational.

Quench your curiosity and your thirst with this chapter's recipes . . . and have some fun in the process!

Lavender Cooler

Lavender flowers provide a subtle purplish color and a refreshing, calming flavor to this summertime cooler. Perfect for a baby shower or an outdoor wedding reception.

3 cups granulated sugar
3 cups water
½ cup dried lavender flowers
4 cups fresh lemon juice
8 cups cold water, regular or sparkling
Ice

Chef's Notes

In Season . . .
Lavender is a relative of mint, with aromatic violet flowers and pale green-gray leaves. Dried lavender flowers are available in bulk in our health and beauty department.

Combine the sugar and water in a medium saucepan. Bring to a boil; reduce heat, stirring often, until sugar is dissolved.

Place the lavender flowers in a large heatproof bowl. Pour the syrup over the dried flowers, pressing down to submerge. Let steep for 2 hours or until completely cool.

Strain the syrup through a fine sieve, pressing gently on the flowers to extract all the liquid. Discard the flowers and cover and refrigerate the syrup for up to 1 week.

When ready to serve, in a *very large* pitcher measure 4 cups of the lavender syrup. Add the lemon juice and the cold water. Stir well to combine. Serve over ice in tall glasses. Serves about 18.

Opposite: Sunrise, Sunset (or both?) . . . The only dilemma this drink presents is when to enjoy it.

Tropical Dream

Escape with a refreshing taste of the tropics.

3.5 oz. pineapple juice
3.5 oz. orange juice
2 oz. frozen banana chunks
3 oz. coconut juice
Orange or pineapple wedge for garnish

Blend together the pineapple juice, orange juice, banana, and coconut juice until smooth. Pour into a 12-oz. chilled glass and garnish with an orange or pineapple wedge. Serves 1.

Sunrise, Sunset

Reminiscent of a beautiful, golden red sunset . . .
This is a juice bar standout!

4.5 oz. pineapple juice
4.5 oz. orange juice
3 oz. strawberry puree
Pineapple wedge for garnish

In a 12-oz. glass, pour the pineapple juice, then the orange juice. With the bottom end of a long-handled spoon, slowly stir strawberry puree into glass, lightly and gently swirling puree into drink. Serve immediate with a pineapple wedge. Serves 1.

Luscious Fruit Smoothie

Tropical fruits wake up your taste buds in this delectable smoothie.

8-oz. can pineapple chunks, juice packed
1 large ripe mango, cut into chunks
1 large ripe banana, peeled and sliced
8 oz. pineapple yogurt
1½ cups ice cubes
Fresh mint leaves and additional cubed
mango for garnish

Chef's Notes

How to Do It . . .
Once peeled and frozen, the banana will turn dark—but this won't affect the overall color or flavor of this smoothie.

Drain pineapple, reserving juice. Cover and chill the juice.

In a medium freezer-proof bowl, combine the pineapple, mango, and banana. Cover and freeze for 2 hours or until firm.

When ready to serve, in a blender combine reserved pineapple juice, frozen fruit, and pineapple yogurt. Blend until smooth.

With blender running, add ice cubes a few at a time through opening in lid. Blend until smooth. Serve immediately, garnishing with fresh mint and cubed mango. Serves 3+ (8-oz. servings).

Sparkling Red Raspberry or Strawberry Lemonade

Perfect for summer sipping and tempting enough to
set up your own lemonade stand!

3 cups freshly squeezed lemon juice (from
about 15 large lemons)
2 tsp. finely chopped fresh mint
1 cup red raspberries or strawberries,
mashed with a fork
1½ cups granulated sugar
3 qt. sparkling water, cold

Stir together the lemon juice, mint, berries, and sugar until the sugar dissolves. When ready to serve, stir in the sparkling water. Pour into pitchers and serve well chilled over ice. Makes about 1 gallon.

Chef's Notes

How to Do It . . .
Garnish with fresh whole raspberries or strawberries, sliced lemons, and mint leaves if desired.

In Season . . .
Not in the mood to juice 15 lemons? Check our grocery aisles for organic 100 percent pure lemon juice—it's the perfect substitute.

Pulp Friction

We also provide a nondairy alternative for our juice bar
customers, using their choice of ice-cream substitutes.

2 scoops vanilla ice cream
3 oz. orange juice
3 oz. pineapple juice
Whipped cream for topping
Pineapple or orange wedge for garnish

In a blender, combine ice cream, orange juice, and pineapple juice, blending well to combine. Pour into 12-oz. glass. Top with whipped cream; garnish with a pineapple or orange wedge. Serves 1.

Berry Delicious

Do we tell you that you'll be at your "berry" best after
enjoying this? Thankfully, no, but we should!

8 oz. apple juice
1 oz. frozen red raspberries
1 oz. frozen strawberries, plus wedge
for garnish
1 oz. frozen blueberries
1 oz. frozen pitted sour cherries

In a blender, combine the apple juice, raspberries, strawberries, blueberries, and cherries. Blend until thick and smooth. Pour into a 12-oz. glass and garnish with a fresh strawberry wedge. Serves 1.

Chef's Notes

How to Do It . . .
All of these frozen fruits should be unsweetened. Frozen pitted Bing (sweet) cherries can be substituted for the sour ones.

Strawberry Green Tea Cooler

Created for a tea class in the cooking school, this is an
often requested, refreshing beverage.

1 pt. fresh strawberries, stemmed and halved,
plus more for garnish
¼ cup honey
6 oz. frozen orange juice concentrate,
partially thawed
2 cups brewed green tea, cooled completely
Fresh mint sprigs

In a blender, combine the strawberries with the honey, blending until smooth. Add the orange juice concentrate and blend until well combined.

Remove from blender and stir mixture into a pitcher with the green tea infusion, stirring to blend well. If desired, cooler can be served over ice. Garnish with a strawberry wedge or fresh mint sprig. Makes 4 servings (¾ cup each).

Chef's Notes

About . . .
Green tea is produced from tea leaves that are steamed and dried but not fermented.

Opposite: A delightful blend of in-season, organic strawberries with green tea . . . and, pun intended, it's a honey of a drink!

Beet Me Up, Scotty!

Live long and prosper . . . and enjoy this juice bar favorite often!

¾ cup stemmed spinach
5 sprigs curly parsley
6 oz. carrot juice
1 oz. beet juice
Lemon wedge or cucumber slice for garnish

Juice the spinach and parsley in a juicer, then combine with the carrot juice and beet juice. Pour into a 12-oz. glass and garnish with a lemon wedge or fresh cucumber slice. Serves 1.

Chef's Notes

How to Do It . . .
Fresh is best, so you'll need a quality juicer to juice just before serving, as we do in our juice bars.

Opposite: Will drinking this help you get your Klingon?!

Cranberry Champagne Sparkler

Cranberry syrup gives this drink color and sparkle. It's the perfect beverage for a special occasion toast or a holiday celebration.

3 cups fresh cranberries, divided
1 large lemon
½ cup granulated sugar
¾ cup water
4 inches stick cinnamon, broken
5 whole cloves
½ cup honey
¼ cup fresh lemon juice
Decorative ice ring
1 bottle champagne, chilled

Reserve ⅓ *cup* of the cranberries for garnish, freezing on a tray until ready to use.

Using a vegetable peeler, remove strips of peel from the lemon. Combine the peel, sugar, water, cinnamon, and cloves in a medium saucepan. Bring to a boil, stirring to dissolve sugar. Add the remaining 2⅔ cups cranberries.

Return mixture just to boiling while stirring constantly. Reduce heat, cover, and simmer 5 minutes. Remove from heat and cool completely to room temperature. Stir in honey and lemon juice. Press mixture through a sieve, discarding solids. Cover and chill syrup at least 1 hour or up to 3 days.

To serve, combine syrup and ice ring in a punch bowl. Slowly add champagne, stirring gently to combine. Ladle into glasses or punch cups. Garnish with reserved frozen cranberries. Serves 4+.

Mulled Wine with Citrus

No matter what your price point, our wine department will
advise you on the perfect wine for this recipe.

750-ml bottle dry red wine
1 cup granulated sugar
½ cup fresh lemon juice
2 lemons cut into ¼"-thick rounds
1 orange cut into ¼"-thick rounds
3 cinnamon sticks, broken in half
20 whole cloves
1 tsp. whole allspice berries

In a large saucepan combine the wine, sugar, juice, lemon rounds, orange rounds, cinnamon, cloves, and allspice. Cook covered over low heat for 1 hour to allow flavors to blend (being sure not to boil). When ready to serve, ladle hot wine into mugs and enjoy. Makes 6+ servings.

Chef's Notes

How to Do It . . .
Place the cinnamon stick pieces, cloves, and whole allspice berries into a cheesecloth tied with twine or a tea-infuser ball, making them easier to get out when the mixture is ready to serve.

Warm Spiced Cranberry Cider

Perfect for a holiday get-together or tailgating party.

Zest and fruit of 1 large navel orange, fruit cut into large chunks, plus slices for garnish
4 cups cider
4 cups cranberry juice
4 cinnamon sticks
¼ cup firmly packed light brown sugar

Chef's Notes

How to Do It . . .
If not using immediately, cool, cover, and refrigerate overnight. Reheat just before serving.

Put orange zest and fruit into a food processor or blender and pulse several times until coarsely chopped.

Place orange mixture, cider, cranberry juice, cinnamon sticks, and brown sugar in a large saucepan. Stirring, heat over medium-high heat until hot.

Strain mixture and return to saucepan to keep warm. When ready to serve, pour into mugs and garnish each serving with an orange wedge. Makes 8 servings (1 cup each).

Hot Strawberry Cider

Since cider and strawberries are not in season at the same time,
frozen strawberries work well in this recipe.

8 cups apple cider
10 oz. frozen sliced strawberries
4" stick cinnamon
1 tsp. whole cloves
Apple slices and cinnamon sticks for garnish

Combine cider, strawberries, stick cinnamon, and cloves in a large saucepan. Bring to a boil, reduce heat, then cover and simmer for 10 minutes. Strain through a cheesecloth-lined sieve.

When ready to serve, pour cider mixture into heat-proof glasses or mugs. Garnish each serving with an apple slice and a cinnamon stick. Makes 8 servings (1 cup each).

White Hot Chocolate

White chocolate elevates that cold weather favorite,
hot chocolate, to the next level.

¼ cup half-and-half
¾ cup coarsely chopped white chocolate
3" stick cinnamon
⅛ tsp. freshly grated nutmeg
2¼ cups milk, whole or 2 percent
1 tsp. pure vanilla extract
¼ tsp. pure almond extract
Ground cinnamon

Combine half-and-half, white chocolate, stick cinnamon, and nutmeg in a medium saucepan, whisking over low heat until chocolate is melted. Remove stick cinnamon. Add the milk, whisking until hot but not boiling.

Remove from heat and stir in the vanilla and almond extracts. Serve warm in cups or mugs, topped with a sprinkling of ground cinnamon. Serves 4.

Chef's Notes

About . . .
When purchasing white chocolate, be sure to read the label. If cocoa butter isn't mentioned, the product is simply an overly sweet, artificial confectionary coating.

How to Do It . . .
To create a foamy layer on top, blend some of the hot chocolate mixture in a blender until frothy and add to each serving.

Opposite: A sweet, satisfying white hot chocolate drink—the perfect way to chase your chills away.

Tofu Oatloaf, served atop greens and often ladled with some vegan gravy, is one of our hearty signature dishes.

MUSTARD SEED MARKET & CAFÉ CLASSICS

Arguably, all the recipes in this cookbook are Mustard Seed Market classics—newly introduced or time-tested and treasured dishes. However, when you mention the collection of recipes in this chapter, everyone (customers and employees) always responds in the same way—"Oh, that's a classic."

So here we present a chapter on our classics, signature items that are loved and treasured, imprints of creative cooks and chefs who have left their mark and taste on Mustard Seed Market & Café.

No-Bull Chili

A flavorful, meatless chili that's a customer favorite. (Face up
to it, doesn't the name just make you smile?!)

¾ lb. chopped yellow onion
¾ lb. chopped carrot
2 tbsp. canola oil
26.5 oz. tomato sauce
½ lb. corn kernels, fresh in season or frozen
½ cup masa harina
1 tbsp. ground cumin
1 tsp. garlic powder
1 tsp. granulated onion
1 tbsp. dried oregano, crushed
1½ tsp. chili powder or more to taste
2 tsp. sea salt
4-5 cups cooked kidney beans

In a large saucepan, sauté the onion and carrot in the canola oil until onion is transparent, stirring often. Stir in the tomato sauce, corn, masa harina, cumin, garlic powder, granulated onion, oregano, chili powder, and salt, blending well to combine. Add the kidney beans and simmer for 1 hour or until desired thickness. Serves 4+.

Chef's Notes

About . . .
Masa harina is flour made from dried masa, the traditional dough used to make corn tortillas.

Tofu Oatloaf

A variation on a meatloaf theme, the oatloaf lends itself perfectly to leftovers, especially in whole-grain sandwiches for tomorrow's lunch.

Canola oil for greasing pan
15 oz. packed refrigerated, firm tofu, drained
1⅛ lb. rolled oats
1⅛ lb. Texturized Vegetable Protein (TVP)
½ cup finely chopped yellow onion
6.5 oz. diced tomatoes
6.5 oz. tomato sauce
½ cup finely chopped fresh Italian (flat-leaf) parsley
¼ cup tamari
¼ cup stone-ground mustard
2 tsp. granulated onion
1½ tsp. garlic powder
½ tsp. freshly ground black pepper
1 tsp. sea salt

Chef's Notes

How to Do It . . .
Restaurant recipes don't easily convert to cups and teaspoons for the home cook. For a more accurate measure, it's best to use a kitchen scale for weighing some of these ingredients.

Heat oven to 325 degrees. Grease a loaf pan.

In a large bowl of an electric mixer, beat tofu on lowest speed until crumbled. Add the oats, TVP, onion, tomatoes, sauce, parsley, tamari, mustard, granulated onion, garlic powder, pepper, and salt. Mix until completely blended, occasionally stopping to scrape down sides of the bowl. Place into greased pan.

Cover with foil and place loaf pan in a larger baking pan. Carefully add hot water to reach 1" up sides of larger pan. Bake/steam in oven for 30 minutes.

Remove from the oven and carefully remove loaf pan from water bath. Return only the loaf pan to the oven and bake for 50 minutes. Uncover and allow to bake for 10 additional minutes. Cool briefly on a wire rack, slice, and serve. Serves 6+.

Chicken Quesadilla

*An assortment of steps goes into our chicken quesadilla . . .
and that's why it's been a longtime café classic.*

Refried Beans

2 cups cooked black beans
1 tsp. chopped fresh cilantro
2 tbsp. finely minced yellow onion
1 garlic clove, pressed
¼ tsp. ground coriander
½ tsp. ground cumin
¼ tsp. chili powder
¼ tsp. sea salt
Pinch of cayenne pepper

Chicken Salad Dressing

1 cup mayonnaise
1½ tsp. stone-ground mustard
½ tsp. sea salt
⅛ tsp. freshly ground black pepper
½ tsp. dried thyme, crushed
½ tsp. dried basil, crushed
¼ tsp. dried oregano, crushed

Chicken Salad

3 cups cubed, cooked chicken breast
¼ cup finely chopped yellow onion
¼ cup finely chopped red onion
¼ cup finely chopped celery
1 tbsp. diced green bell pepper
2 tbsp. diced red bell pepper
1 tbsp. diced yellow bell pepper
¾ cup Chicken Salad Dressing or enough to
moisten Chicken Salad

Quesadilla

2 8" whole-wheat tortillas
5 oz. Refried Beans
5 oz. Chicken Salad
5 oz. cooked short-grain brown rice
1 oz. shredded cheddar cheese
1 oz. shredded Monterey Jack cheese
1 oz. sliced, pitted ripe black olives
1 oz. seeded, chopped tomatoes
½ oz. chopped scallions
2 oz. sour cream
3 oz. salsa

For the Refried Beans: In a medium bowl, mash the cooked beans and combine with the cilantro, onion, garlic, coriander, cumin, chili powder, salt, and cayenne pepper. Cover and refrigerate until needed.

For the Chicken Salad Dressing: Combine the mayonnaise, mustard, salt, pepper, thyme, basil, and oregano in a small bowl, blending well. Cover and refrigerate until needed.

For the Chicken Salad: In a large bowl, combine the chicken, onions, celery, peppers, and Chicken Salad Dressing, mixing well until moistened and well blended. Cover and refrigerate until needed.

For the Quesadilla: Place one tortilla on a work surface and top with ½ cup each of Refried Beans, Chicken Salad, and rice, spreading lightly but evenly to within 1" of the sides. Top mixture with second tortilla, pressing gently to seal. Top with cheeses, olives, tomatoes, and scallions. Place under broiler just to melt cheeses. Cut into fourths and serve with sides of salsa and sour cream. Serves 1 or 2.

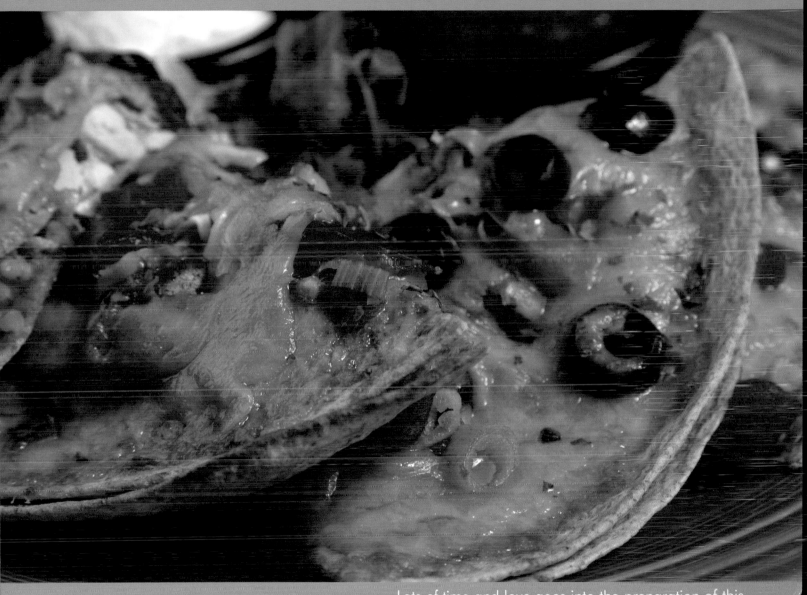

Lots of time and love goes into the preparation of this quesadilla recipe, a longtime customer favorite.

Bulgur Waldorf

Our take on a Waldorf salad. The addition of bulgur to this
Mustard Seed Market classic dish gives it whole-grain goodness.

5 cups apple juice, divided
3 cups seedless raisins
4 cups whole-wheat bulgur
3 cups walnuts, toasted
1 cup maple syrup
½ cup fresh lemon juice
1 tsp. pure vanilla extract
5 large or 8 small crisp, tart apples

In a large saucepan bring the apple juice to a boil. Add the raisins, then remove from heat and allow to cool slightly. Add the bulgur to the saucepan, cover, and set aside for 20 to 45 minutes or until liquid is absorbed.

Coarsely chop the walnuts.

In a medium bowl, whisk together the maple syrup, lemon juice, and vanilla. Core and cut the apples into a ½" dice. Add to the maple mixture, tossing well to coat.

In a large serving bowl combine the raisin/bulgur mixture with the walnuts and the apple mixture. Plate as individual servings. Serves 6+.

Hot Thai Salad

Our customers love the sweet and spicy flavors and the fresh crunch from this market kitchen salad.

Hot Thai Dressing

¾ cup + 2 tbsp. brown rice vinegar
¾ cup sherry wine vinegar
½ cup toasted sesame oil
1½ tbsp. chili oil
¼ tsp. cayenne pepper
⅛ tsp. sea salt

Salad

10 oz. udon noodles, cooked al dente
¼ cup Hot Thai Dressing
2 cups diced red bell pepper
2 cups diced green bell pepper
2 cups diced yellow bell pepper
2 bunches scallions, thinly sliced on
the diagonal
1 cup chopped fresh Italian (flat-leaf) parsley
1 cup black sesame seeds

For the Hot Thai Dressing: In a medium bowl, whisk together the vinegars, oils, pepper, and salt until well blended. Set aside until ready to use.

For the Salad: In a large serving bowl toss together the noodles, Hot Thai Dressing, peppers, scallions, and parsley, mixing until well combined. Toss in black sesame seeds and serve immediately. Serves 4+.

Chef's Notes

About . . .
Chili oil is vegetable oil in which hot red chilies have been steeped to release their heat and flavor.

Tangy Quinoa Salad

A nutty, flavorful grain salad.

Salad

2 cups quinoa
4 cups water
1 cup grated carrot
¾ cup finely chopped celery
2 medium tomatoes, chopped
1 large cucumber, seeded and diced
½ cup finely chopped fresh Italian
(flat-leaf) parsley
½ cup sliced, pitted ripe black olives
½ cup sunflower seeds, toasted or raw

Dressing

⅓ cup canola oil
⅓ cup fresh lemon juice
½ tsp. vegetable seasoning, or
more to taste
3 garlic cloves, minced or pressed, or
more to taste
2 tbsp. shoyu

For the Salad: Rinse quinoa thoroughly in a small strainer for several minutes. Drain. Place water and quinoa in a large saucepan, bring to a boil, reduce heat, and simmer for 20 minutes or until the quinoa is cooked and all the water has been absorbed.

Remove pan from the heat and fluff the grains with a fork. Turn quinoa into a large serving bowl, adding the carrot, celery, tomatoes, cucumber, parsley, and olives.

For the Dressing: Whisk the oil, juice, seasoning, garlic, and shoyu together in a small bowl and toss with salad, mixing gently to blend well. Cover and chill for 30 minutes to allow flavors a chance to blend.

Just before serving, toss in sunflower seeds. Serves 5+.

Chef's Notes

About . . .
Shoyu is Japanese for soy sauce.

Sold under various brands, vegetable seasoning is a salt-free seasoning alternative.

A Trio of Signature Dressings

These café from-scratch dressings are requested not only with our organic greens salads but also make a flavorful addition to freshly steamed veggies and brown rice.

Ranch Dressing

2½ cups buttermilk
2½ cups mayonnaise
½ cup finely chopped curly parsley
½ tbsp. granulated onion or to taste
½ tbsp. garlic powder or to taste
2½ tbsp. canola oil
3 tbsp. honey

Combine the buttermilk, mayonnaise, parsley, granulated onion, garlic powder, oil, and honey in a large bowl, blending well. Store covered in the refrigerator for up to 1 week. Makes about 5¾ cups.

Chef's Notes

How to Do It . . .
When measuring, remember that liquids are fluid ounces and not weights.

Sesame Tahini Dressing

1 cup tahini
1 cup canola oil
1 cup water
1½ oz. tamari
1½ oz. + ⅛ oz. fresh lemon juice
¾ oz. brown rice vinegar
1 scallion, very finely chopped

Combine the tahini, oil, water, tamari, lemon juice, vinegar, and scallion in a large bowl, blending well. Store covered in the refrigerator for up to 1 week. Makes about 4 cups.

Honey Mustard Dressing

2⅔ cups canola oil
⅔ cup stone-ground mustard
⅔ cup honey
1 tbsp. + 1 tsp. poppy seed
1 tbsp. white wine vinegar

Combine the oil, mustard, honey, poppy seed, and vinegar in a large bowl, blending well. Store covered in the refrigerator for up to 1 week. Makes about 4½ cups.

Tempeh Reuben

Seasoned tempeh served grilled on rye with Thousand Island Dressing, sauerkraut, and Swiss cheese with chili-roasted potatoes on the side . . . delicious!

Thousand Island Dressing

1 cup mayonnaise
¼ cup sweet pickle relish
⅓ cup ketchup

Tempeh Reuben

2 tbsp. corn oil
4 oz. veggie burger
2.5 oz. sauerkraut
2 slices rye bread
2 oz. sliced or shredded Swiss cheese
Thousand Island Dressing

For the Thousand Island Dressing: In a medium bowl, combine the mayonnaise, relish, and ketchup, stirring to blend well. Cover and refrigerate until ready to use.

For the Tempeh Reuben: Heat oil in a small sauté pan over medium heat. Sauté veggie burger for 2 minutes per side. Set aside on a paper towel to drain. Place sauerkraut in pan at low heat and warm.

Toast bread, then place Swiss cheese on toasted bread followed by veggie burger, sauerkraut, and enough Thousand Island Dressing to lightly coat. Serve immediately. Serves 1.

Brown-Rice Crust Pizza

We now have many customers who are wheat restricted, but
this crust gives them one of numerous tasty alternatives.

3 cups cooked short-grain or long-grain
brown rice
1 cup grated cheddar cheese
½ cup toasted sesame seeds
2 large eggs, beaten to blend
Favorite pizza sauce
Veggies, thinly sliced
Grated or shredded cheese

Heat oven to 400 degrees

Combine the cooled rice with cheese, sesame seeds, and eggs. Pat mixture onto a lightly greased or sprayed 12" pizza pan. Bake for 20 minutes.

Remove from oven and top with your favorite sauce, veggies, and cheese. Return to oven and continue baking until cheese is bubbly. Let stand 5 minutes, then cut into 8 pieces. Serves 4+.

Pizza, Your Way

This gluten-free crust is a perfect alternative to a wheat pizza crust.

1 tbsp. active dry yeast
⅔ cup brown rice flour, plus extra
for rolling dough
½ cup tapioca flour
2 tbsp. dry milk powder, regular or
nondairy milk powder
2 tsp. xanthan gum
½ tsp. sea salt
1 tsp. unflavored gelatin powder
¼ tsp. dried oregano, crushed
¼ tsp. dried basil, crushed
¼ tsp. granulated garlic
⅔ cup warm water
½ tsp. granulated sugar
1 tsp. extra-virgin olive oil
1 tsp. brown rice vinegar
Nonstick cooking spray
Favorite pizza sauce
Favorite toppings

Chef's Notes

About . . .
Xanthan gum is used as a stabilizer, emulsifier, and thickener and is produced from the fermentation of corn sugar.

How to Do It . . .
The thinner you can press the dough, the crisper and more flavorful it will taste.

Heat oven to 425 degrees.

In a large bowl with an electric mixer, blend the yeast, flours, milk powder, xanthan gum, salt, gelatin powder, oregano, basil, and granulated garlic at low speed. Add warm water, sugar, olive oil, and vinegar. Beat on medium speed for 4 minutes. Add additional water 1 tsp. at a time if needed to form a soft dough.

Drop dough onto a 12" pizza pan that has been lightly coated with cooking spray. Sprinkle some rice flour atop dough, then gently press dough onto pan, continuing to sprinkle dough with flour as needed to prevent your hands from sticking. A slight ridge around the edge will help contain your toppings.

Bake in center of the oven for 10 minutes. Remove from oven. Spread with your favorite sauce and toppings. Bake for an additional 20 to 25 minutes or until top is nicely browned. Serves 4+.

Health Club Wrap

This simple wrap, without high-fat condiments, is crisp and colorful.

1 12" spinach tortilla
1 12" tomato tortilla
½ cup seeded, diced tomato
¼ cup seeded, halved, then thinly
sliced cucumber
½ cup ripe, sliced avocado
4 oz. shredded yogurt cheese
1 oz. sprouts of your choice, washed, then
thoroughly dried

Layer 1 tortilla atop the other. On one half of the tortilla, layer tomatoes, cucumber, avocado, cheese, and sprouts. Roll up (wrap it up!) and enjoy. Serves 1.

Salmon Wrap

A fresh 5-oz. salmon fillet, grilled and wrapped in a spinach tortilla with our
Roasted Garlic Mayonnaise, shredded lettuce, and tomato. A café menu classic!

Roasted Garlic Mayonnaise

¾ cup peeled garlic cloves
1½ cups extra-virgin olive oil
2 cups mayonnaise

Wrap

½ cup extra-virgin olive oil
4 5-oz. pieces Black Pearl Salmon,
skinned and boned
4 12" spinach tortillas
1 cup diced tomatoes
2 cups shredded leaf or romaine lettuce
½ cup Roasted Garlic Mayonnaise

Chef's Notes

About . . .
Black Pearl Salmon is a natural choice for farm-raised salmon. Black Pearl Salmon's feed is free of animal proteins and added pigmenting compounds (colors). No chemicals, antibiotics, or pesticides are used in raising these salmon.

How to Do It . . .
To "roll and fold like a burrito," fold in the sides of the tortilla then roll the tortilla to completely enclose the filling.

Heat oven to 350 degrees.

For the Roasted Garlic Mayonnaise: Place garlic cloves in a 6" ovenproof sauté pan, add oil, and cook in the oven for 15 to 20 minutes or until golden brown. Allow to cool, then remove the cloves from the oil.

Place garlic cloves in a food processor and puree, adding mayonnaise and blending for 1 additional minute. Tightly covered, this will keep for 2 weeks in the refrigerator.

For the Wrap: Brush oil on both sides of the salmon pieces. Place salmon on a hot grill for 5 minutes on each side or until cooked.

While waiting for salmon to finish cooking, place tortillas on a work surface, equally dividing the tomatoes and lettuce between the four tortillas. Spoon the Roasted Garlic Mayonnaise over the tomato mixture, topping with the freshly grilled salmon pieces. Roll and fold like a burrito. Cut in half and enjoy. Serves 2+.

Opposite: Wrap your taste buds around this: freshly grilled salmon, roasted garlic mayo, and a spinach tortilla. Simply irresistible!

Mediterranean Chicken Wrap

Naturally raised boneless, skinless chicken tenders marinated with garlic, olive oil, herbs, and spices, then wrapped in a tomato tortilla with spinach, black olives, tomatoes, and feta cheese. A perfect wrap to lunch on or enjoy over a casual dinner conversation in our café.

Tapenade

½ cup medium dice pitted ripe black olives
½ cup medium dice pitted green olives
½ cup capers, drained
1 small red onion, finely diced
1 scallion, thinly sliced
1½ cups small dice tomatoes
½ cup feta cheese crumbles
½ cup grated Romano cheese
1 tbsp. finely chopped combination of fresh basil, thyme, and oregano
¾ cup extra-virgin olive oil

Wrap

4 5-oz. skinned, boned, split chicken breasts
2 garlic cloves, pressed
1 cup extra-virgin olive oil
1 tbsp. chopped fresh basil
½ tsp. freshly ground black pepper
4 12-oz. flour tortillas, regular, spinach, or tomato
1 cup shredded spinach
8 slices cucumber
1 cup chopped tomatoes
1 cup feta cheese, crumbled
8 oz. Tapenade

For the Tapenade: In a medium bowl, combine the olives, capers, onion, scallion, and tomatoes. Add the cheeses, herbs, and oil, tossing lightly to blend. Cover and refrigerate until ready to use.

For the Wrap: Marinate the chicken in the garlic, olive oil, basil, and black pepper for 30 minutes.

Remove chicken from marinade and place on hot grill. Cook on each side for about 4 minutes or just until cooked through and no longer pink. Cut chicken into strips; set aside.

Grill tortillas for about 15 seconds on each side. Place warmed tortillas on work station and top each with desired amount of shredded chicken strips, spinach, 2 slices of cucumber, 2 tbsp. tomatoes, 2 tbsp. feta, and 2 oz. of the Tapenade. Roll and fold like a burrito, cut in half, and enjoy! Serves 4+.

Persian Rice

*Dates and cashews give this short-grain rice salad a sweet,
pleasant flavor . . . it could easily pass for dessert.*

¼ cup extra-virgin olive oil
½ cup canola oil
⅓ cup fresh lemon juice
1 tbsp. dried dill weed, crushed
4 cups short-grain brown rice, steamed
⅓ lb. roasted, salted cashew pieces
½ lb. pitted dates, chopped
1 bunch scallions, finely chopped

In a medium bowl whisk together the oils, lemon juice, and dill weed.

In a large serving bowl, combine the rice, cashews, dates, and scallions. Pour oil mixture atop rice blend and toss gently but thoroughly to combine. Serves 4+.

Chef's Notes

How to Do It . . .
Chop dates by snipping them with a sharp pair of kitchen scissors dipped frequently in hot water.

This sweet Cookie Basket with Fruit and Creamy Amaretto Sauce has it all: texture, flavor, and a burst of color. Sharing is optional!

SWEET SOMETHINGS

All of us have some degree of a sweet tooth, and whether you love to spend all day baking an elaborate dessert, prefer one you can plan ahead and do your baking in stages, or want to whip up a quick sweet thing, explore this tasty chapter.

The desserts in this chapter reflect a certain sensibility. Once again, there are layers of flavors and textures perhaps you had not previously thought of. Sweet things elevated by the finest ingredients to appeal to an assortment of tastes:

• Homey desserts (Bittersweet Blueberry Clusters)
• Snacks or lunchtime treats (Giant Ginger Cookies)
• Share-with-company desserts (Cookie Baskets with Fruit and Creamy Amaretto Sauce)

Make them with love, then share and enjoy them!

Pumpkin "Gelato"

This is so simple, but students in Italian-themed
cooking classes love its simplicity and flavor.

1 qt. premium vanilla ice cream,
organic preferred
¾ cup pumpkin puree
1 tsp. ground cinnamon
Pinch ground cloves
Pinch ground ginger
Pinch ground allspice
1 tbsp. pure vanilla extract

Chef's Notes

About . . .
This is superb served atop a square of our bakery's
gingerbread.

Let the ice cream soften slightly at room temperature
for 10 to 15 minutes. Transfer the ice cream to a mixing bowl. With an electric mixer, beat the ice cream
just until creamy.

Add the pumpkin, cinnamon, cloves, ginger, allspice, and vanilla; blend on low speed until evenly
distributed. Working quickly, scrape the ice cream
into a serving bowl, using a large rubber spatula to be
sure you don't miss anything!

Refreeze for at least 6 hours before serving. This
freezes to a soft consistency. Makes about 1½ qt.

Dairy-Free Pumpkin Pie with Whole-Wheat Crust

Although especially popular in the fall, our vegan customers love these pies all year long.

Whole-Wheat Crust

¾ cup whole-wheat pastry flour
¾ cup white whole-wheat flour
1½ tsp. ground cinnamon
⅛ tsp. freshly grated nutmeg
Pinch of sea salt
¼ cup trans-fat-free shortening, cold
⅓ cup ice water
1 tbsp. fresh lemon juice or rice vinegar

Dairy-Free Pie Filling

18 oz. silken extrafirm tofu
2 cups pumpkin puree
⅔ cup honey or maple syrup
½ tsp. pure vanilla extract
2 tsp. ground cinnamon
½ tsp. freshly grated nutmeg

For the Whole-Wheat Crust: In a medium bowl, sift together the flours, cinnamon, nutmeg, and salt. Cut in the shortening, tossing until coarse crumbs form. Combine water with juice/vinegar and toss in only enough of the liquid to form a soft dough that holds together. Form into a flat disc and wrap in plastic wrap. Refrigerate for 30 minutes.

Drain tofu for the Filling in a colander while rolling Crust. Remove dough from refrigerator and roll into a 12" circle atop waxed paper. Gently place on baking sheet and refrigerate for 40 minutes to prevent dough from shrinking.

When ready to bake, heat oven to 350 degrees. Place dough in a 9" pie pan and crimp edges. Lightly pierce dough all over, then partially bake for 12 minutes. While baking, prepare filling.

For the Dairy-Free Pie Filling: In a food processor or blender, blend drained tofu until smooth. Add the pumpkin, honey/maple syrup, vanilla, cinnamon, and nutmeg. Pour into partially baked pie crust. Bake for 1 hour; filling will be soft but will firm as it chills. Chill at least 4 hours and serve. Serves 6+.

Honey Cake with Honey-Orange Syrup

A satisfying, rich, moist cake.

Honey-Orange Syrup

½ cup honey
3 tbsp. orange juice concentrate, thawed
1 tbsp. finely grated orange zest

Honey Cake

1 cup honey
1 cup unsweetened applesauce
3 large eggs, lightly beaten
1½ cups unbleached, all-purpose flour or
whole-wheat pastry flour, plus additional for
dusting pan
¾ tsp. baking soda
¼ tsp. sea salt
½ tsp. freshly grated ginger
¾ cup toasted walnut pieces, finely ground

Heat oven to 350 degrees. Grease and flour a 9" springform pan; set aside.

For the Honey-Orange Syrup: In a small bowl, whisk all ingredients until well blended. Set aside.

For the Honey Cake: In a large bowl, stir together the honey, applesauce, and eggs, whisking until blended.

In a medium bowl, whisk together the flour, baking soda, and salt; stir in the ginger. Add to the honey mixture and fold in the walnuts.

Pour batter into prepared pan and bake until a toothpick inserted in the center comes out clean, 40 to 45 minutes.

Transfer pan to a wire rack and let cool for 30 minutes. Run a knife around inside edge of springform pan, then gently remove ring side. While cake is still warm, gently spread Syrup over top. Serve warm. Serves 8+.

Apples with Cinnamon Cider Dip

The perfect party appetizer, tailgate sweet, or after-dinner conversation starter!

2 tbsp. cornstarch or arrowroot
1 tbsp. firmly packed light brown sugar
1¼ cups apple cider
3 tbsp. honey
2 tsp. fresh lemon juice
½ tsp. ground cinnamon
⅛ tsp. ground cloves
1 tbsp. unsalted butter
4 crisp, tart apples, cored and sliced

In a medium saucepan, stir until blended the cornstarch/arrowroot and brown sugar. Stir in the apple cider, honey, lemon juice, cinnamon, and cloves. Cook and stir until thickened and bubbly, then stir for 2 more minutes.

Remove from heat. Add butter, stirring until melted. Serve dip warm with sliced apples. Makes 4+ servings.

Bittersweet Blueberry Clusters

An unexpected complement to fresh, seasonal tart-sweet
blueberries. Caution: flavors will explode in your mouth!

12 oz. bittersweet chocolate, coarsely chopped
¼ cup trans-fat-free shortening
2 cups fresh blueberries, rinsed, drained, and
gently patted dry

Chef's Notes

How to Do It . . .
For white-chocolate blueberry clusters, follow directions, except substitute white chocolate (with cocoa
butter) for bittersweet chocolate.

In a small saucepan over low heat or in the top of a
double boiler over simmering water, melt the chocolate and shortening, stirring often until blended and
smooth. Remove from heat.

Gently fold blueberries into chocolate mixture until
well coated. Drop by teaspoonfuls into small paper
candy cups or onto a wax-paper-lined baking sheet.
Chill for 20 to 30 minutes or until chocolate is set.
Eat immediately! But if you're called away, candies
may be kept at room temperature for about 1 hour.
Makes about 2½ dozen clusters.

Fresh organic blueberries waiting to be harvested.
Advice from the cooking school: It's easier to coat
these with bittersweet chocolate *after* they're picked!

Fresh Seasonal Strawberries, Two Ways

★

Both of these offer great in-the-kitchen action, fun to prepare with your guests.

Orange-Marinated Strawberries

These orange-kissed berries are perfect on their own or served spooned atop your favorite ice cream.

2 qt. fresh, juicy strawberries, cleaned, hulled, and halved
2 tbsp. granulated sugar
1 tbsp. finely grated orange zest
⅓ cup fresh orange juice
1 tbsp. orange liqueur

Arrange the strawberries in a single layer in a shallow serving dish. In a small bowl, whisk together the sugar, zest, juice, and liqueur. Pour over the berries and let them marinate covered at room temperature for 15 to 30 minutes. Serves 6+.

Strawberries in Lavender Syrup

Lavender flowers add a sweet, relaxing aroma and beautiful color to fresh strawberries.

3 tbsp. granulated sugar
⅓ cup water
¼ cup dried lavender flowers
1 qt. fresh, juicy strawberries, cleaned, hulled, and thickly sliced

In a small saucepan, make a sugar syrup by cooking sugar in the water over medium heat until sugar dissolves. Add the lavender flowers, pressing into syrup until wet. Remove from heat, cover, and let steep for 30 minutes to 1 hour.

Strain syrup and gently toss with strawberries in a medium serving bowl. Let marinate for 15 to 30 minutes. Serve as is, over our bakery's angel food cake, or with ice cream. Serves 4+.

Chef's Notes

How to Do It . . .
Don't make these more than 30 minutes in advance or the berries will lose their color and texture.

Chef's Notes

How to Do It . . .
Ditto: don't make these more than 30 minutes in advance or the berries will lose their color and texture.

Cherry Bruschetta

Cooking cherries in red wine and sugar is a time-honored tradition in Italy.
Have our wine department help you pick out the perfect bottle for this recipe.

¾ cup granulated sugar
1 cup red wine
1 tsp. lemon zest
1½ lb. pitted sweet cherries, in season or frozen,
thawed, and drained
4 thick slices artisan bread
1½ tbsp. unsalted butter, room temperature

In a medium saucepan, combine the sugar, wine, and zest, cooking and stirring over medium heat until the sugar dissolves. Add the cherries, stirring gently. Bring mixture to a boil over high heat, then reduce to low and simmer uncovered for 15 minutes.

Lightly grill or toast the bread, then spread with the butter. Place the bread on individual serving plates with an edge. Spoon the cherries and their juices over the bread. Serve warm. Makes 4 servings.

Chef's Notes

About . . .
This recipe is easy to pass over . . . Cherry Bruschetta?! Trust me, if you want to put the "wow" in your friendships, surprise them with this sweet thing!

This is definitely not a "walk around while I'm wearing my best whites" dessert (or even appetizer), but something to indulge in and enjoy at a table.

How to Do It . . .
Be sure to measure frozen cherries while still frozen, then thaw, draining juices before using.

Cranberry-Lemon Bars

▼

This makes for a centerpiece holiday dessert. The colors glisten!

Cranberry Puree

2½ cups fresh or frozen cranberries
½ cup water
½ cup granulated sugar

Crust

1½ cups unbleached, all-purpose flour
¼ cup + 2 tbsp. confectioners' sugar, sifted
¾ cup unsalted butter, cut into cubes then softened to room temperature

Lemon Filling

2 large eggs
¾ cup + 2 tbsp. granulated sugar
½ tsp. baking powder
Pinch salt
2 tbsp. grated lemon zest
2½ tbsp. fresh lemon juice

Chef's Notes

How to Do It . . .
Cranberry puree may be made 1 day ahead, then covered and refrigerated until ready to use. Bring to room temperature before using.

In Season . . .
You'll miss them when they're gone, so freeze some fresh cranberries directly in their bags for six to eight months and use as desired.

Heat oven to 350 degrees.

For the Cranberry Puree: In a small saucepan, combine the cranberries and the water. Bring to a boil over medium heat. Stir and cook until the berries burst and the mixture reduces to about ¾ cup (this takes at least 10 minutes).

Remove saucepan from heat and stir in the sugar until sugar dissolves. Strain through a sieve into a medium bowl, pressing to extract as much fruit mixture as possible.

For the Crust: Mix the flour and confectioners' sugar in a medium bowl. Using a pastry blender or two forks, cut in the butter until mixture resembles coarse crumbs. Press the crust evenly into an ungreased 11x8" tart pan with removable bottom. Build a ½" edge up the sides of the pan. Bake for 18 minutes, then carefully remove the tart pan to a wire rack.

For the Lemon Filling: With an electric mixer, beat the eggs and sugar until they are light lemon in color. Add the baking powder, salt, zest, and juice and beat until the mixture is very light and frothy, about 4 minutes. Pour filling evenly over the partially baked crust.

Return the pan to the oven and bake until the top is set and golden, 15 to 20 minutes. Cool completely on a wire rack.

When ready to spread Cranberry Puree atop cooled lemon bar mixture, lightly whip the Puree in a small bowl with a fork. (This makes mixture easier to spread.) Gently spread atop lemon filling in pan. Refrigerate for 30 minutes, then cut into bars and enjoy. Makes about 16 pieces.

Layers of tart sweet upon tart sweet . . . If the beautiful
jeweled colors don't convince you to indulge, one
taste will!

Light and Lemony Bars

One of two of our favorite versions of a very satisfying, tart treat.

Crust

½ cup white or brown rice flour
¼ cup potato starch
¼ cup tapioca flour
½ cup unsalted butter, cold, plus more for greasing pan
⅓ cup confectioners' sugar, sifted, plus additional for serving

Filling

1 cup granulated sugar
½ tsp. baking powder
2 large eggs, lightly beaten
¼ cup fresh lemon juice
1 tbsp. finely chopped lemon zest

Heat oven to 350 degrees. Grease an 8" square cake pan with butter.

For the Crust: In a small bowl, mix together the rice flour, potato starch, and tapioca flour. Measure ⅔ *cup* of the mixed flours; set remainder aside.

In a food processor, combine the butter, the ⅔ cup of the flours, and the confectioners' sugar; pulse until mixture is crumbly. Press into prepared pan and bake for 20 minutes or until crust is set. Cool completely on a wire rack.

For the Filling: In a medium bowl, whisk together the remaining flour mixture, granulated sugar, baking powder, eggs, lemon juice, and zest. Pour over crust and bake for 20 to 30 minutes or just until set. Cool completely on a wire rack.

When ready to serve, cut into pieces and dust each piece with additional confectioners' sugar as desired. Serves 8+.

Winter Fruit Compote

Sometimes, a simple fruit dessert is all that's required.

4 fresh tangerines or mandarins, peeled, sectioned, and seeded
1 cup seedless red or green grapes
1 cup frozen whole unsweetened red raspberries
⅓ cup slivered, blanched almonds
1 cup dried cranberries
2 tbsp. crystallized ginger, finely chopped

In a large serving bowl, combine the sectioned citrus, grapes, raspberries, almonds, dried cranberries, and crystallized ginger. Serves 4+.

Chef's Notes

How to Do It . . .
Perhaps you're looking for the remainder of the instructions . . . but this recipe is simple and the only remaining instruction is to enjoy.

Take this from a dessert to an appetizer by serving this compote with a triple cream cheese (such as St. Andre) and whole-grain crackers.

In Season . . .
When fresh satsuma oranges (what we know as canned mandarins) are in season, snatch these seedless jewels up and don't stop enjoying them until the season ends!

Cookie Baskets with Fruit and Creamy Amaretto Sauce

Almost too pretty to eat . . . but our café invites you to dig in and enjoy!

Baskets

1 cup unsalted butter
1 cup granulated sugar
½ cup light corn syrup
1¾ cups tapioca flour
2 tsp. ground ginger
Fresh seasonal berries

Creamy Amaretto Sauce

1 lb. cream cheese, softened to
room temperature
½ lb. sour cream
¾ cup firmly packed light brown sugar
¼ cup fresh lemon juice
½ cup + 1 tbsp. Amaretto liqueur

Chef's Notes

About . . .
Tapioca flour is a starchy substance extracted from the root of the cassava plant.

How to Do It . . .
Remember that when you're moving and molding the cookies that they're hot—they just came out of the oven. However, working with the hot cookies is imperative: they're pliable and moldable when they're hot, and crisp and crackly when they're not!

Heat oven to 350 degrees. Line baking sheets with parchment paper.

For the Baskets: Melt butter in a small saucepan. Add the sugar, syrup, flour, and ginger, mixing well to blend.

Drop tablespoonfuls of dough onto cookie sheets, leaving plenty of space in between each to allow for spreading. Bake for 7 to 10 minutes or until the cookies are golden brown. Remove from oven and allow to cool for 1 minute, then gently remove cookies and place each over an inverted small bowl. This will allow cookies to mold into a basket shape. Allow to cool before carefully removing. Makes 6+ baskets.

For the Creamy Amaretto Sauce: In a large bowl of an electric mixer, combine the cream cheese, sour cream, sugar, juice, and liqueur. Mix at low speed until liquid is incorporated, then increase speed to medium and beat for 2 minutes until smooth and well combined. Chill mixture before serving. Leftovers may be refrigerated covered for 10 days. Makes about 2½ cups.

When ready to serve, invert and fill cookie baskets on individual serving plates with fresh seasonal fruit. Serve with a side of Creamy Amaretto Sauce.

Flourless Chocolate Espresso Cake with Red Raspberry Fool

Dense chocolate flavors with a jolt of espresso, topped with
a burst of red raspberry flavor.

Cake

12 oz. semisweet chocolate, coarsely chopped
4 oz. unsweetened chocolate, coarsely chopped
1 lb. unsalted butter, diced
1 cup freshly brewed espresso or 1 tbsp. instant
espresso powder dissolved in 1 cup hot water
1 cup firmly packed light brown sugar
8 large eggs, lightly beaten

Raspberry Fool

3 cups chopped fresh red raspberries, divided,
plus additional whole raspberries for serving
¾ cup granulated sugar
1 tbsp. arrowroot or cornstarch
1 cup heavy (whipping) cream, whipped

Chef's Notes

About . . .
Although we all know a few fools, this one refers to
an old-fashioned English dessert made of cooked,
pureed fruit that is sometimes strained, chilled, and
folded into whipped cream. Covered and refrigerated, this fool keeps for no more than 2 days.

Heat oven to 350 degrees. Lightly grease then line
bottom of a 9x2" round cake pan with a parchment
paper circle.

For the Cake: Place all of the chocolate in a large bowl.
In a medium saucepan, bring the butter, espresso, and
sugar to a boil, stirring to dissolve the sugar. Pour atop
the chocolate, let sit for 2 minutes, then whisk until
smooth. Cool slightly. Whisk in eggs until blended.

Pour batter into prepared pan. Place cake pan in a
roasting pan and pour enough hot water into roasting
pan to come halfway up sides of cake pan. Bake until
center of cake is set and tester inserted into center
comes out with a few moist crumbs attached, about 1
hour. Remove pan from water bath. Cool cake completely on a wire rack, then refrigerate overnight.

Cut around pan sides to loosen cake. Using oven mitts
to protect yourself, hold pan bottom over low heat for
15 seconds to warm slightly to help release cake. Place
large plate over cake, invert, and gently peel off parchment. Invert cake back onto a serving platter.

For the Raspberry Fool: Place *half* of the chopped
raspberries in a food processor; process until smooth.
In a small saucepan, combine the sugar and arrowroot/cornstarch, mixing well. Add the raspberry
puree. Bring to a boil over medium heat, stirring constantly until thickened. Boil 1 minute.

Transfer to a medium bowl. Add remaining chopped
raspberries; mix well. Refrigerate until thoroughly
chilled. Fold chilled raspberry mixture into whipped
cream just until blended.

Serve cake slices with a generous dollop of the
Raspberry Fool and a garnish of fresh raspberries.
Serves 61.

Chocolate Hazelnut Tart

For those with a sweet tooth and a love of chocolate, this tart is for you. You need to plan ahead, however, as this tart does not firm up until it has had a chance to chill overnight.

Sugar Dough

1 lb. unsalted butter, softened
1¼ cups granulated sugar
1 large egg, lightly beaten
2 oz. or 3 large egg yolks
3⅔ cups unbleached, all-purpose flour

Chocolate Hazelnut Filling

1 cup coarsely chopped toasted hazelnuts
6 oz. milk chocolate, coarsely chopped
2 cups skinned, toasted hazelnuts
4 tbsp. honey
4 tbsp. light corn syrup
⅛ tsp. sea salt
1 cup granulated sugar
4 tbsp. water, plus more if needed
1¼ cups heavy (whipping) cream

Chocolate Mousse Topping

10 oz. milk chocolate, coarsely chopped
1 cup + 4 tbsp. heavy (whipping) cream

Chef's Notes

How to Do It . . .
Extra dough can be frozen for 2 to 4 months if well wrapped.

Skinning hazelnuts is a relatively easy task. Place them on a baking sheet and roast at 350 degrees until lightly golden, about 12 minutes. Shake the pan or stir once or twice during roasting. While the nuts are still hot, place them on a clean towel and rub to remove the skin (it's okay if some pieces of the skins remain). Set hazelnuts aside to cool completely.

For the Sugar Dough: In a large bowl of an electric mixer, cream together the butter and sugar until light and fluffy. When mixture is well combined, scrape sides of bowl, then add the egg and egg yolks, blending well.

Add the flour all at once and mix only until incorporated. Divide dough into 4 pieces, then shape and gently pat into discs. Wrap in plastic wrap and refrigerate until ready to use. Enough for 4 12" tart shells.

When ready to make a tart, heat oven to 350 degrees. Remove 1 disc of dough and allow to soften slightly at room temperature. Roll dough thinly and place in a 12" tart pan with removable bottom. Lightly pierce bottom and sides of dough with a fork, then bake for 20 minutes until golden and dough is dry and lightly crisped. Set aside to cool completely on a wire rack.

For the Chocolate Hazelnut Filling: Spread the cup of chopped hazelnuts on the baked crust.

In a medium bowl combine the milk chocolate pieces, 2 cups skinned hazelnuts, and honey; set aside.

In a large saucepan, combine the corn syrup, salt, sugar, and just enough water to cover the bottom of the pan. Bring to a boil and boil gently until mixture caramelizes and turns very dark, but not burned, stirring only occasionally with a wooden spoon.

When mixture is thick and dark, remove from heat and carefully whisk in the cream to make a caramel. Add caramel mixture to the chocolate mixture, blending gently. Fill tart shell. Chill 30 minutes.

For the Chocolate Mousse Topping: Melt chocolate in a double boiler over simmering water; when melted, remove from heat and allow to cool for 10 minutes. Whip heavy cream and fold into cooled chocolate, one third at a time. Decoratively pipe Topping atop partially chilled tart using a plain round tip and pastry bag, filling top completely. Allow tart to chill overnight before cutting and serving. Serves 8+.

Chocolate . . . oh, you sweet thing! Rich and creamy and nutty and chocolaty . . .

Triple Chocolate Biscotti

Chocolate, chocolate, and more chocolate . . . Fair trade, bittersweet, and artisan . . . To snack on or turn into finger-food desserts like this one!

⅓ cup unsalted butter
⅔ cup granulated sugar
¼ cup unsweetened cocoa powder, sifted
2 tsp. baking powder
2 large eggs, lightly beaten
1¾ cups unbleached, all-purpose flour
4 oz. white chocolate, coarsely chopped
3 oz. bittersweet chocolate, coarsely chopped

Chef's Notes

How to Do It . . .
Biscotti is not an exact science as far as shaping and baking, so use these instructions as your guide.

Heat oven to 375 degrees.

In a large bowl of an electric mixer, beat butter until softened. Add sugar, cocoa powder, and baking powder, beating until combined. Beat in the eggs, then add in the flour. By hand, stir in the chocolate pieces.

Divide dough in half and shape each portion into an 8 to 10" log. Place the two logs about 4" apart on a parchment-paper-lined baking sheet. Flatten slightly until about 2" wide. Bake for 25 minutes; cool on a wire rack for 30 minutes. Lower oven temperature to 325 degrees.

On a cutting board with a serrated knife, cut each log crosswise into ½"-thick slices. Lay slices cut side down on an ungreased cookie sheet. Bake for 8 minutes, then turn slices and bake for an additional 10 to 13 minutes or until biscotti are dry and crisp. Do not overbake.

Cool completely on a wire rack. Store biscotti in an airtight container at room temperature. Makes about 2 dozen.

Vegan Chocolate Cake

Our bakery's vegan chocolate cakes are difficult to keep in stock . . . especially when they're frosted and decorated with all-natural food colors. Our bakers are artists!

Nonstick cooking spray
3 cups unbleached, all-purpose flour
⅔ cup cocoa powder
2 tsp. baking soda
1 tsp. sea salt
1 cup granulated sugar
1 cup vegetable oil
1 cup cold, organic brewed coffee
1 tsp. pure vanilla extract
¼ cup brown rice vinegar

Heat oven to 375 degrees. Spray 2 10" cake pans with nonstick cooking spray and line with parchment paper.

In a medium bowl, sift together the flour, cocoa, baking soda, salt, and sugar.

In another medium bowl, combine the oil, coffee, and vanilla. Stir into dry ingredients until well incorporated. Add the vinegar and mix well.

Divide batter evenly between the 2 pans. Bake 20 to 30 minutes or until a toothpick inserted in the center comes out clean. Cool on a wire rack for 20 minutes. Invert, remove parchment paper, and invert again on a rack to cool completely. Yields 2 individual plain cakes or 1 filled and frosted 10" layer cake.

Soft Vegan Oatmeal Cookies

A satisfying, soft, gooey oatmeal cookie that keeps well.

12.3 oz. of silken firm tofu, drained
1 cup firmly packed light brown sugar
⅓ cup canola oil
1 tbsp. pure vanilla extract
1¾ cups old-fashioned rolled oats
½ cup unbleached, all-purpose flour or white whole-wheat flour
½ cup whole-wheat flour
½ tsp. sea salt
1½ tsp. ground cinnamon
1 tsp. baking powder
½ cup seedless raisins or dried cranberries

Chef's Notes

About . . .
Vegans are the purists of the vegetarian world, refusing to eat all animal-derivative foods, including butter, cheese, eggs, and milk.

Heat oven to 375 degrees. Line cookie sheets with parchment paper.

In a blender or food processor, puree tofu. Transfer tofu to a medium mixing bowl and stir in the sugar, oil, and vanilla. Add oats, stirring to combine.

In a small mixing bowl, combine the flours, salt, cinnamon, baking powder, and raisins/cranberries, mixing well to blend. Add the dry ingredients in thirds to the tofu mixture, mixing well after each addition until all ingredients are moistened.

Roll or scoop a generous tablespoonful of dough into a ball, placing on cookie sheets. Lightly flatten cookies before baking. Bake for 12 to 14 minutes or just until golden. Makes about 3½ dozen cookies.

Tofu Cheesecake

This creamy, dense cheesecake keeps well in the refrigerator for several days.

15 small oat bran or amaranth graham
crackers, coarsely ground
½ tsp. ground cinnamon
3 tbsp. soy margarine, melted
3½ lb. soft tofu, drained and
coarsely crumbled
⅔ cup plain or vanilla soy milk
¼ cup tahini
¾ cup maple syrup
2 large egg whites
1½ tsp. pure vanilla extract
2 tbsp. fresh lemon juice
Fresh seasonal fruit such as grapes,
blueberries, apricots, or peaches

Heat oven to 350 degrees.

Place the cracker crumbs, cinnamon, and margarine in a small mixing bowl, stirring to combine. Press onto the bottom of a 9" springform pan.

In a blender, puree tofu in batches until smooth, adding a portion of the soy milk with each batch. Scrape mixture into a large bowl. Stir in the tahini, syrup, egg whites, vanilla, and lemon juice, mixing well.

Scrape into pan, smoothing the top with a spatula. Bake 35 to 40 minutes or until the filling is set and the top begins to turn golden. Cool completely on a wire rack, then cover and refrigerate until chilled.

When ready to serve, arrange fruit on top in any fashion that pleases you. Serves 6+.

Ginger-Syrup-Glazed Tofu

A creamy custard dessert that will surprise (and please) even non-tofu eaters!

4 navel oranges
¾ cup granulated sugar
1 cup water
⅓ cup finely slivered fresh ginger, plus
more for garnish
1-lb. block of silken firm tofu, drained
¼ cup crystallized ginger, coarsely chopped

Chef's Notes

About . . .

Silken tofu is rich, unstrained soy milk mixed with a natural coagulant, then poured into aseptic cartons that are then placed in water and heated. The finished product is soft and smooth.

Peel the oranges, then cut between the membranes to release the orange sections. If you do this over a bowl you can capture the fresh orange juices. Set aside.

In a large saucepan, combine the sugar, water, and ginger. Bring to a boil over medium-high heat, then reduce the heat to medium, cover, and simmer for 8 minutes.

Halve the tofu horizontally and place the two halves in a single layer in a baking dish. Pour the syrup over the tofu and let sit covered for 12 minutes to infuse the tofu with ginger flavor.

Cut the tofu into 4 even slices and carefully transfer them to rimmed serving bowls. Spoon the ginger syrup atop each serving of tofu. Garnish with the orange sections and some crystallized ginger. Makes 4+ servings.

Giant Ginger Cookies

These large cookies have a kick and a bite!

4½ cups unbleached, all-purpose
flour or whole-wheat pastry flour
4 tsp. ground ginger
2 tsp. baking soda
1½ tsp. ground cinnamon
1 tsp. ground cloves
¼ tsp. sea salt
1½ cups unsalted butter
2 cups granulated sugar
2 large eggs, lightly beaten
½ cup molasses
1 tsp. finely chopped crystallized ginger
¾ cup coarse sugar

Chef's Notes

About . . .
Molasses is a thick, strong-tasting cane-sugar syrup, a byproduct of making sugar.

How to Do It . . .
Do not overbake or the cookies will not be chewy.

Heat oven to 350 degrees.

In a medium mixing bowl, stir together the flour, ginger, baking soda, cinnamon, cloves, and salt. Set aside.

In a large bowl of an electric mixer, beat the butter until softened. Gradually add the granulated sugar, beating until fluffy. Add eggs, molasses, and crystallized ginger; beat well to blend. Add *half* of the flour mixture, beating until combined. Stir in remaining flour (using a wooden spoon if this dough is too heavy for your mixer at this point).

Using a ¼-cup scoop, shape dough into 2" balls. Roll in the coarse sugar. Place on an ungreased cookie sheet about 2½" apart.

Bake for 12 to 14 minutes or until cookies are light golden brown and puffed. Let stand for 2 minutes before removing from cookie sheets and cooling on a wire rack. Makes about 2 dozen large cookies.

Baguette Bread Pudding with Choice of Two Toppings

At our house, there's always half a baguette from our bakery left after dinner. It's almost planned, since we love to make this bread pudding with it.

4 tbsp. unsalted butter, melted, divided
2 tbsp. firmly packed light brown sugar
6 cups 1" cubes day-old baguette
2 cups milk, whole or 2 percent
2 large eggs, lightly beaten
⅓ cup granulated sugar
2 tbsp. apple juice
1 tbsp. pure vanilla extract
1 medium-size crisp, tart apple, peeled,
cored, and chopped

Heat oven to 350 degrees. Brush a 13x9" baking dish with *1 tbsp.* of the melted butter. Sprinkle the brown sugar evenly over the bottom of the dish. Set aside.

In a large bowl, combine the bread cubes and the milk. Pressing down, let the bread soak until it has absorbed most of the milk, about 5 minutes.

In a medium bowl, whisk together the eggs, sugar, juice, vanilla, and remaining butter. Pour over the bread, tossing in the apples and stirring gently to mix well.

Pour mixture into the prepared baking dish, scraping all the liquid out of the mixing bowl. Cover the baking dish with foil and bake for 50 minutes. Remove the foil and continue baking for 15 additional minutes, until the pudding is fluffy with a golden crust. While the pudding is baking prepare your choice of two toppings (or both!). Bread pudding serves 5+.

Chef's Notes

About . . .
Brown rice syrup, with a gentle, sweet flavor, is one of the most balanced unrefined sweeteners available.

Coffee Whipped Cream

1 cup heavy (whipping) cream
1 tbsp. instant coffee powder
2 tbsp. granulated sugar

In a bowl, combine the cream, coffee powder, and sugar, then chill the mixture, stirring once or twice to dissolve the sugar and the coffee powder. This will take about 15 minutes to dissolve. Remove the mixture from the refrigerator and beat with an electric mixer until cream holds soft peaks, then transfer the whipped coffee cream to a serving dish. Serve a generous dollop atop the warm bread pudding. Makes about 1 cup.

Cranberry Caramel Sauce

½ cup unsalted butter
1¼ cups firmly packed light brown sugar
2 tbsp. brown rice syrup
1 cup fresh cranberries, cleaned
½ cup heavy (whipping) cream

In a medium saucepan, melt the butter. Stir in the brown sugar, syrup, and cranberries. Bring to a boil; cook until sugar dissolves and the cranberries pop, stirring constantly. Stir in the cream and return to a boil. Remove from heat, let cool slightly, then serve a generous spoonful atop the warm bread pudding. Makes about 2¾ cups.

Spice Snack Cake

A sweet treat to snack on for our gluten-free friends,
developed in the cooking school.

1 cup brown rice flour
⅔ cup potato starch
⅓ cup tapioca flour
1 tsp. xanthan gum
1¾ tsp. baking soda
¾ tsp. sea salt
1 tsp. ground ginger
1 tbsp. ground cinnamon
1 tsp. freshly grated nutmeg
¼ tsp. ground cloves
¼ tsp. ground allspice
1½ cups milk (cow, soy, rice, or nut)
1½ cups firmly packed light brown sugar
¼ cup unsalted butter, plus more for
greasing pan
¼ cup corn oil
⅓ cup molasses
1 tsp. gluten-free vanilla
2 large eggs, lightly beaten

Heat oven to 325 degrees. Grease a 9" round cake pan with butter. Line bottom with parchment paper.

In a large mixing bowl, sift together the rice flour, potato starch, tapioca flour, xanthan gum, baking soda, salt, ginger, cinnamon, nutmeg, cloves, and allspice.

In a small saucepan, combine the milk and brown sugar and bring just to a boil over medium heat. Remove from heat; whisk in the butter, oil, molasses, and vanilla until butter is melted.

Add the liquid mixture to the flour mixture, stirring until blended. Add eggs and mix until well blended. Pour the batter into the prepared pan and bake for 45 minutes or until a toothpick inserted in the center of the cakes comes out clean.

Cool cake completely on a wire rack. Run a thin knife around the edge of cake, then invert onto a large plate, gently peeling off parchment paper. Invert onto a serving plate. Cut into pieces. Serves 4+.

BIBLIOGRAPHY

Editors of Sunset Books. *Fresh Produce A to Z*. Menlo Park, CA: Lane Publishing Company, 1987.

Herbst, Sharon T. *Food Lover's Companion*. 2nd ed. Hauppauge, NY: Barron's Educational Series, 1995.

Jacobi, Dana. *The Natural Kitchen: Soy!* Rocklin, CA: Prima Publishing, 1996.

National Audubon Society. *Seafood Lover's Almanac*. New York: National Audubon Society's Living Oceans Program, 2000.

Peterson, James. *Vegetables*. New York: William Morrow, 1998.

Sass, Lorna. *The Complete Vegetarian Kitchen*. New York: Hearst Books, 1992.

Shaffer, Bev and John. *No Reservations Required*. Wooster, OH: The Wooster Book Company, 2003.

Wood, Rebecca. *The New Whole Foods Encyclopedia*. New York: Penguin Books, 1999.

INDEX

Gluten-Free Index

The recipes that follow were written and prepared gluten free; as always, be sure to check ingredients for known offenders. Many other recipes in this cookbook could be adapted for a gluten-free diet.

Vegetarian Index

The recipes that follow were written
and prepared vegetarian; as always, be sure
to check ingredients for known offenders.
Many other recipes in this cookbook could
be adapted for a vegetarian diet.